SAGE was founded in 1965 by Sara Miller McCune to support the dissemination of usable knowledge by publishing innovative and high-quality research and teaching content. Today, we publish more than 750 journals, including those of more than 300 learned societies, more than 800 new books per year, and a growing range of library products including archives, data, case studies, reports, conference highlights, and video. SAGE remains majority-owned by our founder, and after Sara's lifetime will become owned by a charitable trust that secures our continued independence.

Los Angeles | London | Washington DC | New Delhi | Singapore | Boston

'AD'APTING
to MARKETS

'ADAPTING
to MARKETS

Repackaging Commercials in Indian Languages

Sunitha Srinivas C.

www.sagepublications.com

Los Angeles • London • New Delhi • Singapore • Washington DC • Boston

First published in 2015 by

 SAGE Publications India Pvt Ltd
B1/I-1 Mohan Cooperative Industrial Area
Mathura Road, New Delhi 110 044, India
www.sagepub.in

SAGE Publications Inc
2455 Teller Road
Thousand Oaks, California 91320, USA

SAGE Publications Ltd
1 Oliver's Yard
55 City Road
London EC1Y 1SP, United Kingdom

SAGE Publications Asia-Pacific Pte Ltd
3 Church Street
#10-04 Samsung Hub
Singapore 049483

Published by Vivek Mehra for SAGE Publications India Pvt Ltd, typeset in 10/12 pt Utopia by Emaptis, Chennai and printed at Sai Print-o-Pack, New Delhi.

Library of Congress Cataloging-in-Publication Data

Sunitha Srinivas, C.
  'Ad'apting to markets : repackaging commercials in Indian languages / Sunitha Srinivas C.
    pages cm
  Includes bibliographical references and index.
  1. Advertising—India. 2. Advertising—Language. 3. Psycholinguistics. 4. Sales promotion. I. Title.
  HF5813.I4S86   659.10954—dc23 2015   2015010158

ISBN: 978-93-515-0240-1 (HB)

The SAGE Team: Shambhu Sahu, Isha Sachdeva, Nand Kumar Jha and Rajinder Kaur

For my parents

Thank you for choosing a SAGE product!
If you have any comment, observation or feedback,
I would like to personally hear from you.
Please write to me at **contactceo@sagepub.in**

Vivek Mehra, Managing Director and CEO,
SAGE Publications India Pvt Ltd, New Delhi

Bulk Sales

SAGE India offers special discounts
for purchase of books in bulk.
We also make available special imprints
and excerpts from our books on demand.

For orders and enquiries, write to us at

Marketing Department
SAGE Publications India Pvt Ltd
B1/I-1, Mohan Cooperative Industrial Area
Mathura Road, Post Bag 7
New Delhi 110044, India

E-mail us at **marketing@sagepub.in**

Get to know more about SAGE

Be invited to SAGE events, get on our mailing list.
Write today to **marketing@sagepub.in**

This book is also available as an e-book.

Contents

Acknowledgements

I express my gratitude to all those friends and colleagues who supported and encouraged me and saw me through this book; and to all those who provided support, talked things over, read, wrote, offered comments and assisted me in editing and proof-reading. I also acknowledge the enormous part played by the University Grants Commission (UGC) in providing financial assistance for a research project, leading to the creation of this book.

Introduction

Advertising is a prominent, powerful and ubiquitous medium in which language is used skillfully. Its seductive and controversial quality has attracted constant and intense attention across a range of academic disciplines including linguistics, media studies, politics, semiotics and sociology. Television advertising is an environment in which the lines between entertainment and promotion have not just been blurred, but have been almost completely removed. The concept of advertainment (a portmanteau of the words *advertising* and *entertainment*) incorporates advertising that seduces by engaging users' game-playing instincts and immersing them in worlds of embedded content, by means of prizes, coupons and other enticements. It combines elements of entertainment, information and reward which, when applied to any kind of marketing or advertising content (for any product, service, brand, audience, etc., in any type of media), renders the content highly *magnetic*—and prone to audience response. The combination of these elements (within a permission-based structure) compels an individual with a resonant interest or passion, to engage with the content, with a significantly higher level of attention and response. Advertising is one of the most visible activities of business. By inviting people to try their products, companies risk public criticism and attack if their advertising displeases or offends the audience or if their products do not measure up to the advertised promise. Proponents of advertising point out that it is safer to buy advertised products because when a company's name and reputation are at stake, it tries harder to fulfil its promises. The advertainment structure anticipated that by adding exponential value through relevant prizes and incentives, consumers would be motivated to buy.

Advertising is both applauded and criticized not only for its role in selling products but also for its influence on the economy and society. For years, critics have denigrated advertising for a wide range of sins—real as well as notions formed without much reflection. In the mid-1960s, the psychologist Ernest

Dichter asserted that a product's image, created in part by advertising and promotion, is an inherent feature of the product itself. Subsequent studies showed that while an advertisement may not address a product's quality directly, the positive image conveyed by advertising may imply quality. Moreover, by simply making the product better known, advertising can make the product more desirable to the consumer. In these ways, advertising adds value to the brand. Consumers can choose the values they want in the products they buy. For low price, they can buy an inexpensive economy car. If status and luxury are important, they can buy a limousine, a sedan or a racy sports car. Many of the consumer wants and needs are emotional, social or psychological rather than functional. One way we communicate who we are (or want to be) is through the products we purchase and display. By associating the product with some desirable image, advertising offers people the opportunity to satisfy those psychic or symbolic wants and needs. In terms of our economic framework, by adding value to products, advertising contributes to self-interest—for both the consumer and the advertiser. It also contributes to the number of sellers. This increases competition, which also serves the consumer's self-interest. Advertising can help get new products off the ground by giving more people a higher level of *complete information*, thereby stimulating primary demand—demand for the entire product class. In declining markets, when the only information people want is about price, advertising can influence selective demand—demand for a particular brand. John Kenneth Galbraith, a perennial critic of advertising, concedes that by helping to maintain the flow of consumer demand (encouraging more buyers), advertising helps sustain employment and income. Advertising stimulates a healthy economy. It also helps create financially healthy consumers, who are more informed, better educated and more demanding. As a result, consumers demand that manufacturers are held accountable for their advertising. This has led to an unprecedented level of social criticism and legal regulation. For advertising to be effective, consumers must have confidence in it. So, any kind of deception not only detracts consumers from the complete information principle of free enterprise but also risks being self-defeating. The fact is that advertising, by its very nature, is not complete information. It is biased in favour of the advertiser and the brand. People expect advertisers to be proud of their products and probably do not mind if they puff them a little. But, when advertisers cross the line between simply giving their point of view and creating false expectations, people begin to object and resist.

The television is a convenient and flexible advertising medium, owing to its widespread popularity and the ease with which a message can reach millions of viewers internationally and nationally. Television advertising allows advertisers the flexibility to use various approaches and different combinations of audio, video and text to make adverts memorable and emotional, depending on the product or service or the target audience. It uses audio and visual effects to create a lasting impact. Marketers employ colour, sound, sight, drama and motion to ensure that their message is strong and persuasive. Additional tactics and props, such as attractive models, elaborate sets, enchanting graphics and audio-visual effects further enhance impact. Companies spend untold billions every year on advertising. Television has gradually become one of the best and effective advertising mediums owing to its widespread reach. Highly engaging, it has the ability to make instant connections with the audience. Advertising on television gives one the opportunity to communicate with local, national and even international audiences. This is done in just a short amount of time. Businesses segment organize their advertisements according to their target market. It can get them the attention they need as well as increase brand awareness for their business. Television advertisements use audio-visuals and actions to convey the message which easily catch the attention of consumers. Scores of television advertisements feature songs or melodies (jingles) or slogans designed to be striking and memorable, which may remain in the minds of television viewers long after the span of the advertising campaign. Some of these ad jingles or catch-phrases even take on lives of their own, spawning gags that appear in films, television shows, magazines, comics or literature. Advertising agencies also use humour as a tool in their creative marketing campaigns. Psychological studies have attempted to demonstrate the effects of humour and their relationship to empower advertising persuasion. When messages are conveyed successfully, the ad becomes more credible to the audience. Television's influence is a factor in the child's construction of social reality. Prior to the prevalence and pervasiveness of the mass media, children were socialized primarily through family and community. The basic structure of family and community having been changed, no longer are they the only major influences that socialize children. Now, children receive more socializing messages from a mass medium than from parents, school, church or the community. Business is interested in children and adolescents because of their buying power and because of their influence on the shopping habits of their parents. As children are easier to influence, they are especially targeted by the advertising business. Accordingly, television plays a major role in the process of enculturation—to be a medium of the socialization of most people into their cultural roles and standardized behaviour. Critics claim that advertising manipulates us into buying things by playing on our emotions and promising greater status, social acceptance and sex appeal. While the clutter problem is irksome to viewers and advertisers alike, most people tolerate it as the price for free television, freedom of the press and a high standard of living. However, with the proliferation of new media choices, this externality is only likely to get worse. Virtually, every popular website is cluttered with advertising banners, and the e-mail boxes are flooded with advertising messages on a daily basis. Advertising has long been criticized for insensitivity towards minorities, women, immigrants, the disabled, the elderly and a myriad of other groups— that is, for not being *politically correct*. The very presence of advertising affects the nature of our culture and environment, even when we do not want it. Marketing professionals earnestly believe in the benefits that advertising brings to society. Advertising, they say, encourages the development and speeds the acceptance of new products and technologies. It gives consumers and business customers a wider variety of choices. By encouraging mass production, it helps keep prices down. It stimulates healthy competition between producers as well, which benefits all buyers. Advertising, it has been pointed out, also promotes a higher standard of living. It pays for most of our news media and subsidizes the arts and supports freedom of the press. It also provides a means to disseminate public information about important health and social issues. While ethical advertising is doing what the advertiser and the advertiser's peers believe is morally right in a given situation, social responsibility means doing what society views as best for the welfare of people in general or for a specific community of people. Together, ethics and social responsibility can be seen as the moral obligation of advertisers not to violate the basic economic assumptions, even when there is no legal obligation. Advertising gives consumers complete information about the choices available to them, encourages added sellers to compete more effectively and thereby serves the self-interest of both consumers and marketers. It is a key element in the promotional mix. Effective advertising works towards fulfilling the marketing or corporate objectives set by an organization. Creative advertising uses many forms of advertising appeals that consumers respond to. These appeals are conveyed in advertising through various forms of conventional media such as print, television, radio, the Internet and various forms of unconventional media such as promotional events, van-operations and fairs, to name a few. Indian culture is reflected in Indian advertising, where an ideal world tends to be portrayed through the depiction of a loving husband, wife, mother and child, success, love, achievement, fantasy, family unity and other consumer aspirations. Advertising reflects the lifestyle, popular culture and aspirations of a consumer while communicating the value proposition of the product. The Indian consumer's culture is influenced by many factors, including diversity in religion, geographic location, social class, family structure, occupation and economic status. Advertising has a major impact on society because adverts help in establishing norms in a society and the social and ethical responsibility of advertisers—be it advertisement agencies or the marketing departments of organizations. Culture is also conveyed in advertising through the use of symbols and logos (McDonald's golden arches are viewed as symbolizing American culture and associations of individualism). Culture is not only about beliefs, values and norms of a social group, but it also provides individuals with an interpretive frame to construct meanings and form social impressions and judgements.

Advertising is a form of communication intended to persuade an audience to purchase products, ideals or services. While advertising can be seen as necessary for economic growth, it is not without social costs. Unsolicited commercial emails and other forms of spam have become so prevalent that they are a major concern to users of these services, as well as a financial burden on the Internet service providers. Advertising increasingly invades public spaces and frequently uses psychological pressure (like appealing to feelings of inadequacy) on the intended consumers, which may be harmful. Criticism of advertising extends to audio-visual aspects (cluttering of public spaces and airspace), environmental aspects (pollution, oversize packaging, increasing consumption), political aspects (media dependency, free speech, censorship), financial aspects (cost) as well as ethical/moral/social aspects (subconscious influencing, invasion of privacy, increasing consumption and waste, target groups, certain products and honesty). As advertising has become prevalent in modern society, it is increasingly being criticized. Advertising occupies public space and more of it invades the private sphere of people. It is hard to escape from advertising and the media. Public space, it has been pointed out, is increasingly turning into a gigantic billboard for products of all kinds. The most important element of advertising is not information but suggestion—making use of associations, emotions and drives in the subconscious, such as sex drive and herd instinct; desires, such as happiness, health, fitness, appearance, self-esteem, reputation, belonging, social status, identity, adventure, distraction and reward; fears, such as illness, weaknesses, loneliness, need, uncertainty, security, or of prejudices, learned opinions and comforts. All human needs, relationships and fears—the deepest recesses of the human psyche—become sheer means for expansion of the commodity universe under the force of modern marketing. With the rise to prominence of modern marketing, commercialism—the translation of human relations into commodity relations—although a phenomenon intrinsic to capitalism, has expanded exponentially. Cause-related marketing in which advertisers link their products to some worthy social causes has also boomed. Advertising uses the model role of celebrities or popular figures and makes deliberate use of humour as well as associations with colour, tunes, certain names and terms. These are examples of how one perceives himself and one's self-worth. In his description of *mental capitalism*, Georg Franck says, 'the promise of consumption making someone irresistible is the ideal way of objects and symbols into a person's subjective experience' (Shamiyeh, 2005:98–115). Evidently, in a society in which revenue of attention moves to the fore, consumption is drawn by one's self-esteem. As a result, consumption becomes *work* on a person's attraction. From the subjective point of view, this *work* opens fields of unexpected magnitude for advertising. For advertising critics, another serious problem is that the long-standing notion of separation between advertising and editorial/creative sides of media is rapidly crumbling, and advertising is increasingly hard to tell apart from news, information or entertainment. The boundaries between advertising and programming are becoming blurred. Advertising draws heavily on psychological theories about how to create subjects, enabling advertising and marketing to take on a *more clearly psychological tinge*. Increasingly, the emphasis in advertising has switched from providing *factual* information to symbolic connotations of commodities, since the crucial cultural premise of advertising is that the material object being sold is never in itself enough. Even those commodities providing for the most mundane necessities of daily life must be imbued with symbolic qualities and culturally endowed meanings via the *magic system* of advertising. In this way and by altering the context in which advertisements appear, things can be made to mean *just about anything* and the *same* things can be endowed with different intended meanings for different individuals and groups of people, thereby offering mass produced visions of individualism. Before advertising is done, market research institutions need to know and describe the target group to exactly plan and implement the advertising campaign and to achieve the best possible results. A whole array of sciences directly deals with advertising and marketing or is used to improve its effects. Focus groups, psychologists and cultural anthropologists are de rigueur in marketing research. Vast amounts of data on persons and their shopping habits are collected, accumulated, aggregated and analysed with the aid of credit cards, bonus cards, raffles and Internet surveying. With increasing accuracy, this supplies a picture of behaviour, wishes and weaknesses of certain sections of a population with which advertisement can be employed more selectively and effectively. The influence of advertisers is not only with regard to news or information on their own products or services but it also expands to articles or shows not directly linked to them. In order to secure their advertising revenue, the media have to create the best possible *advertising environment*. Television shows are created to accommodate the needs of advertising (like splitting them up in suitable sections). Their dramaturgy is typically designed to end in suspense or leave an unanswered question in order to keep the viewer attached. The movie system, which was once outside the direct influence of the broader marketing system, is now fully integrated into it through the strategies of licensing, tie-ins and product placements—to aid in the selling of the immense collection of commodities. The prime function of many Hollywood films today is to aid in the selling of the immense collection of commodities. Performances, exhibitions, shows, concerts, conventions and most other events too can hardly take place without sponsoring. Artists are graded and paid according to their art's value for commercial purposes. Corporations promote renowned artists, thereby getting exclusive rights in global advertising campaigns. Advertising itself is extensively considered to be a contribution to culture. It is integrated into fashion. On many pieces of clothing, the company logo is the only design or is an important part of it. There is only a little extent left outside the consumption economy, in which culture and art can develop independently and where alternative values can be expressed. Every visually perceptible place has the potential for advertising. Especially urban areas with their structures and also landscapes in sight of thoroughfares are more and more turning into media of advertisements. Signs, posters, billboards and flags have become decisive factors in the urban appearance and their numbers are still on the rise. Outdoor advertising has become unavoidable. Traditional billboards and transit shelters have cleared the way for more pervasive methods such as wrapped vehicles, sides of buildings, electronic signs, kiosks, taxis, posters, sides of buses and so and so forth. Digital technologies are used on buildings to sport *urban wall displays*. In urban areas, commercial content is placed at our sight and in our consciousness every moment we are in public space. Over time, this domination of the surroundings has become the *natural* state. Through long-term commercial saturation, it has been implicitly understood by the public that advertising has the right to own, occupy and control every inch of available space. The steady normalization of invasive advertising dulls the public's perception of their surroundings, re-inforcing a general attitude of powerlessness towards creativity and change. Thus, a cycle develops enabling advertisers to slow-ly and consistently increase the saturation of advertising with little or no public outcry. The massive optical orientation to-wards advertising changes the function of public spaces which are utilized by brands. Urban landmarks are turned into trade-marks. The highest pressure is exerted on renowned and highly frequented public spaces which are also important for the iden-tity of a city. Urban spaces are considered public commodities and in this capacity they are subject to *aesthetical environment protection*, mainly through building regulations, heritage pro-tection and landscape protection. These spaces are peppered with billboards and signs; they are remodelled into media of ad-vertising. According to advertising critics like Sut Jhally, it is not surprising that something this central, and so much being ex-pended on it, should become an important presence in social life. Indeed, commercial interests, with intent on maximizing the consumption of the immense collection of commodities, have colonized more and more spaces of our culture. For in-stance, almost the entire media system (television and print) has been developed as a delivery system for marketers and its prime function is to produce audiences for sale to advertisers. Both the advertisements it carries and the editorial matter that acts as a support for it, celebrate the consumer society. According to crit-ics, the total commercialization of all fields of society, the priva-tization of public space, the acceleration of consumption and waste of resources including the negative influence on lifestyles and on the environment has not been noticed to the necessary extent. The hyper-commercialization of culture is recognized and roundly detested by public. The men and women involved in advertising lend their intellect, voices as well as their artis-tic skills to purposes which shatter and ultimately destroy the confidence in the existence of meaningful purposes of hu-man activity and respect for the integrity of man. The struggle against advertising is, therefore, essential if we are to overcome the pervasive alienation from all genuine human needs that cur-rently play such a corrosive role in the present society. Advertis-ing may seem at times to be an almost trivial if omnipresent as-pect of our economic system. *Subvertising*, culture jamming and

adbusting have become established terms in the anti-advertis-
ing community. Critics like Naomi Klein and Noam Chomsky
have criticized the complete occupation of public spaces,
surfaces, the airspace, the media, schools, etc., and the constant
exposure of almost all senses to advertising messages, an invasion of privacy. Mostly, consumers are unaware that they themselves to some extent bear the cost of advertising in the price
paid for the product. Clutter of ads is to be strictly avoided. Advertising clutter refers to the proliferation of advertising that
produces excessive competition for viewer attention, to the
point that individual messages lose impact and viewers abandon the adverts (via fast-forwarding, changing channels, quit-
ting viewing, etc.), thereby reducing the effect of any particular
advertisement. Ad clutter is perhaps the most potentially vexing
problem that advertisers and networks face. Commodity
aesthetics involve the promise of happiness engineered by advertisers through the consumption of images which appeal to
human needs and sensuality.

India is known for its highly traditional culture, where communities live according to the rules set by generations. However,
within these behavioural patterns, there exists an aspiration to
be modern and cosmopolitan in outlook and is the image which
advertising in India tends to depict consumers as. Media that
allows for segmentation (like a regional television channel or
a religious channel) does have advertising with cultural cues.
Along with this are festivals in every state of the nation, usually
celebrated together as symbols of social cohesion and solidarity.
However, such festivals, like Onam in Kerala, get celebrated by
all communities, although having Hindu roots. The influence of
the rituals of religion becomes a strong cultural force, influencing Indian markets and the visual impact of advertising. Hindu
festivals like Diwali and Dussehra, thus, become important
in a multireligious context like that of India. Symbols like the
marriage chain (*mangalsutra*), red vermilion powder (*kumkum*)
on the parting line of a married woman's hair and dot on the
forehead (*sindoor*/*bindi*) all symbolize a married woman. Advertising uses these appeals. A man applying the red vermilion on
a woman's parting of hair on the day of wedding, symbolizing
protection—is used smartly by ICICI prudential life insurance,
with *we cover you at every step*. The ads have models using In-

dian style of dressing like the sari for women or the traditional Indian male attire (like the dhoti). This is really not surprising, since Western clothing is becoming more popular in India, especially in the metropolitan milieu. Western clothing has come to represent *new modern* attire, and since advertising tends to appeal to the aspirations of consumers (their contemporaneity), the advertisements tend to have the models dressed in Western clothing. Film celebrities have high fan following and are commonly used in Indian advertising. The viewers have a *prestige bias* that makes them emulate those they view as prominent and influential. Film celebrities, as depicted in the ads, are often not what the average Indian consumer is like—celebrities being usually fair in complexion, most Indians on the other hand are shades of brown. The lifestyle depicted in ads (like polo, sailing, mountain climbing) is often not understood by many, and overall the Western looks depicted in the adverts are not usually what most Indians look like. However, the Bollywood world of magic is a means of escapism from relatively difficult living conditions and plays a key role in making consumers feel that this is a culture which they aspire. The concept of family in India is not limited to the nuclear family, but includes uncles, aunts, cousins and the extended family. The joint family is also popularly depicted in Indian cinema, television and advertising to depict the melodrama of members all living together under one roof. Parents are given importance in the Indian culture. MasterCard credit card had a famous advertisement in their global 'Priceless' campaign of a son gifting a vacation to his parents. Raymond's suiting shows a mother stressed out because of her grown-up son going away from her as he has got a job abroad, but becomes happy on seeing that her son has organized her travel papers to accompany him. This would mean a *Mama's boy* in many cultures, but not in India. He becomes a complete man—where it becomes a part of Raymond's very famous *Complete Man* advertising campaign that has run for over decades. Family is, therefore, an important appeal in Indian advertising. With the boom in Information Technology and in mobile phone usage, the touch of technology plays a key role in Indian lifestyle. Advertisements of high-technology products like computers and mobile phones tend to visually depict the product details. Consequently, the appeal of technology is being used in advertisements, especially in high involvement rational products. India is emerging as one of the largest consumer markets in the world, with a sizable and educated middle class that continues to grow affluent and demands Western-style consumer and durable goods. Changes in economic landscape in India have also resulted in changes in the cultural and social landscape. As Indians embrace Western lifestyles, concerns have been expressed about transferring predominantly Western ideologies and social conventions through advertising and other modes to India (Schwartz, 2003). Common concerns about the Western influence pertain to a promotion of excessive consumerism, overemphasis on the self as opposed to the common societal good, issues pertaining to morality and gender stereotyping.

The concept of adaptation versus standardization is one of the most common concepts discussed in international marketing, with some arguing that products and services should be adapted to meet the needs of foreign markets, and others arguing that in an increasing global world, the need to adapt is becoming less important. Others have tended to argue that the degree to which a company might adapt a product or service depends on a variety of factors including the nature of the product (or service), the markets being targeted and the level of interaction between the foreign market and the home market. Despite the considerable level of research on this issue, there remains a high level of debate and argument about this important yet troublesome concept. Global marketers need to understand consumer attitudes in different cultures and countries in order to craft effective marketing strategies. It is well documented that attitudes towards advertising influence consumer exposure and attention to advertisements. Understanding maternal communication patterns and media-related attitudes and behaviours is important for advertisers who are interested in reaching out to both adult and young viewers. This area has received considerable attention in both academic and practitioner research, particularly in the Western world, but few studies have been conducted in developing countries like India. India is a country with diverse cultures and many languages. Advertising is usually created in English or Hindi or in the regional language where the advertisement is produced. These advertisements are usually translated in 12–16 languages and sometimes in dialects (especially in rural communications). When *Hinglish* is used in advertisements, there tends to be a greater local flavour in the English communications, and the message becomes more appealing. Advertising is a marketing phenomenon which has major social implications and influences our wants, beliefs and values. It has the potential of political power and, thus, may affect rules of the market. Advertisers keep experimenting with a wide array of solutions, many of which have been around since the advent of television broadcasting. The politics of linguistic transmission has now evolved into a politics of cultural transmission in which translators, and translations, perpetuate or contest values and ideas that represent particular cultures. Hence, there arises the necessity of positioning translation within cultural studies. In order to facilitate global advertising, advertising agencies have begun to conduct cross-cultural research studies of consumer behaviour. Through advertising, the producer informs the innovators that the product exists and makes claims about its quality. There comes up the question as to what extent a company should adapt a luxury product or service to meet the local conditions. The design of a firm's symbols and icons through the colour and form and often the appearance of specific words and/or numbers act as indicators (even in localized adverts) for people. While some core elements of foreign products need to be promoted on the basis of their degree of Westerness, it is also important to modify promotional images and messages to build a link or a bridge between the product and local consumers. The level and degree of promotional adaptation may be quite discrete but nonetheless important. Visual aspects influence perceived similarity of advertising. But not all types of pictures are universal in their meanings and some may not be an effective means of communicating with the non-literate market segments. Therefore, though pictures are more universal than words, international marketers still have to do a research of their markets before attempting to communicate with them through pictures. It is necessary for advertisers to first decide on the image or symbolic meanings that are important to the target consumers for a certain product, service or company. As Chandler puts it, 'Signs take the form of words, images sounds, odours, flavours, acts or objects but such things have no intrinsic meaning and become signs only when we invest them with meaning' (2002:17). Anything can be a sign 'as long as someone interprets it as *signifying* something—referring to or *standing for* something other than itself' (Chandler, 2002:17). No sign makes sense on its own but only in relation to other signs. A sign has no *absolute* value independent of its context. While signification clearly depends on the relation between the two parts of the sign, the value of a sign is determined by the relationships between the sign and other signs within the system as a whole (Sassure, 1983:112–113). The relationship between intertextuality and adverts is also significant.

> In order to make sense of many contemporary advertisements... one needs to be familiar with others in the same series. Expectations are established by reference to one's previous experience in looking at related advertisements. Modern visual ads make extensive use of intertextuality in this way. Sometimes there is no direct reference to the product at all. Instant identification of the appropriate interpretative code serves to identify the interpreter of the advertisement as a member of an exclusive club, with each act of interpretation serving to renew one's membership. (Sassure, 1983:200)

Subsequently, which celebrity best projects the desired meaning or image is to be located and engaged. Then, an appropriate ad campaign must be designed in such a way that it captures the image in the product or service and transfers it to the consumer. How an advertising message is presented is critically important in determining its effectiveness. According to Grant McCracken (1989), the effectiveness of the celebrity endorser depends on culturally acquired meanings that a consumer brings to the endorsement process (Bootwala, 2007:108).

This book has its origin in a project funded by the UGC and deals with advertising, its socio-cultural implications as well as the localization process implied or seen in television advertisements (on which the book focuses). The book also discusses the manner in which the local market is approached (through localization) by adverts to woo the consumer and increase sales, the various ways in which localization is achieved, and the visual as well as linguistic *translation* that localized adverts involve. It maps out the process of localization as well as the problems of *translation* (visual/linguistic) involved. The transfer of advertising campaigns across the globe is a process that does not proceed smoothly, continuously and incrementally. As a social construction, advertisement *translation* calls for a socio-cultural–linguistic approach.

As its focal point, the book has television advertising and the process of localization that advertisements go through to reach the varied, large multitudes. Chapter 1 deals with the impact of advertising. Within the context of consumer culture, advertising can be seen to shape and reflect social reality by drawing upon patterns of meaning within the social and cultural world to construct symbolic associations for consumer goods. Chapter 2 is on advertising and advertisements and refers to how advertising manipulates people's needs and lures consumers to buy products and consume certain products that depict a way of life. People seek various products from which they derive actual gratifications. Market research measures provide insight into what is working in an advert in any country or region. Consumer sovereignty exerts tremendous influence over the market. They no longer absorb standardized products in a passive way. Chapter 3 deals with the different aspects of adverts—semiotics, ecology and landscape, gender issues in advertising, issues around postcoloniality, corporate social responsibility and translation/localization. Issues of cultural transmission implicated in advertising are taken up in Chapter 4, which deals with the variable codes in television advertising. Language is a major vehicle of socio-cultural interaction. Translation plays an indispensable role in transferring messages across languages and cultural barriers. Those who import texts from one culture to another through translation perform an act of transfer. The *texts* become an integral part of the home repertoire of the target culture. Advertisement (television) translation (linguistic/graphic from one culture to another) also addresses a new audience and cultural situation, and involves a *rewriting* of an original *text*. The whole visual presentation has to be *translated* to adapt to the target culture addressed. As its target audience, advertising has (in different times/epochs) people belonging to different cultures. The historicity as well as the culture is required while creating an advert. Chapter 5 takes up issues of *translation*/localization in the analysis of television advertisements. Advertisement *translation* (visual/aural/linguistic) plays a significant role in business communications and international marketing. Communication becomes effective in a *foreign* environment only when the message has been translated. The responsibility for achieving the goals in a competitive market, to a large extent, rests with the translator/localizer. Chapter 6 analyses television advertisements from different segments (appearing on various Indian television channels, in different languages and visually diverse at times), their *translation* into different cultures. Chapters 7 and 8 provide a glimpse of the new/social media and issues of localization therein. Chapter 9 provides an overview of the localization process involved in advertising.

The World of Advertising

*The personality of a product is an amalgam of many things—
its name, its packaging, its price, the style of its advertising
and above all, the nature of the product itself.*

—*David Ogilvy*

Advertising is defined as messages, paid for by those who send
them, intended to inform or influence people who receive
them. It is any paid form of non-personal communication, presentation and promotion of ideas, goods or services by an identified sponsor. These images permeate society, and they consist
of text and image(s) organized in a manner that strengthens
the interplay between the verbal and non-verbal elements.
Advertisements may be commercial (consumer, trade and corporate advertising), non-commercial (government or charity
advertising) or for socially relevant causes (promotion of family planning, fighting social evil, polio vaccine, save petrol, etc.).
Through television, newspaper, popular magazines and radio
commercials and in the form of hoardings and posters, when
on the streets or while travelling, companies vie hard to capture an increasingly larger market share. Advertising through

powerful media is an effective and legitimate tool to rally public opinion. It gives product information, helps public to make a free choice and creates a competitive environment essential for the improvement of the quality of the products which are to be made available at fair prices. Advertisements reflect the value system of a society and offer freedom of choice (to make an intelligent choice) to consumers from among the products available. The advertiser has to minutely know the attitudes, beliefs and motives of the target audience. As a basic tool of marketing, it increases competition and kindles demand. The advertiser reaches public through the media, and the media depend on advertising for survival. Advertising has an acknowledged dialogical and intertextual structure which draws upon a multitude of cultural codes, ideologies and discourses to construct meaning. Within the context of consumer culture, advertising can be seen to shape and reflect social reality, by drawing upon patterns of meaning within the social and cultural world to construct symbolic associations for consumer goods. These commodity discourses become ingrained within popular psyche and shape consumer experiences of social reality. Advertisements have become an integrated part of the popular culture (which they even parody). By drawing upon socially situated codes, myths, cultural discourses and national ideologies to develop resonant associations for consumer goods, advertisements both constitute prevailing ideologies and construct new mythologies and ideologies for commodities through these dialogical and intertextual relationships (Sherry, 1987:441–461).

According to James Webb Young (2007:5), advertising works in five ways:

1. By making the product/service familiar
2. By reminding people about the product/service
3. By spreading news about the product/service
4. By overcoming inertia in potential customers
5. By adding value to a product that is not in the product

Modern advertising is said to have developed in the late 19th and early 20th centuries. Egyptians used papyrus to make sales messages and wall posters. Commercial messages and political campaign displays have been found in the ruins of Pompeii and ancient Arabia. Advertising on papyrus was common in ancient

Greece and Rome. A wall or rock painting for commercial advertising is another manifestation of an ancient advertising form. Out-of-home advertising and billboards are considered the oldest forms of advertising. Images associated with the trade gradually came to be used along with signs. Street callers (town criers) announced the sellers' whereabouts for the convenience of the customers. As reading and printing developed, advertising expanded to include handbills. In the 17th century, in England, advertisements started to appear in weekly newspapers. False advertising and so-called *quack* advertisements became a problem, which ushered in the regulation of advertising content. As the economy expanded during the 19th century, advertising grew alongside. The 1960s saw advertising transform into a modern approach in which creativity was allowed to shine, producing unexpected messages that made advertisements more tempting to consumers' eyes. It ushered in the era of modern advertising by promoting a *position* or *unique selling proposition* designed to associate each brand with a specific idea in the reader or viewer's mind. The growing popularity of the Internet drew audiences away from advertisers populating just the television platform. Marketing through the Internet opened new frontiers for advertisers. At the turn of the 21st century, a number of websites (including the search engine Google) started a change in online advertising by emphasizing contextually relevant, unobtrusive adverts intended to help, rather than inundate, users. This led to a plethora of similar efforts and an increasing trend of interactive advertising. Communication has been a part of the selling process ever since there has been the need to exchange goods from one person to another. The development of technology and research has led to increased sophistication in advertising. The recorded history of advertising covers a long span including the modern satellite and Internet age.

The advertisements in the pre-independence era in India were mainly addressed to the affluent class. The situation changed after independence as advertisers started focusing on the middle class. The rapid strides in technology have had their impact on advertising. A single commercial uses a combination of communicating mediums—the visual and the verbal. Both these should convey the same unique message and connotative meaning to build a complete communication image. Advertising in India is a highly competitive business. Advertising agencies take care of consumer needs and provide creative designs with concept and ideas. An Indian advertising agency has to take a lot of factors into consideration, taking care not to cross the line of discomfort for the consumers. There has been a long tradition of advertising in India since the first newspapers published in India in the 19th century carried advertising. The first advertising agency was established in 1905, B. Dattaram and Company, followed by the India Advertising Company in 1907, the Calcutta Advertising Agency in 1909, S.H Bensen in 1928, Hindustan Thomson Associates in 1929, Lintas in 1939 and McCann Erikson in 1956. The first advertising appeared on the state television in 1976. In the mid-1990s, there was a massive expansion in advertising in India, and the increased competition among multinationals made big budgets a necessity. The profile of advertising agencies in India changed dramatically during this period. Advertising industry has expanded rapidly in recent years; the growth being driven by television advertising, especially satellite channels. The period also witnessed increased government spending on advertising in areas such as tourist promotion, AIDS awareness and army recruitment. The usage of different advertising media has changed in recent decades, largely due to changes in technology. Some of the largest advertisers in India are exploring different strategies and media to attempt to enter the rural consumer market. Media alternatives such as video vans and point of purchase video display were an attempt by major advertisers to communicate to rural purchasers in their local language, rather than Hindi and English, the main languages on television.

There have been significant changes in recent years, and no longer does successful advertising focus on product benefits only, but also works through values and value change. In the advertisement planning phase, the marketing group draws out a plan for advertising based on a well-defined marketing strategy and analysis. They conduct product targeting analysis and customer targeting analysis. Based on the results of these analyses, they come out with a plan that specifies the decisions related to the media and publisher selection, presentation approach, targeted audience, posting schedule and advertisement content. An advertisement design allows a designer to plan and implement the necessary stages such as designing, creation and modifications for a specific advertisement. Advertisers do conduct campaigning for each advertisement that features in an advertisement campaign. They interact with selected publishers to find the desirable advertisement spaces and available schedules. Then, they negotiate with publishers to reach a business deal. As a result of their negotiation, an advertising contract is generated for each schedule ad space. It specifies the advertisement space selection, schedule, payment method and cost. Later, the created ads are delivered to publishers for posting in case of online adverts. During advertisement measurement, the collected performance data of advertisements are analysed and evaluated to check their problems and effectiveness to online viewers. After ad posting, advertisers make the payment transactions to publishers for the posted advertisements based on a contracted payment method. For the last many years, companies have relied on traditional advertising in the form of catchy jingles, television commercials, billboards and print ads in newspapers, magazines and direct mails. The technique in advertising is to interrupt a radio listener, television viewer or magazine reader with an attention-grabbing ad that compels the consumer to buy the company's product or at least have the product closer to the forefront of his or her mind the next time the individual is making a decision to buy a product. In most instances, advertising is acceptable to the consumer. Most people do not mind seeing ads while watching television, listening to the radio or reading magazines—or at least they understand that these ads are necessary in order to receive the content they are seeing, reading or hearing. While some technologies challenge advertisers to come up with new methods of advertising, others (such as Internet, television) require users to watch a 30-second advertisement prior to the start of a show. The rise of new media has increased communication between people all over the world and the Internet. It has allowed people to express themselves through blogs, websites, pictures and other user-generated media. As a result of the evolution of new media technologies, globalization transpires.

The Illusion Industry: Advertising on Television

The study of advertising brings together many of the key social and political concerns of our times, such as new capitalism, globalization, overconsumption, cultural and individual identities, communication revolution and so on. It provides insight into the ideologies and values of contemporary societies. Cultural values reflected in advertising messages are considered to have a powerful influence not only on consumers' product choices but also on their motivations and lifestyles. Advertising's creative use of language makes it a particularly rich site for language and discourse analysis. Operating in all media and exploiting the interaction among word, sound and image, it provides a key location for studies of multimodal communication. Ever since the intensification of advertising in the 1950s, leading scholars have analysed its use of language. Though user habits are rapidly changing, television advertising has long been considered the most effective mass-market advertising format.

A substantial literature has developed that examines and questions the role of mass communications and advertising within the institutional structures of contemporary capitalist societies. In contrast to media studies that focus on how to use mass communications within the given political economic order to influence audiences and sell products, critical research has addressed the social and cultural effects of mass communications and their role in perpetuating an unjust social order. One facet of critical analysis of advertising has examined the content and structure of advertisements for their distorted communications and ideological impact. Employing semiotics and/or content analysis, numerous critical studies working at the micro level have examined how advertising's mass communications persuade or manipulate consumers. By contrast, others present broader historical analysis that locates advertising and mass communications within the history of contemporary capitalism and examines their impact on the larger social and political economic structure. Studies such as these have probed how advertising and mass media have contributed to the development and reproduction of an undemocratic social order by concentrating enormous economic and cultural power in the hands of a few corporations and individuals. These numerous facets of critical media studies have generated numerous insights into the conservative social functions and ideological effects of mass communications that were ignored by those which tended to focus on the effects that mass communication had in carrying out certain specific tasks. Very rarely, it has been pointed out, have critical studies of advertising and mass communications adequately articulated the linkage between the macro political economic structure of mass media and the micro mass communication forms and techniques so as to reveal both the socio-economic functions of advertising and the ways that advertisements actually shape and influence perception and behaviour which reproduce the existing social system. The failure to clearly and comprehensively articulate this linkage has often generated an implicit conspiracy theory suggesting that a few elites in control of the mass media consciously conspire to manipulate culture and consciousness. This deficiency has plagued critical analyses of advertising and communications which have generally failed to explain how mass communications, in general, and advertising, in particular, can exercise the power and impact that critical theorists suggest. Several recent studies on advertising take an explicitly critical sociological orientation towards advertising as a means of reproducing the existing capitalist society. This literature argues that not only does advertising carry out crucial economic functions in managing consumer demand and in aiding capital accumulation, but it also helps produce the sort of ideological ambience required by consumer capitalism, thus linking, more or less successfully, macro- and micro-analysis. It provides illuminating historical framing of the history of advertising and the consumer society as well as provides sociological analysis, cultural and ideological critique and political proposals to regulate or curtail advertising in contemporary capitalist societies.

Adverts inform, persuade or may do both. John Wilmshurst (1978:12–13) speaks about the different views regarding advertising:

> Galbraith's view that advertising creates or changes the tastes, reflects the psychological theory of behaviourism. Kirzner's view that advertising reveals opportunities for satisfying tastes is consistent with Gestalt psychology. Shackle's emphasis on imagination is closer to the psychoanalytic view, and suggests a role for advertising in stimulating the creation of opportunities for satisfying tastes. For both Shackle and Kirzner, but in contrast to Galbraith, advertising certainly affects behavior, but it does not *determine* it. It is an *aid* to choice rather than a substitute for it. The consumer is an *active* rather than *passive* participant.

The medium of advertising is a vehicle for carrying the sales message of an advertiser to a prospective buyer. The advertising techniques used to promote commercial goods and services can also be used to inform, educate and motivate the public about non-commercial issues, such as HIV/AIDS, political ideology, energy conservation and deforestation. Virtually any medium can be used for advertising. The array of commercial advertising media includes magazines, newspapers, radio, cinema and television adverts, text messages, direct mails, banners, mobile telephone screens, wall paintings, billboards, printed flyers, colourful posters, shopping carts, web pop ups, skywriting, bus stop benches, human billboards, town criers, sides of buses/vehicles, subway platforms and trains, air terminals, in-flight advertisements on seatback tray tables or overhead storage bins, highway advertising, taxicab doors, roof mounts and passenger screens, musical stage shows, elastic bands, doors of bathroom stalls, stickers in supermarkets, shopping cart handles, the opening section of streaming audio and video, and the backs of event tickets and supermarket receipts. Any place an identified sponsor pays to deliver or transmit its message through a medium is advertising. Advertising agencies undertake the task of planning and executing the advertisement programmes on behalf of their clients. It helps to achieve the marketing objectives and marketing plans of an organization. An organization has to identify the segments of the market it intends to serve, and the product should be with a suitable promotion strategy. The idea of the high quality and prestige of the product is reinforced when a firm introduces it by associating it with prestigious people, places and events. Right advertising is essential. It is a creative/ business approach. A creative mind is essential for the effectiveness of advertising.

The narrative structure of an advertisement provides the opportunity to show a change of state (a *before* and *after* effect) and how the product brings this about. A synecdochic or metonymic relation operates—the product being represented as an intrinsic part of the characteristic and elegant lifestyle that the advertisement typically portrays. Though advertisements are criticized of creating false needs, aspirations and wants, they reflect the essence of the social structure and cultural identity of a country or specific society. Narrative advertisements influence and perpetuate ideas and values and also create needs that are indispensible to a specific economy. They have to raise the product's selling point within the limits of a temporally and spatially restricted storyline. It relies on the sender (teller), a message (tale) and an addressee. Advertising is vital in India and, like anywhere else, creates demand for consumer goods. It sustains competitive activity, boosts demand and, used rightly, facilitates the consumer's choice of the right product. Advertisements should establish a brand image and conform to and respect the prevailing norms of ethics and morality. The advertiser is to have a fair knowledge of his product, consumer habits, behaviour as well as market. The reach of the advertisement, the use of colours and the positioning are important. The advertisement is not to wear out, nor the audience to get bored.

Television is an all pervading medium to reach the people with purchasing power. Michel Foucault asserts that television and cinema act as effective means of reprogramming memory in which 'people are shown not what they were but what they must remember having been'. He further points out, 'Since memory is a very important factor in struggle ... if one controls people's memory, one controls their dynamism' (Foucault, 1996:92). Theorists have perceived television as a liberating medium, with vast educational and innovative potential. Contemporary societies are about 'creating an image, refining a *look*, presenting a *style*' (Abercrombie, 1996:38), and this preoccupation with surface appearance is closely linked with consumerism as people are encouraged to buy an image (Jameson's notion of *depthlessness*, a superficial culture reflected in and promoted by television). As Baudrillard puts it, the modern consumer '...sets in place a whole array of sham objects, of characteristic signs of happiness, and then waits ... for happiness to alight' (Lane, 2003:70). Television adverts show people whose lives are made happier because of the expensive consumer items they possess. It proves the efficaciousness of the consumer object. Baudrillard argues that the media does not present us with reality, '...but the *dizzying whirl of reality*' (Lane, 2003:72). The media is the site to play out one's desires, protecting him/her at the same time from confronting the everyday realities of a dangerous and problematic world. The individual attempts to find personal satisfaction in the consumption of goods. In the postmodern world, one is thus involved in the empty and meaningless play of the media. Human beings are expected to be passive consumers, subjected to mass advertising, especially to advertising and whole systems of consumption. Baudrillard also speaks about (a) the first-order simulation, where the representation of the real is obviously just an artificial representation (a painting, a map); (b) the second-order simulation, which blurs the boundaries between reality and representation and (c) the third-order simulation, which produces a hyperreal or a real without origin or reality (Lane, 2003:86). John Fiske in his *Television Culture* attempts to analyse the viewer's interpretation. Although acknowledging that television produces an ideologically dominated society, Fiske's analyses of television elaborates a position from which the *subordinate decoders* (the viewers who are supposedly just watching passively) can produce resistant readings and refuse ideological manipulation (as a sort of *resisting reader*)—how the viewer manages to negotiate the conflicting images and ideologies without becoming a mere puppet of the televisual medium. It, thus, seeks to move away from how texts position the viewer towards what viewer does with the text. He perceives television as a contradictory medium, a state which allows it to promote the hegemonic ideology while at the same time promoting an oppositional and different cultural value for the marginalized sections of society. Television is a site where conflicting power interests coalesce—'Far from being the agent of the dominant classes, it is the prime site where the dominant have to recognize the insecurity of their power, and where they have to encourage cultural difference with all the threat to their own position that this implies' (Lane, 2003:326). For those like Arthur Kroker and David Cook, television is synonymous with postmodernity—'In postmodernist culture, it is not TV as a mirror of society, but just the reverse: *it's society as a mirror of television*' (Kroker, 1988:269).

Companies may opt for in-house advertising or delegate the job to an advertising agency. The message has to be expressed clearly. As Russel Colley puts it:

All commercial communications that weigh on the ultimate object of a sale must carry a prospect through four levels of understanding.

The prospect must first be *aware* of the existence of a brand or company. He must have a *comprehension* of what the product is and what it will do for him. He must arrive at a mental suspicion or *conviction* to buy the product. Finally, he must stir himself to *action*. (Wilmshurst, 1978:200)

The Defining Advertising Goals for Measured Advertising Results (DAGMAR) recognizes the need to take account of the recipients' reactions and does not deal purely with the message as such yielding an automatic response. Appropriate advertising approach is necessary for different countries:

First comes the obvious differences of language, culture pattern, distribution methods, advertising media and the like. Second there is a difference that is not so obvious and therefore much more important to come to terms with—...the 'self-reference criteria' [i.e. seeing things from a particular view point, according to our own cultural background]. (Wilmshurst, 1978:200)

Creative talent, visualization, tone and layout are important in advertising. It should command attention, sustain interest, be memorable and highlight product features. Memorable words and expressions which draw mental pictures, music and sound mixed with jingles and the product features have to be highlighted. The background, caption, border, heading, slogan and text form a part of the layout which is to attract, arouse interest and conviction. Positioning is important to emphasize the salient point of an advert. The different units of the layout should be so placed as to create an impression of completeness. Pictorial devices achieve more effect than words to set background and atmosphere. Illustrations quickly gain attention and they may be symbolic, a comparison and contrast, feature oriented, use oriented, the product shown alone or in-use, and product magnified in detail or compressed. Casting the product against a proper background facilitates the visual communication process to boost marketing. Jingles (short songs that convey the advertising messages) are either original tunes or adaptations of popular tunes. Television adverts feature catchy jingles or catch phrases that generate sustained appeal, which may remain in the minds of viewers long after the span of the advertising campaign. In addition to reaching the audience with sound and motion, television adverts differ from print advertisements in that they are structured in time (as opposed to being structured in space). Colour is an important visual element to create stunning visual impact. Culture, personal factors, changing trends, opinion, family, society and lifestyle are some other influencing factors. Advertising is to speak not only in the language of each country (at times particular region of the country) but also in the idiom and thought patterns within which the people of the country express themselves. Use of visuals varies. The products, services, documentation, customer support, maintenance procedures and marketing of a company must reflect the needs of the local market in terms of culture, language and business requirements. Television shows a significant advantage over other media as it combines sight and sound. An advertising concept combines the video and the audio. The words describe what the basic idea is and the visuals reinforce what the words say, and render it more powerful. Television can produce a variety of appeals and executions not possible with print. The video consists of the sight or the visual, and the audio of spoken words, music or other sounds/special sound effects and voices. The two components must work in a synergistic manner to produce the desired impact. The visual elements should be successful in attracting the viewer's attention and communicating the desired image, idea or message. The audio/voice could include two or more persons appearing in the commercial who are involved in a conversation or it could be a single individual appearing as a spokesperson or it could be a voice-over (the message is delivered or the action sequence is described by an unseen presenter). Jingles and catchy songs, built around the product or service, that communicate the advertising theme and messages are the other important musical elements of commercials. A creative advertising concept captures attention as well as gets across the main selling point and the brand name. The advert itself has a variety of elements: headlines, illustrations, copy, logotype, a sub-headline as well as several other illustrations of varying importance. An advertisement slogan sums up the theme, the essence of the product position and delivers an easily remembered message in few words etched in every consumer's mind. Used more often on television and radio than in print, slogans are combined with a catchy tune to make a jingle. Music is the cutting edge that helps to etch a commercial into long-term memory.

The textual and visual level of advertising communication (the psychological as well as the physical properties of products to prospective buyers) presents an intelligent processing of an arrangement of sign. Advertising texts are remembered easily and are more evocative than explicit. The text is generated as a fusion among a benefit, an offered value and a sensory fact or promise highlighted. A link exists between the text and the advertising image. Visibility is important—encompassing the specific typefaces for the logo and slogan, specific colours and textures for the letters, different orientation of text within the page. The focal point is visual which is highlighted by the textual, non-verbal (signified by movement) and the passing time. The contents of advertisement communication are reflective of the prevailing attitudes and values of society. Mass media not only reflect the values of society but also influence them. Commercial advertisers seek to generate increased consumption of their products or services through branding, which involves the repetition of an image or product name in an effort to associate related qualities with the brand in the minds of consumers. The television commercial is generally considered the most effective mass-market advertising format. Infomercials describe, display and often demonstrate products and their features, and commonly have testimonials from consumers and industry professionals. With the dawn of the Internet arose many new advertising opportunities. Mobile advertising, advergaming, email advertisements (often being a form of spam) and social network advertising have emerged in the present century. Significant trends like the rise of entertaining advertising and the growing importance of the niche market using niche or targeted adverts indicate the future of advertising. Advertising on consumer-generated media is termed as consumer-generated advertising. They are sponsored content on blogs, wikis, forums, social networking websites and individual websites. This sponsored content is also known as sponsored posts, paid posts or sponsored reviews. The content includes links that point to the home page or specific product pages of the website of the sponsor. A communal marketing (used to refer to a marketing practice that incorporates public involvement in the development of an advertising/marketing campaign) campaign invites consumers to share their ideas or express their articulation of what the brand means to them through their own personal stories, with the use of print media, film or audio. The result of this is showcased, often in a cross-media campaign, to invite the extended community of like-minded individuals to share the results, thereby creating a communal bond between the brand champions as advertisers and other individuals who have a natural affinity with what the brand has to offer. The result provides the brand with a way to create a deeper connection with their core market, while also opening up new pathways to extend the relationship to new customers. Consumer-generated marketing is different from viral marketing or word-of-mouth advertising; however, it achieves a high level of publicity within high-relevance communities. The very act of reaching out to consumers to invite them as co-collaborators and co-creatives is a fundamental component of the marketing campaign. The construct naturally lends itself to other consumer-marketing activities, such as communal branding and communal research. Any time a brand reaches out to its audience to invite them to become co-collaborators in the development of an advertising campaign, they are participating in a *communal branding* effort. Whenever marketing decisions are the result of communing with the brand's audience to help drive the development of a campaign, they are engaging in *communal research*. The practice of consumer-generated marketing has been in use for several years with the emergence of communal forms of information sharing including weblogs, online message boards, podcasts, interactive broadband television and other new media that has been adopted by consumers at the grass-root level to establish community forums for discussing their customer experiences.

Just as Horkheimer and Adorno discussed *the culture industry*, and Enzensberger *the consciousness industry*, Wolfgang Fritz Haug (1986:121–122) criticizes the *illusion industry*, or *distraction industry*, for being tools of domination which exploit people's needs and manipulate them into accepting consumer capitalism:

> Since the vast majority of people can find no worthwhile goal within the capitalist system, the distraction industry appears to be a good investment for the system as a whole, as well as for competently run private capital. ... With shades and shadows the illusion industry populates the spaces left empty by capitalism, which only socialism can fill with reality.

Haug's critique is grounded in the analysis of the ways in which the capitalist economy uses advertising to maximize profit, and this focus on the fundamental processes of capitalist production separates his analysis from those who criticize only appearances and techniques of advertising and obscure their relation to normal capitalism. Haug argues that what he calls commodity aesthetics shape the values, perceptions and consumer behaviour of individuals in contemporary capitalist societies so as to integrate them into the lifestyles of consumer capitalism. The concept of commodity aesthetics emerges within the problem of realization (i.e., capital accumulation, the realization of surplus value) and the tension between *use-value* and *exchange-value*. The concept describes the ways that aesthetics is integrated into the production, distribution and marketing of commodities. More specifically, commodity aesthetics refers to 'a beauty developed in the service of the realization of exchange value, whereby commodities are designed to stimulate in the onlooker the desire to possess and the impulse to buy' (Haug, 1986:8). In other words, commodity aesthetics uses aesthetics to sell products and consumer capitalism in the form of advertising, packaging, marketing and display. Much like Baudrillard, Haug emphasizes the importance of image and appearance in contemporary society and reveals how they are connected to the sales effort and to the capitalist political economy. A central part of Haug's historical critique of capitalism and analysis of manipulation involves the moulding of sensuality and 'how human need and instinct structures are altered under the impact of a continually changing prospect of satisfaction offered by commodities' (Haug 1986:45). The drive for exchange value propels a concern with the appearance of commodities that culminates in the technocracy of sensuality involving 'the domination over people that is affected through their fascination with technically produced artificial appearances' (Haug 1986:45). This process 'turns the sensual being ... into a dependent variable of the capital valorization process' (Haug, 1986:80). Selling commodities requires a promise of use-value that involves images that appeal to consumer's senses and needs. Moreover, these needs can never be fully satisfied if capital accumulation is to continue. Thus emerges aesthetic innovation, planned obsolescence and fashion, all engineered to keep individuals on the consumption treadmill so essential to continued capital accumulation. 'The appearance always promises more, much more, than it can ever deliver. In this way the illusion deceives' (Haug, 1986:50). The major strength of Haug's critique of advertising is both the rigorous theoretical apparatus with which he conceptualizes advertising within the process of capitalist society and the wealth of concrete detail concerning how advertising, packaging, sales and manufacture of fantasies and illusions actually take place. For Haug, many current analyses of advertising are flawed by assuming that an evil conspiracy on the part of marketers is the cause of advertising excesses. The real cause of commodity aesthetics lies not in individual motivations or conspiracy but is a logical result of an unrestrained economic function (Haug, 1986:108) that has been developing historically, that is, the pressure to maximize capital accumulation or to go out of business. Haug's key insight is that manipulation is less a technique than a historical process, whereby the capitalist system forces corporations to maximize their profits by all means available and to create needs to buy products that individuals do not really need. Against standard critiques which associate advertising with manipulation and the production of *false consciousness* and *false needs*, Haug argues that 'manipulation could only be effective if it *somehow* latched on to the *objective interests* of those being manipulated' (Haug, 1986:6). Following this line of inquiry, he attempts to demonstrate the ways that advertising distorts needs for sensual gratification, human interaction and a sense of self-worth by providing dubious role/gender models, anxieties and fantasies. He claims that advertising and commodity aesthetics take these genuine needs, and through a moulding of sensuality shape human needs so that they 'are now estranged and distorted beyond recognition' (Haug, 1986:6). In contrast to critics such as Vance Packard and Wilson Bryan Key, who suggest that single advertising messages are powerful and manipulative, Haug views manipulation as a more subtle historical process which is all the more insidious because it is less visible at any given moment. Indeed, Packard, Key and those who argue that advertising directly and immediately influences consumer behaviour are assuming the validity of the old *bullet*, or *hypodermic*, theory of communication which claims that communication messages directly and immediately shape thought and behaviour. Haug argues by contrast that advertising is more significant for its long-term effects on thought and behaviour than its short-term impact on consumer behaviour. This position provides a useful corrective to those who dismiss claims concerning the power of advertising simply because there is no conclusive evidence that advertising works immediately and directly to induce consumers to buy a specific product as a specific and ascertainable result of exposure to advertising. There are both interesting similarities and differences between Haug's theory and that of French theorist, Jean Baudrillard. Baudrillard focuses his early works on analysis of the system of objects and signs which constituted the consumer society. Haug's theory of how commodity aesthetics induce individuals to desire or purchase certain products is similar to Baudrillard's theory of how the political economy of the sign helps integrate individuals into the consumer society. Furthermore, Haug's description of the incorporation of aesthetics into advertising, packaging and display runs parallel to Baudrillard's analyses of how the implosion of aesthetics and commodification in contemporary capitalist societies provides an aestheticization of commodities and a commodification of art and aesthetics. This phenomenon is certainly manifest in advertising which employs the most advanced aesthetic techniques to sell commodities and promote consumption as a way of life. Haug's analysis of commodity aesthetics is particularly useful in concretely demonstrating how aesthetics is embodied in the advertising, packaging, production, display and selling of commodities.

Advertising critics such as Sut Jhully place advertising within the larger structure of a market-industrial economy where the institutions of media, industry and advertising converge. In the process, from the origins of the consumer culture and the transition from industrial to consumer society, the communications media and advertising agencies evolved hand-in-hand into the modern advertising industry where advertising is a central institution of the market-industrial economy. There is an increasing trend that involves a shift of emphasis within advertisements away from communicating specific product information towards communicating the social and symbolic uses of products. Jhally expanded the category of information within advertising to include not just functional product information, but social symbolic information as well. It is in this sense that goods function as communicators and satisfiers—they inform and mediate social relations, telling individuals what they must buy to become fashionable, popular and successful while inducing them to buy particular products to reach these goals. However, in the consumer society, commodities are important adjuncts to interpersonal relations because they communicate social information to others. They serve as a projective medium into which we transfer the intricate webs of personal and social interactions. The consumer society has caused a profound transformation in social life involving 'the change in the function of goods from being primarily satisfiers of wants to being primarily communicators of meanings' (Haug 1986:238). Advertising is significant because, in consumer capitalism, individuals depend on it for meaning— a source of social information embedded in commodities that mediate interpersonal relations and personal identity. Advertising should, therefore, be conceived as an important institution in the consumer society because it produces patterned systems of meaning which play a key role in individual socialization and social reproduction. Consequently, the *marketplace* should be seen as a cultural system and not just as a mechanism for moving commodities and money. Furthermore, it is cultural symbolism and images that provide crucial insights into the nature and functions of advertising. The persuasive form of modern advertising indicates how cultural forms of social communication create meanings through non-discursive visual imagery which come to shape consciousness and behaviour subtly by sanctioning some forms of thought and behaviour while delegitimating others. For instance, advertising conveys through its images positive presentations of assertive masculine behaviour and images of well-groomed and fashioned men and women. Advertising presents proper and improper images of behaviour and role models for men and women. The result is a culture where image plays a more important role than linguistic discourse, for while verbal imagery is discursive, visual imagery is non-discursive, emotional, associative, iconic and fictive. Advertising plays a key role in the transition to a new image culture, and thus in the transition from a discursive book/print culture to a figurative media culture. In this media culture, domains of social life ranging from religion to politics fall under the sway of the reign of images. The iconic representation, or persuasive images, have a greater impact in decision-making, effective opinion and behaviour than verbal discourse and can be absorbed without full conscious awareness and without being translatable into explicit verbal formulations. Advertising is a form of social communication which promotes non-communication, or what Habermas calls, systematically distorted communication. Distortions result from techniques that are irrational, illogical and imagistic and that affect individuals subliminally and unconsciously. Advertising promotes commodity fetishism and a fetishized consciousness that invests goods, services and individuals with symbolic properties, associating products with socially desirable traits. In the consumer society, individuals define themselves as consumers and gain fundamental modes of gratification from consumption. Hence, marketers and advertisers generate systems of meaning, prestige and identity by associating their products with certain lifestyles, symbolic values and pleasures.

The growth of the Internet and rapid changes in technology have made the market volatile and changed the ways in which consumers communicate about products. Today's increasingly global business environment requires incorporation of a glocal perspective into all aspects of a company. Most adverts are the product of a process involving research, positioning, media selection and composition of the advertisement. The advertiser must position his product so that the buyer decides to choose the seller's particular product or service, from among similar goods and services. To position the product successfully and to reach the buyer successfully, the advertiser tries to understand the consumer behaviour. How an advertising message is presented is critically important in determining its effectiveness. Celebrity branding is a type of branding, or advertising, in which a celebrity becomes a brand ambassador and uses his or her status in society to promote a product, service or charity, and sometimes also appears as a promotional model. A number of advertisements employ a celebrity spokesperson to endorse a product or brand to the extent that it has become a global phenomenon today. Subsequently, it is to be determined which celebrity best projects the desired meaning or image. A study by Friedman revealed that although the image of the celebrity may not necessarily spill over onto the product, celebrities still serve as attention-getters, sources of credibility, aids to recall and/or reference group identifiers. Moreover, physically attractive celebrities can significantly enhance measures of spokesperson credibility and attitude of consumers towards an ad, especially for an attractiveness related product. The process of social influence explains the way in which source characteristics of celebrities could affect a change in perceptions and attitudes of consumers. According to Grant McCracken (1989), the effectiveness of the celebrity endorser depends on culturally acquired meanings that a consumer brings to the endorsement process—'Celebrities draw their powerful meanings from the roles they assume in their television, movie, military, athletic and other careers. Each new dramatic role brings the celebrity into contact with a range of objects, persons and contexts. Out of these objects, persons, and contexts are transferred meanings that then reside in the celebrity' (Bootwala, 2007:108). The celebrities at times position themselves as a sensitive and liberal star when the product he/ she endorses cashes in on the widely prevalent prejudice (fair skin as against dark in the country). The danger of them being accused racist, colour prejudiced and socially irresponsible arises when they endorse these products. Celebrity branding can take several different forms, from a celebrity simply appearing in advertisements for a product, service or charity to a celebrity attending PR events, creating his or her own line of products or services, and/or using his or her name as a brand. The most popular forms of celebrity brand lines are for clothing and fragrances. Many singers, models and film stars now have at least one licensed product or service which bears their name. Lately there has been a trend towards celebrity voice-overs in advertising. Some celebrities have distinct voices which are recognizable even when they are not present on-screen (like Amitabh Bachchan). This is a more subtle way to add celebrity branding to a product or service. The use of a celebrity or sports professional can have a huge impact on a brand. For example, sales of Nike golf apparel and footwear is said to have doubled after Tiger Woods was signed up on a sponsorship deal. More recently, advertisers have begun attempting to quantify and qualify the use of celebrities in their marketing campaigns by evaluating their awareness, appeal and relevance to a brand's image and the celebrity's influence on consumer-buying behaviour. A particular public figure is to motivate consumers who see them in an ad to purchase the product advertised. Celebrity branding is a global phenomenon, and it assumes paramount importance in countries like India where celebrities are given the status of demi-gods by the masses. There is a certain correlation between successful celebrity branding and brand endorsements. With the increased visibility of social networking, celebrities are being created in new mediums daily. Cyber celebrities often use the Internet as a resource to follow celebrity branding trends. The surreal world of celebrity branding is exposed in this provocative and fascinating look into how personalities evolve into iconic brands that are worshiped by millions. The importance of creating a larger-than-life image in retaining admiration and adoration for a star is revealed through a careful investigation of the role of television, film, music videos, magazines and tabloids in celebrity branding. Celebrities like Jennifer Lopez, Tina Turner, David Bowie, Madonna and Prince uncover the methods and significance of maintaining a lifestyle that fans wish to emulate. An intimate look at what it takes to create an icon raises the curtain on how public image can be designed to appeal to the public's deepest emotional needs, desires and ego.

Advertising manipulates people's needs and lures consumers to products and consumption as a way of life. People seek various products, from which they derive actual gratifications. Advertising research is the key to determining the success of an advert in any country or region. The ability to identify which elements and/or moments of an advertisement contribute to its success is essential. Market research measures provide insight into what is working in an advert in any country or region. Consumer sovereignty exerts tremendous influence over the market. They no longer passively absorb standardized products.

Making Sense of Advertisements: Reading Ads Theoretically

...the meaning is not lying there on the page, one has to make an effort to group it.

—William Leiss

Advertising, in its non-commercial guise, is a powerful tool capable of reaching and motivating large audiences. The word *advertise* comes to us from Latin *advertere* meaning to turn towards or to pay attention. It has to avoid use of objectionable appeals, technique, excessive repetition of messages, loud volume as well as silliness of presentation. Advertising involves visual persuasion. Consumers are exposed daily to advertising, an important component of mass media. According to Duncan Barry (1988), the media construct reality, have their own forms, codes and conventions, and present ideologies and value messages, and media are businesses that have commercial interests. It *constructs* the product, creating a world that is exciting and entertaining enough to keep audiences interested. The construct is based on factors like culture, social understanding and our unique experiences. The notions of reality are reinforced or affected by what the media places before us. Public service advertising, non-commercial advertising, public interest advertising, cause marketing and social marketing are different aspects of the use of sophisticated advertising and marketing communication techniques. The customer profiles as well as the growing popularity of niche content brought about by everything from blogs to social networking sites, in the present times, provide advertisers with audiences that are smaller but much better defined, leading to ads that are more relevant to viewers and more effective for companies' marketing products. These advertisements are targeted to a specific group and can be viewed by anyone wishing to find out more about a particular business or practice at any time, right from their home. This causes the viewer to become proactive and actually choose what advertisements they want to view. An appropriate ad campaign must be designed in such a way that it captures the image in the product or service and transfers it to the consumer. The advertising image can condition perception of objects before they are actually seen. It is designed to mould opinion and not to offend anyone in the market, designed for maximum visual impact. A blend of text and imagery is used to promote product/services. Good products have to be complemented by consistent communication of high quality and reliability. Advertisements have been analysed from different perspectives, each contributing towards the world of advertising and its understanding. The ad-saturated landscape, the global scenario, the visual signs and culture codes (from a semiotic point of view), along with the gender, ecological, postcolonial standpoints as manifested in an advertisement have also been subject to scrutiny.

Adverscapes

Contemporary life is to a large extent enveloped, even engulfed by *adverscapes*—a landscape covered with advertisements one sees around him/her, through its display in print, on television, Internet and other media. Choosing from the wide range of products, one's purchase affects the choices on offer and determines what succeeds and fails in the market. Advertising is an industry which wields considerable power—being linked to a chain of marketing practices which function to sustain the flow of goods on which the economic system depends. Within cultural theory, advertising has often been seen as emblematic of the culture in which it has become all pervasive. For F.R. Leavis, advertising epitomized the exploitation of the cheap response which characterizes contemporary mass civilization. Theodor Adorno and Max Horkheimer argued that advertising pervades the culture industry subsiding the ideological media and turning culture into an assembly-line whose standardized products it furnishes with artificial differences. For contemporary theorists too, advertising functions in an emblematic way, creating an ideology of its own. The French philosopher Jean Baudrillard argues how it invades everything. Both public and private spaces disappear, as does the separation between them, to be replaced by 'great screens on which are reflected atoms, particles, molecules in motion', in the *era of hyperreality*. He claims in his influential *Simulacra and Simulations* that communication technologies, capable of infinite replication and wide dissemination of information, have initiated *a world of simulation* that now functions to supplant the real world. In the postmodern world, mass reproduced representations lose their originals and the *real* is scarcely discernible. Baudrillard coined the term *hyperreal* to describe the way in which the media now dominate our perception of the outer world. A media representation becomes a hyperreality (a reality that is more real than that which we can directly experience in the outside world) with the reality encountered in the world itself, a pale shadow of this.

Adverscapes engender an *imaginary real* that reflects nuances of popular culture and discourse. These socially constructed *unreal*/digitally manipulated images (established through advertising) fill the consumer with a desire to *possess* the product, its consumption, maintaining and ensuring the continuity of the *unreal* and the manipulated. The term *mediascape* (used by Arjun Appadurai to describe and situate the role of electronic and print media in global cultural flows, which are fluid and irregular as they cross global and local boundaries) describes the way that visual imagery (also visual culture) impacts the world. Such imagery comes from books, magazines, television, cinema and advertising (adverscapes) that can directly impact the landscape and also subtly influence, through persuasive techniques and an increasingly pervasive presence, the way people perceive reality. Mediascape indexes the electronic capabilities of production and dissemination, as well as 'the images of the world created by these media'. They are characterized by being image-centred, narrative-based and by their ability to offer a 'series of elements ... out of which scripts can be formed of imagined lives' (*Disjuncture and Difference*). Emerging as an instance/means of popular discourse, adverscapes (as a part/subsystem of the existing mediascape) target a mass audience, envelop and *create* new images of culture. It contributes towards the construction of an *imagined community* (*imagined* to mean *perceived*—the perception of space (an *imagined geography*—a tool of power) created through certain images, texts or discourses (advertising/adverscapes) that gorges on the images constructed by the media, for its existence and happiness. These cultural images forged by adverscapes contribute towards the hyperreal existence. Appadurai articulated a view of cultural activity known as the *social imaginary* (from the original notion of psychoanalyst and theoretician Jacques Lacan that indicated the cultural practices and values of a particular culture/community). Drawing on Lacan, Appadurai conveyed that the imagination is an organized field of social practices that exists as social facts, social structures and/or cultural norms that are external in relation to the individual (*Disjuncture and Difference*).

Mediascape contextually describes the visual culture. As a part of the mediascape, advertising intrudes on the surrounding landscape with bright colours, lights and large fonts. Adverscapes in general contribute negatively to the mental climate of a culture by promoting products as providing feelings of completeness, wellness and popularity to motivate purchase. The lines between the real and the fictional landscapes become blurred in advertising, with the result that the further away these audiences/consumers are from the direct experiences of metropolitan (modern) life, the more likely they are to construct imagined worlds which are chimerical and aesthetic. It is resuscitated, energized and maintained by advertising/adverscapes. Mediascapes are results of the diffusion of the ability to produce media images and the global spread of media images themselves. They are deemed to provide large and complex repertoires of images (of beauty/fairness, status, masculinity/femininity, culture and class) and narratives to local groups around the world, which are used in creating local narratives, and towards providing metaphors through which people live—seen in adverts for cosmetics, automobile, jewellery, etc. The media environment we occupy affects our life. Advertising occupies a pivotal role in the social construction of reality—as a cultural artefact, a social fact and a meme (an idea, behaviour or style that spreads from person to person within a culture)—a reality with inherently conflicting elements of heterogeneity and global homogeneity, an imaginary social. It subtly influences through persuasive techniques and an increasingly pervasive presence, the way people perceive/create reality. Instances of cultural jamming disrupt the unconscious thought process that takes place when most consumers view popular advertising and bring about a *detournement*, trying to evoke reaction. People have a motivational drive to reduce cognitive dissonance (as in subvertising which attempts to cut through the glitz of a mediated reality and, momentarily, reveals a deeper truth within) by altering existing cognitions or adding new ones to create consistency (a *recuperation* wherein the subversive, conflicting thought, radical ideas and images become safe and commodified). With passing time, the sophistication of advertising methods and techniques has advanced, enticing, shaping and even creating consumerism and needs where there has been none before, or turning luxuries into necessities. The overwhelming amount of advertising and its prevalence in mass media leaves no doubt that advertising leaves an indelible imprint on our social and cultural values. Advertising has become a kind of social guide, depicting us in all the myriad situations possible to a life of free choice. It provides ideas about style, morality and behaviour.

Adverts cater to all sections of society and address varied themes. Advertising affects the whole world and India is no exception to it. It has re-engineered the mindset. In the present era, advertisement agencies are redefining the laws of living for Indians. The TV screen spells a soothing escape from inadequacies and is a harried existence that busy enticing viewers in seeing a world that arises essentially out of their make-believe assumptions. Advertisements not only play a crucial role in defining the patterns of understanding but they are also focused on changing the reactions that such perception arouses in people. Good at reading the pulse of the masses, they are replacing the good old passions with new found *obsessions*. It is through advertisements that the good old sweets are getting replaced by chocolates—*kuch meetha hojaye*. While the advert from Bhima (jewellery) says *pennayal ponnu venam ponninkudamayidenam*, Manappuram (gold loan) says *veetil swarnam vachitenthinu nattil kenunadapu*. Deftly, advertisements mesmerize the present as well as the prospective customers. Advertising is suggestive of an alternative life in action. It also attempts to convert the very ethos and concept of a society which ostensibly manifests the tendencies and attitudes that are capitalistic in tone and tenor. Adverscapes, therefore, focus not on what does good but what looks and feels good physically and sensually—the imagery of perfect body that is drilled into the young minds through adverts being an instance. The advertisements today promote the sale of a product as well as force a paradigm shift in the thinking patterns of the people. Much of the controversy over advertising stems from the ways many companies use it as a selling tool and form its impact on society's tastes, values and lifestyles. The images created by adverscapes reveal (the *depthlessness*) notions (and cohabitative character) of Indian values *vis a vis* a globalized existence—a superficial culture reflected in and promoted by advertising. As pointed out by Appadurai, the polarization models (producers/consumers; centre/periphery) can no longer be used to explain the global cultural economy. Paradoxically, the tug between the *global* and the *local* becomes an adjunct to global homogenization, subspeciating into debates on commodification and inadvertently leading to a hegemonic relationship between the producer and the consumer/s and between consumers themselves. Concomitantly, the consumer is reduced to the *status* of the consumed (indicative of the insecurity of power). Global cultural flows occur in and through the growing disjunctures between these various areas (landscapes) resulting in a deconstruction of established binaries (contradictorily revealing the power invested in them). In such a scenario, power exists in a state of fluidity, going through shifts and counter-shifts.

The renowned literary critic, Northrop Frye, likens the subtle working of advertising to the experience of a twilight train trip. As one's eyes are passively pulled along a rapidly moving landscape, it turns darker and one begins to realize that many of the objects that appear to be outside are actually reflections of what is in the carriage. As it becomes entirely dark, one enters a narcissistic world, where except for a few lights here and there, we can see only the reflection of where we are. An analysis of the working of advertising and propaganda in the modern world will show us how successful they are in creating a world of pure illusion. The illusion of the world itself is reinforced by the more explicit illusions of advertising in a society that is becoming more and more dependent on televisual constructions for its sense of social/cultural identity. Far from simply hyping particular products, advertising *creates* a world for us.

Memeplexes

Ideas and how they propagate in human culture is the concern of memetics. Memes exemplify a self-replicating unit with potential significance in explaining human behaviour and cultural evolution. Culture is composed of atoms like memes, which compete with one another. A meme is a unit of information in a mind whose existence influences events such that more copies of the same get created in other minds. They spread by being passed down from mind to mind and those successful works behind the creation of cultures. The word *meme* (from *mimeme*, modelled on *gene*) was coined by Richard Dawkins in *The Selfish Gene* as a concept for discussion of evolutionary principles in explaining the spread of ideas and cultural phenomena. The term was used to describe a unit of human cultural transmission (as well as information) analogous to the gene (a genetic unit that is small enough to last for a large number of generations and to be distributed around in the form of many copies), arguing that replication also happens in culture, albeit in a different sense. A meme is, thus, an idea, behaviour or style that spreads from person to person within a culture. It operates as a unit for carrying cultural ideas, symbols or practices that can be transmitted from one mind to another through writing, speech, gestures, rituals or other imitable phenomena. Memes self-replicate (as replicators or entities that are capable of being transmuted from one brain to another), mutate and respond to selective pressures. Like genes, it refers to whatever is copied (with variation) from one person to another by imitation, whether habits, skills, songs, stories or any other kind of information. Memes like genes are active agents working purposcfully (through various mediums, one being adverts) for their own survival. Dawkins contended that the meme is a unit of information residing in the brain and is the mutating replicator in human cultural evolution. It is a pattern that can influence its surroundings and can propagate. He initially defined meme as that which 'conveys the idea of a unit of cultural transmission, or a unit of *imitation*'. They compete for space in our memories and for the chance to be copied again, as only some of the variants can survive. Large groups of memes that are copied and passed on together are called co-adapted meme complexes, or *memeplexes*. Memes in advertisements become evolutionary models of cultural information transfer. They have an independent existence, are self-replicating and are subject to selective evolution through environmental forces.

Adverts infect people with memes illuminating consciousness about the memes that form it, parasitizing people into propagating them and consume the product. Those memes, in turn, influence the infected people's behaviour so that they help perpetuate and spread the virus. Each of these admeme entities exist in the form of lots of copies of the same advert in different languages and on different channels), and at least some of the entities are potentially capable of surviving—in the form of copies—for a significant period of evolutionary time. Admemes, like genes, are the replicators and man their survival machines. Some of these varieties of admemes lose the power of self-replication, and their kind ceases to exist when they themselves cease to exist. Others still replicate but, at times, less effectively. Yet other/new varieties turn out to be even better self-replicators than their predecessors and contemporaries. The admeme replicators survive, not only by virtue of their own intrinsic properties, but also by virtue of their consequences (which may be direct or even quite indirect, and boosting sales in the case of advertisements) on the world. They function as cultural replicators. The success that an admeme replicator has in the world will depend on what kind of a world it is—the pre-existing conditions. An advert is a meme enclosing within it memeplexes that function as mind parasites that make certain their copying. Just as genes propagate themselves in the gene pool by leaping from body to body via sperms or eggs, so admemes in the form of catch phrases, tunes and ideas propagate themselves in the *meme pool* by leaping from brain to brain via a process (which, in a sense, can be called imitation, ensuring its replication). The survival value of the (god meme, for example) meme in the pool often results from its great psychological appeal. Adverts focus on city life (as meme) as incarnating the loneliness and alienation of capitalist modernity. It explores not only the liveliness of the big city, but also the depths of moral corruption to which human beings can be reduced. With their representations of life in the city, the adverts became powerful socialization agencies, indirectly educating, through memeplexes, their audiences in the ways of the world, emphasizing the rules and norms of urban life, presenting model situations, model forms of behaviour and so on. The female viewer mimicks femininity and identifies with the passive, conventional versions of women (fair, lovely and docile) on screen. A fertile meme when planted in a mind literally parasitizes the brain, turning it into a vehicle for its propagation in just the way that a virus may parasitize the genetic mechanism of a host cell. The ideas get readily copied by successive generations of individual brains. In a conducive ambience, they replicated making copies of themselves. Whenever conditions arise in which a new kind of replicator makes copies of itself, the new replicator will tend to take over and start a new kind of evolution of their own. However, just as not all genes that can replicate do so successfully, so some memes are more successful in the meme-pool than others. Some of the admemes, like some of the genes, achieve brilliant short-term success (like popular jingles and videos) in spreading rapidly, but do not last long in the meme pool. Others may continue to propagate themselves in altered form. There is a continuous mutation and blending in admemes; both the ad and the meme mutually assisting in their survival. Fashions in dress and diet, ceremonies and customs, art and architecture, and engineering and technology, all evolve (the change may be progressive) in historical time in a way that looks like highly speeded genetic evolution. Admemes establish themselves in a culture in numerous forms and are transmitted verbally or by action from one mind to another, rooting and assisting their survival in the pool.

Recurrence of memes occurs in adverts. The same ad may be watched several times, the audience same or different. Replication of memes is made possible on a massive scale by adverts. They are created by carriers (human beings) of memes who inadvertently help perpetuate/replicate them. These established memes appeal to a large audience at a single moment. A single advert may be a meme pool (a single advert conveying Indian notions of family, tradition as well as modernity) where memes compete with each other for survival in the minds of the audience/viewer (already a carrier of memes). This becomes more complicated as, on the one hand, there is the existing meme in the viewer/audience facing that on screen as well as the creator's memes trying to project, imprint and replicate itself (those that survive). At times the memes may be shared ones trying to root themselves firmly in the viewer/audience and, thus, the social fabric. Adverts ensure the survival of memes, its replication as well as establishing of new ones in the viewer/audience. The imaginative world and the meme created before him/her inadvertently functions (though the audience is aware of what the film is getting at or the politics behind it) to mirror the existing society as well as firmly roots them there through the thinking as well as docile viewer. It becomes a manifestation of *power* or control emerging from culture. The notion of spectator is passivity brushed aside here for there exists an intertextual relay. Emergence, sustenance, replication of a meme or meme pool may be traced retrospectively to social factors. The ideological implications also shift. The meme is *selected* to register these concerns at that historical juncture. Personas adopted by the actors (and so does the meme) play a particularly significant part in ideological reproduction. The look or the gaze of the viewer helps in replicating it into many. The viewer becomes a part of the memeoid, which has been taken over by a meme to the extent that its own self, its existence, becomes inconsequential. Admemes occupy a pivotal role in the social construction of reality—as a cultural artefact, a social fact, a meme (an idea, behaviour or style that spreads from person to person within a culture).

Through localization, new memes are implanted in the target local culture, which alters a few essential tendencies of that culture. When an international brand gives its ads and boosts its sales in a certain culture, it does not require the product at all. The advert (uses the language and backdrop of the target culture) induces the local culture to readjust for the new meme. In a certain sense, localization becomes a misnomer here. For the ad is not localized *per se* because the local that the advert imagined did not exist prior to the arrival of the advert; it creates the *local* using a set of sememes that existed already in the culture.

Semiotics

Semiotics studies sign process (semiosis) or signification and communication, signs and symbols. It includes the study of how meaning is constructed and understood and can be applied to anything which can be seen as signifying something to everything which has meaning within a culture. It can be applied to the analysis of any media texts, making explicit what is usually only implicit. A *text* (an advert) is in itself a complex sign containing other signs. Semioticians classify sign systems in relation to the way they are transmitted. This process of carrying meaning depends on the use of codes that may be the individual sounds or letters that humans use to form words, the body movements they make to show attitude or emotions or even something as general as the clothes they wear. Semiotic methods are more often than not used to reveal different levels of meaning and at times hidden motivations. Semiotics analyses visual media, mass media as well as advertising. Visual signs and cultural codes in advertising too come under the purview of semiotics. Ferdinand de Saussure stressed that signs are not meaningful in isolation, but only when they are interpreted in relation to each other. Since the meaning of a sign depends on the code within which it is situated, codes provide a framework within which signs make sense. Semiotics can be applied to anything which can be seen as signifying something—to everything which has meaning within culture. It can be applied to the analysis of any media text making explicit what is only implicit. Social identities get communicated through talk, work, clothes, hairstyle, food habits and so on. Semioticians classify sign systems in relation to the way they are transmitted. This process of carrying meaning depends on the use of codes that may be in the form of individual sounds or letters that humans use to form words, the body movements they make to show attitude or emotion, or even something as general as the clothes they wear. Manipulations take place at numerous levels because of the desire to sell products. Issues of technological determinism in the choice of media and the design of communication strategies assume new importance in this age of mass media. Semiotics has been applied to diverse areas as movies, art, advertising, fashion as well as visuals. Advertisements generally share three basic patterns which, following Greimas, occur in all narratives, namely (a) desire, search or aim (involving a subject and an object); (b) communication (involving a sender and a receiver) and (c) auxiliary support or hindrance (involving a helper and/or an opponent). The narrative structure provides the opportunity to show a change of state (a *before* and *after* effect) and how the product brings this about. Advertisements for luxury products tend to be more descriptive and the emphasis is on the product and no longer on narrators or characters. Changing the form of the signifier while keeping the same signified can generate different connotations. The choice of different typefaces as well as words often involve connotation. Linguistic codes serve as indicators not only of social class but also of sexual orientation. Codes are variable not only between different cultures and social groups but also historically. Familiarity with particular codes is related to social position in terms of such factors as class, ethnicity, nationality, education, occupation, political affiliation, age, gender and sexuality. The world is read in terms of codes and conventions dominant within the specific sociocultural contexts and roles within which one is socialized. Culture-specific cultural codes are to be read in a like manner. This becomes a necessity in the case of texts produced within and for a different culture, such as advertisements produced indigenously in a different country from our own for the domestic market in that country. Interpreting such texts in the manner intended may require cultural competency relevant to the specific cultural context of that text's production, even where the text is largely visual. The semiotic analysis of cultural myth involves an attempt to deconstruct the ways in which codes operate within particular popular texts or genres, with the goals of revealing how certain values, attitudes and beliefs are supported while others are suppressed. Texts are rewritten, if only unconsciously, by the societies which read them. One is conscious of the contexts in which the text has been reproduced, drawn upon, alluded to, parodied and so on. The concept of intertextuality indicates how each text exists in relation to the other. Some texts allude directly to others. Texts provide contexts in which other texts may be created and interpreted. They draw upon multiple codes from other contexts, both textual and social. In the case of contemporary television adverts, the audience have to make sense of allusions which offer them the pleasure of recognition—a mediated reality which runs counter to the reality which focuses on persuading the audience to believe in the ongoing reality of the narrative. Adverts make extensive use of intertextuality. To understand an ad, one has to adopt the identity of a consumer who desires the advertised product. Value of a sign depends on its relations with other signs within the system. A sign has no absolute value independent of this context. In advertising, what matters in positioning a product is not the relationship of advertising signifiers to the real-world referents, but the differentiation of each sign from the others to which it is related. Although advertisements do not physically represent the product, they provide an iconic representation of both the product and what the product should stand for. The visual imagery generates the appropriate signified concepts or emotional overtones which promote the image of the product. While adverts exhibit Indian overtones, symbols are understood only by those who share a culture. Google has taken the emotional route to market the power of search. Its new TVC shows a young girl reuniting her grandfather with an old friend with the help of the search engine. It opens with the old man narrating his childhood stories to his granddaughter. He talks movingly about a beloved friend in Lahore, whose contact he lost after partition. Through Google, the girl manages to connect with the man in Pakistan and invites him over to Delhi to surprise her grandfather on his birthday. The effectiveness of this

3–5 minutes ad lies in its ability to tap a country's history. An advert is constructed with the aim of targeting the product at an audience familiar with and sympathetic to its relevant cultural signifiers. They often use shared prior cultural experience to attribute meaning to its symbolic representation of the product. The positioning and appearance of the subjects act as signifiers which help to describe the image and, therefore, of the product. The relation between sign and text is mutually dependent, since the reader/viewer may judge the advert by its context and vice versa. The connotative meaning of the product is conveyed through the subject. The visual image manipulates the viewer's knowledge and experience of the product. The signifiers are designed to give a favourable and appropriate image of the product. These signifiers are also to have a strong relationship with the textual context in which the signs were located. The advert consists of the overall impression a reader gets from quickly studying it, the sales message the advertiser tries to convey and the strategy behind it, as well as the cultural knowledge and background of the viewer, for the viewer makes sense of the ad by relating it to his/her culture and to the shared belief systems. Erving Goffman in his analysis looks at the specific codes present in advertisements and considers what they say about society and social relationships. He focuses on minute details of adverts, visual composition of ads as well as the presence of specific social themes in ads. A majority of advertisements stress upon specific visions of society and focus on how the products produce happiness in consumers and project a vision of the future. The viewer will bring his/her own interpretation to the texts by drawing on his or her own cultural values and perceptual codes. As Chandler puts it, decoding involves not simply basic recognition and comprehension of what a text says but also the interpretation and evaluation of its meaning with reference to relevant codes. The semiological approach:

> ...suggests that the meaning of an advertisement does not float on the surface just waiting to be internalized by the viewer, but is built up out of the ways that different signs are organized and related to each other, both within the ad and through external references to wider belief systems. More specifically, for advertising to create meaning, the reader or the viewer has to do some 'work'.

Because the meaning is not lying there on the page, one has to make an effort to group it. (Leiss, 1986:201–202)

The nature of a product is tied directly to identity. Products like Hidesign, Gucci, Tissot, Prada and their identity-image advertisements exist at the top of the socioeconomic spectrum. These are aimed at a select few (the high-income consumers of High Fashion products) because of high cost. It tells the public the cultural and socioeconomic significance of their clothing. Many corporations use symbols and icons as a means of establishing some kind of corporate identity, as it is easy to remember a symbol or icon. These icons and symbols through the use of colour and form, and often the appearance of specific words, give people a sense of what the corporation is like. Viewers pay a great deal of attention to things like hairstyle, clothing and shoes of the actors or models appearing before them in mass-mediated texts like advertisements. Music and sound effects are used to generate certain responses in audiences—based in large part on culturally acknowledged associations between given sounds and certain emotions. As Umberto Eco (1976:7) has suggested, if signs can be used to tell the truth, they can also be used to lie:

Semiotics is concerned with everything that can be taken as a sign. A sign is everything which can be taken as significantly substituting for something else. This something else does not necessarily have to exist or to actually be somewhere at the moment in which a sign stands for it. This semiotics is in principle the discipline studying everything which can be used in order to lie. If something cannot be used to tell a lie, conversely it cannot be used to tell the truth; it cannot be used 'to tell' at all.

The Althusserian concept of Interpellation is used by Marxist media theorists to explain the political function of mass media texts. According to this view, the subject (viewer, listener, reader) is constituted by the text, and the power of the mass media resides in their ability to position the subject in such a way that their representation is taken to be reflections of everyday reality. Television makes people visually available and not in the frozen modality; in movement and action. Socio-historical factors play an important role in shaping how different media are used and their status within particular cultural contexts. There takes place interaction with each individual viewer as commercials include direct address. In visual media, the represented physical distance between the observer and the observed often reflects involvement or critical detachment in the viewer. Semioticians refer to advertising posters as *texts* and to *reading* television (regarded as being in some respects like *language*). Certain binary distinctions are loaded with cultural significance. They are made into the prototype symbols of the good and the bad, the permitted and the forbidden. It is used in relation to mass media texts as well. Binary opposition can be traced even in visual images (the logos of Apple and IBM). The gender-differentiated use of production features which characterize commercials, furthermore, reflect a series of binary oppositions—fast and slow, abrupt and gradual, excited and calm, active and passive, detached and involved (lined up consistently together as masculine and feminine qualities). A printed advert is a syntagm of visual signifiers. Advertisers use visual metaphors. They differentiate similar products from each other by associating a product with a specific set of social values (creating distinct signifieds for it). The formal frame of visual image functions as a synecdoche in which it suggests that what is being offered is a slice of life and that the world outside the frame is carrying on in the same manner as the world depicted within it. Synecdoche invites or expects the viewer to fill in the gaps, and advertisements frequently employ this trope.

Cultural meanings are attached to words and other forms of communication. It revolves around discovering the connotations of objects and symbolic phenomena and of the actions and dialogue of the characters in texts—that is, the meanings these may have for audiences—and tying these meanings to social, cultural, ideological and other concerns. The *codes* (highly complex patterns of association that all members of a given society and culture learn) in people's minds, affect the ways that individuals interpret the signs and symbols they find in the media and the ways they live. As Eco points out, codes and subcodes are applied to the message (text) in the light of a general framework of cultural references, which constitutes the receiver's patrimony of knowledge; his ideological, ethical, religious standpoints, his psychological attitudes, his tastes, his value systems and so on (1976:115). Television uses verbal language, visual images and sound to generate impressions and ideas in people. Meaning can be extracted from the way a certain food has been prepared and the context in which it is served. Food as in advertising too can be symbolic of certain social codes. If food is treated as a code, the messages it encodes will be found in the pattern of social relations being expressed. The message is about different degrees of hierarchy, inclusion and exclusion, boundaries and transactions across boundaries (Douglas 1971: 61–82). The lighting techniques and the use of colour, sound effects and music—all are signifiers that help a viewer to interpret what he/she sees. Advertising often uses stereotype gender-specific roles of men and a woman reinforcing the existing clichés, and it has been criticized as inadvertently or even intentionally promoting sexism, racism, heterosexualism, ableism, ageism and so on. It often reinforces stereotypes by drawing on recognizable *types* in order to tell stories in a single image or 30-second time frame. In addition, people are reduced to their sexuality or equated with commodities and gender-specific qualities are exaggerated. Not only sexualized female bodies, but increasingly also males serve as eye-catchers. The well-crafted images contribute to the formation of gender concepts and establishment of self image. In advertising, it is usually a woman that is depicted as a servant of men and children that reacts to the demands and complaints of her loved ones with a bad conscience and the promise for immediate improvement (wash, food), a sexual or emotional play toy for the self-affirmation of men, a technically totally clueless being that can only manage a childproof operation, female expert, but stereotype from the fields of fashion, cosmetics, food or at the most, medicine, as ultra thin, doing ground-work for others, for example, serving coffee while a journalist interviews a politician. A large portion of advertising deals with the promotion of products in a way that defines an *ideal* body image. This objectification greatly affects women; however, men are also affected. Women and men in advertising are frequently portrayed in unrealistic and distorted images that set a standard for what is considered *beautiful*, *attractive* or *desirable*. Such imagery does not allow for what is found to be beautiful in various cultures or to the individual. It is exclusionary, rather than inclusive, and consequently, these advertisements promote a negative message about body image to the average person. Because of this form of media, girls, boys, women and men may feel under high pressure to maintain an unrealistic and often unhealthy body weight or even to alter their physical appearance cosmetically or surgically in minor to drastic ways. Advertising images offer a sense of identity to their so-called target audiences in the form of observable behaviour patterns and in the social connotations of prestige and status often attached to ownership of the product. Gender manifests itself through behaviour patterns. Advertisements lean heavily on socially generated notions of gender as a means of targeting products at appropriate consumer sectors, appealing to the individual and casting the product in the image of the user. The formal features seen in adverts convey and reinforce some of the messages in the context. These gender *performances* are understood by and accepted in society. Each individual is not only a receiver but also a creator of meaning. The gender patterns are formulated in ads and targeted directly at the viewer in the form of powerful commercial messages. Multiple discourses work within an advertisement. The material culture is replete with oppositions (male–female, work–home, production–consumption and so on) which serve the purpose to enhance and naturalize categories that are inherent in the culture. Oppositional pairs are rarely equally weighted—a hierarchical relation exists between the two. *Woman* is aligned with a number of products (like hair dryers, make up and household machines). Those products not only appear as natural in their contexts but also reinforce the *womanness* of the person. Design is important in constructing identity. Media images of women are confined to the traditional archetypes treating women in their domestic roles and sexual appeal. In advertising, particular women are shown either as housewives whose interests are limited to domestic needs, or else as sexually allowing background which makes consumer goods more attractive by association and reinforce stereotypes. The year 2013 is seen as the year when Indian advertising caught up with the Indian woman. The latest Tanishq jewellery commercial (launched in the middle of the wedding season) hints at the change in contemporary society, and shows a dusky, not-so-young woman, bedecked in jewels, walk around the fire in a traditional Indian wedding ceremony, with her young daughter joining in the ceremony at the behest of her new *daddy*. A dusky bride puts on jewellery before her wedding. A little girl runs up to her excitedly, and they walk to the *mandap* together. The girl wants to participate in the pheras. The bride shushes her but the groom, seeing her disappointment, carries the little girl through the pheras. The little girl then asks the groom if she can call him *daddy*. Tanishq has broken through the clichés to create an ad that is both refreshing in its simplicity and yet boldly manages to convey a message about the changing perception of women in India. Targeting a progressive mindset, it indicates that the second wedding of a divorcee need not be a diluted occasion but a celebration steeped in tradition. Titan is not alone in its quest to appeal to the progressive consumer. Ad film makers and clients across consumer industries are out to change the stereotypical portrayals targeting the *progressive female* (in Bournvita's *Tayyari jeet ki* commercial, or Tata Docomo commercial *Open Up to Honesty*). When the father in HDFC Life's (2013) new television commercial asks his daughter what she wants for her birthday, he does not expect a laundry list that begins with a princess doll but covers another six products before going on to talk about a trip to Disneyland. In these politically correct times, the mother is here obviously smarter and better prepared and so quickly butts in to say everything, including a holiday in the US and higher studies, is already planned for. The relieved father nods, if a trifle disbelievingly, and the advertisement ends with the happy family celebrating the child's birthday, secure in the knowledge that the mother (and HDFC) has got the future mapped. The Bournvita mother-and-child journey continues (2013) in the second *Tayyari jeet ki* film. A mother watches, and helps with the preparations, as her child practices boxing against a bigger opponent. A voiceover explains the need to prepare with someone better than oneself in order to be able to face unequal battles in the future. The young one's helmet comes off and one sees a young girl boxing with a bigger male opponent. Still, she convincingly defeats her opponent under her mother's watchful gaze. The film ends with the mother and child headed home, and the voiceover declaring that only a mother knows the value of good practices, which is why she gives her child Bournvita. The adverts are a reflection of the changing situation and the hypercompetitive nature where winning is all that matters. This is true not just of women-focused categories like jewellery and children's products, but from paints to cars to telecoms. Adverts, in principle, are imperative messages that consist of text and image(s) structured in a manner which strengthens the interplay between the verbal and the non-verbal elements so as to affect a desired action. In the process of coding this message, they necessarily draw from the manner of social structuring and constituting of cultural identity of a given society. What is beautiful in one language is often barbarous, even nonsense in another. Hence, it is unreasonable to limit a translator to the narrow compass of his author's words. He will have to choose some expression which does not vitiate the sense. Close analysis helps the reader to be aware of the way language choices may serve the interest of some to the detriment of others. Amidst the infinite set of possible readings, each reader interprets a text differently from others. The internalized ideas of what is typical for a man or woman also enters the readings indicating how ingrained are the stereotypes of gender. Hero Maestro's *Such a Boy Thing* television commercial though funny is sexist enough to make women uncomfortable. The film shows Ranbir Kapoor picking up his girlfriend on his Hero Maestro. She is clearly uncomfortable with the relationship and wants to talk about it, but everything she says is interpreted by him to relate to the scooter (comfort, journey, breaks). It ends with her smiling at his boyish antics, and the two head for the event they have come to attend. The voice-over concludes *Boys ki life and Maestro ki ride easy hai.* It signs of with 'Maestro. Such a boy thing'. Image illustrates the text and makes it clearer. The text loads the image, burdening it with a culture, a moral and an imagination. The text amplifies a set of connotations that already exist in it. Sometimes the text produces an entirely new signified which is retroactively projected into the image, so much as to appear denoted there. Sometimes the text can even contradict the image so as to produce a compensatory connotation. In advertising, the signification of the image is undoubtedly intentional; the signifieds of the advertising message are formed *a priori* by certain attributes of the product and these signifieds have to be transmitted as clearly as possible. The viewer perceives at one and the same time the perceptual message and the cultural message. The text directs him/her through the signifieds of the image, causing him to avoid some and receive others; by means of an often subtle dispatching, it remote controls him towards a meaning chosen in advance. 'While content analysis involves a quantitative approach to the analysis of the manifest *content* of media texts, semiotics seeks to analyse texts as structured wholes and investigates latent connotative meanings' (Chandler, 2002:8–9). While content analysis focuses on explicit content and tends to suggest that this represents a single fixed meaning, semiotics studies focus on the system of rules governing the *discourse* involved in media texts, stressing the role of semiotic context in shaping meaning. The meaning of a sign is not in its relationship to other signs within the language system but rather in the social context of its use. As semioticians point out, meaning is not *transmitted* to us. It is actively created according to a complex interplay of codes or conventions of which we are normally unaware. 'Signs take the form of words, images sounds, odours, flavours, acts or objects but such things have no intrinsic meaning and become signs only when we invest them with meaning' (Chandler, 2002:17). 'Anything can be a sign as long as someone interprets it as "signifying" something—referring to or *standing for* something other than itself' (Chandler, 2002:17). No sign makes sense on its own but only in relation to other signs. A sign has no *absolute* value independent of its context. While signification clearly depends on the relation between the two parts of the sign, the value of a sign is determined by the relationships between the sign and other signs within the system as a whole (Saussure, 1983:112–113). The intertextuality of adverts is also noteworthy:

> In order to make sense of many contemporary advertisements ... one needs to be familiar with others in the same series. Expectations are established by reference to one's previous experience in looking at related advertisements. Modern visual ads make extensive use of intertextuality in this way. Sometimes there is no direct reference to the product at all. Instant identification of the appropriate interpretative code serves to identify the interpreter of the veradvertisement as a member of an exclusive club, with each act of interpretation serving to renew one's membership. (Saussure, 1983:200)

Meaning is not *transmitted*; it is actively created according to a complex interplay of codes or conventions of which the viewer is normally unaware. As part of its social use within a code, every sign acquires a history and connotation of its own

which are familiar to members of the sign-users' culture. Any
means of expression accepted in a society rests in principle
upon a collective habit, or on convention. The symbol is connected with its object by virtue of the idea of the symbol using
mind, without which no such connection would exist. Contemporary visual adverts are a powerful example of how images
may be used to make implicit claims which advertisers often
prefer not to make more openly in words. As Derrida puts it,
'[T]he materiality of a word cannot be translated or carried over
into another language. Materiality is precisely that which translation relinquishes'. Each medium has its own constraints and,
as Umberto Eco points out, each is already charged with cultural signification. Syntagmatic relations are the various ways
in which elements with the same text may be related to each
other. A printed advert is a syntagm of visual signifiers. A syntagmatic analysis of a text involves studying its structure and
the relationships between its parts. Changing the setting used in
an ad contributes to changing the meaning. The binary oppositions which we employ in our cultural practices help to generate
order out of the dynamic complexity of experience. In order to
communicate, a producer of any text must make some assumptions about an intended audience. Reflections of such assumptions may be discerned in the text (ads). In order to make sense
of many contemporary advertisements, one needs to be familiar with others in the same series. Expectations are established
by reference to one's previous experience in looking at related
adverts. Semioticians classify sign systems in relation to the way
they are transmitted. This process of carrying meaning depends
on the use of codes that may be the individual sounds or letters that humans use to form words, the body movements they
make to show attitude or emotion, or even something as general
as the clothes they wear.

Postcoloniality

It is difficult, if not impossible, for a postcolonial consumer, the
receiving end of almost all late-capitalist ideological circuitry,
to locate a culturally stable sense of self in the indigenous
context, as against the *othered identities* constructed and

offered by the postmodern market and visual media. As Jean Baudrillard rightly says, the contemporary subject is perpetually implicated in the empty and meaningless play of the postmodern media. The postmodern consumer, then, is naturally expected to be a baffled and passive self, subjected to the operative intervention of mass advertising and the systems of consumption it endorses. Not surprisingly, the many routes to self-hood and identity, tabled by the late-capitalistic marketing campaigns in the Third World betray an inherent complicity with the divisive social myths perpetuated during the colonial period. While colonialism legitimized the conviction that the systems of the Invader were superior to those of the Occupied, postcolonialism contests the residual effects of colonialism on indigenous cultures and subverts the Western way of thinking, generating space for the subaltern. The discourse of contemporary visual-media advertisements infiltrates this context with prominently colonial logistics. The discursive project of modern advertisements in the postcolonial audience communities is to promote the construct of a desirable subject position vis-à-vis an *ideal consumer*, by recycling the erstwhile colonial binary of the Self and the Other. The present-day signification processes of the tri-continental mass media is to a large extent, an extended version of the global nexuses of communication and exchange that the networks of colonial trade first facilitated (Boehmer, 1890–1920:112). These nexuses and the consequent cultural edifices were substantially glossed by the early 20th century theorizations of mass culture, especially in the efforts of the Frankfurt School. The most important advocates of the school, Theodore W Adorno and Max Horkheimer, established that the phenomenon of mass culture inevitably carries a political implication, that all the many forms of popular culture are a single culture industry whose purpose is to ensure the continued obedience of the masses to imperialistic market interests—a single marketplace in which the best or the most popular works succeed. Power tends to get centralized in the hands of the few remaining multinational corporations that control production and distribution. In extension, the postcolonial media-culture too draws from the value-system of the colonizer, albeit its neocolonial interpretations. In fact, it is possible to look at the postcolonial subject as futilely vying for the colonizer's normative subject positions in all her claims to identity in terms of modernity. The proclivity to be dubbed *modern* along the lines of their colonizers, in the societies of the Third World (though the Third World modernity, in itself, is a heavily hybridized idea), has necessarily rendered their mass media to behave consequent with the nocuous logics of colonial hierarchization. Modernity, as interpreted by the mass media, is functional only when the subject consents to the *value* of commodities and *buys* the identity created through this new faith; this faith-in-market, it is made to believe, elevates one to a desirable subject position. Through its seamless web, the mass media in the Third World is propagating that the subject needs to, most primarily, be a *buyer*. Visual media and, especially, advertisements, have a vital role to play in forging this faith.

Commodity, in order to derive its transcendental value, has to first be a *spectacle* that thwarts its use-value and, thus, supplants its banality. In this cause, it has to be *exhibited* and its existence-in-itself (as contrasted to existence-for-someone's-use) ratified—this, then, is the discursive space of advertisements. The culture of exhibiting so as to invest a surplus of symbolic value in the commodity necessitates an ideological leaning to the discourse of advertisement, as it happens in any system (say organized religion or monarchy) where symbolism (not physical reality) determines its operative logic. Moreover, the evolution of the advertisement industry in the colonial paradigm, right from the Victorian Great Exhibition, has always stressed on selling difference, or rather, the means to alleviate the difference: the desire of the colonized subject for identity has been deftly converted to the demand for the commodities (Gleason, 1983:64–69). The use of commodities, the advertisements seem to profess, takes the subject closer to her mother culture; the difference between you and your ruler is slightly lesser now that you have shopped; the subject is slowly learning to belong to the upper crust by buying what the world of the colonizer recommends, and the erstwhile signs of her inferiority, namely skin colour, lacuna in scientific understanding or insufficient understanding of the progressive and welfare-oriented modern institutions are gradually being repaired; she must, then, continue to buy to progress in the transformational—or to put it in the colonial terminology, civilizational—process, and sign her faith to the discourse of advertisements. In her insightful and refreshing study of the history of the soap-industry, Anne McClintock observes the manifold ways that connect the world of commodities and their exhibition/display (whose modern extension is the advertisement industry) to the sense of *self* of the colonizer.

The triumph of advertising (semantically polymorphic) in the culture industry is that the consumers feel compelled to buy and consume (*eat McDonald's* or *Dominos,* for instance) its products even as they see through them. It invades the subject's psyche (the domination at the heart of colonial experience) and casts people in roles not of their own making. The ideologically manipulative agenda in moulding the consumer behaviour, stimulating empty needs and imposing social conformity in terms of gender, class, ethnicity and age has been pointed out by theorists like Adorno. The commercial relationship between things being traded begins to dominate and restructure human behaviour and reconstruct social relations. Baudrillard uses commodity fetishism (a central idea in the literature of the neo-Marxist Frankfurt School) to explain subjective feelings towards consumer goods in the realm of circulation (among consumers)—therelationships between people constantly being mediated by the relationships between things. The cultural mystique added to objects by advertising encourages consumers to purchase them as aids to the construction of their identity (and *other*ness). Personal identity comes to be defined and expressed by what the person owns and buys (explicit in the visuals of a sedan to a limousine—Nano, Ritz, Polo, Wagon R, Aveo, SX4, Jetta, Linea, Manza). The neocolonial turn is also noticeable in the *stay-connected* campaign of mobile/Internet technology (Idea, Vodafone, Reliance and so on). These, as well as competency in English language are crucial for the construction of the contemporary Third World subject's identity. One's *status* (and *to belong*) comes to depend on the possession of commodities (*lack*, creating anxiety)—overt in Raymond, Reid and Taylor adverts. The *masks* (submitting to the power of abstract/impersonal market forces which rule the mind) are controlled by the business relationships (and legal/political interests) between things being traded. The manufactured product/object becomes more important than the consumer/possessor who gets embroiled in the imperialistic design which confers him special powers. The most intimate reactions of human beings are thoroughly *reified*. Personality signifies little more than sets of shining white teeth and freedom from body odour, and, at a deeper level, a dissociation from honest emotional responses (in the case of advertisements of products like Close Up, Colgate, Pepsodent, Rexona or Axe). Colonization and its methods of direct and ideological slavery came to associate dark skin with *uncivilized* and *inferior*, and as subordinate to fair skin. A colonial residue (traces of the imperial hegemony), a binary racial classification system, has divided people wholly in terms of a simple binary: light-skinned (a symbol of desirability, wealth, happiness and success through the developing world) and dark-skinned (as ugly and dull) categories. Every dark-skinned subject, occupying a subaltern space, is a *potential* winner (of wealth, success or desirability) *if* they resort to buying and consuming the product. In consuming, in enjoining the market, the consumer *earns* a position in the social ladder—and as s/he refines the *taste* in selecting his/her *brand*, they move up the rungs. Most Indian advertisements show charcoal coloured or chocolate-skinned girls using the product to dramatically alter their colour to near-white and consequently improving their miserable life. Intense competition in the fairness products market ensures that consumers are bombarded with ads at every turn, which translates into high visibility for brand ambassadors.

Advertisements compel the dark skin to believe that its legitimate existence is that of a *consumer*—an ideal subject must consent to this *consumerhood*. Consumerhood provides a *raison d etre* for the embattled subject: 'at long last, for the dark-skinned loser', the message seems to say, 'There is a way to exist and succeed'. These racial stereotypes constructed on skin colour and perpetuating the noxious social myths about worth, beauty and desirability persistent in mass media and popular culture reinforce the colonial conceits on the inferiority of the colonized. The unseen expanse of this socially constructed *reality* (skin whitening, hair colouring and a subsequent total eradication of physical ethnic identity) is exemplified and reiterated in adverts of cosmetic products like Fairever, Fair and Lovely and Fair and Handsome (another binary at play), wherein exists a construction of *fair pride* (a system of privilege *drilled* into our minds). The racialized body is indicative of the *civilizing strategy*, as well as the stereotyped ways of *looking at things*, in L'Oreal lightening and whitening skin tone/hair colour ads featuring actors like Diana Hayden, Lara Dutta, Priyanka Chopra, Aishwarya Rai, Sonam Kapoor and Freida Pinto. They act as pointers towards (the psychodynamic levels at which the overt message can be interpreted) the Western ideal of beauty prevalent within the culture. Marshall McLuhan has implicated psychoanalysis as working complementarily to Marx's idea of commodity fetishism in advertisements, that is, adverts work on an unconscious association—a technique of juxtaposition which enables the advertiser to pass the censor of consciousnesses. While markets cater to an ideal consumer and offer the promise of an enhanced individuality; however, in reality, the project of the contemporary mass advertisement industry is regressive, with the consumer passively operating in or caught within roles over which s/he has little control. This commodity bulimia makes the punter gorge on the products around so that the act (of shopping/consuming) imparts a specious sense of normalcy to the embattled subject and replaces his/her anxiety over a breached and incomplete identity.

Advertisements are criticized because it creates false needs, aspirations and wants. More generally, adverts reflect the essence of the social structure and cultural identity of a country or specific society. Acceptable narrative structures of racial and gender expectations shape our interpretations of experience and the way we explain our own lives. Advertising has to increase demand and establish a brand image. It is used by sellers to influence buyers to select their products or services. The choice is made from among similar goods and services. The Internet has emerged changing the market and the ways in which consumers communicate about products, and these changes occur at great speed. Language, the most powerful communication system, is necessary for ads apart from the visual communication that is involved. Manipulations are carried out because of the desire to sell products. Issues of technological determinism in the choice of media and the design of communication strategies assume new importance in this age of mass media. As Maya Pines notices:

> Everything we do sends messages about us in a variety of codes, semiologists contend. We are also on the receiving end of innumerable messages encoded in music, gestures, foods, rituals, books, movies or ads. Yet we seldom realize that we have received such messages, and would have trouble explaining the rules under which they operate. (Berger, 2011:59)

To produce an attractive identity, products with an affluence of money and artistic talents become the aim. Though the different brands compete with each other in ads of similar products, they are unified in promoting the set of values and lifestyle connected with high fashion. Advertising uses persuasive language and creates image-based identity in the minds of the viewers. Many corporations use symbols and icons as a means of establishing a corporate identity. A musical phrase or a sound is a signifier and the emotion it generates is the signified. Codes and conventions make the signs in a narrative understandable. Cultural meanings are attached to words and other forms of communication. Global characteristics of icons render it more important. The use of advertising within a virtual world is a new idea. As businesses compete in the real world, they also compete in the virtual world. Increase in buying and selling products online (ecommerce) force businesses to adjust, to accommodate the new market. Advertising focuses ones thoughts on the object for sale, the competitors communicating to consumers in their advertising campaigns. Competitive and cultural context needs to be analysed. In-depth analysis of the local cultural context becomes a necessity. The product becomes a *text* with multiple levels of meanings. Products that belong to the same paradigm perform the same function in a given context. The product one chooses is shaped by socially defined, shared classification systems, some of them being personal taste. The paradigmatic level belongs to product positioning.

Advercology

Popular culture and the mass media play an enormous role in shaping people's perception and understanding of environmental issues. The communication of environmental ideas is integral to visual media as well. Environmental issues are framed and represented by various media—how these images and representations are used and contested by a variety of cultural communities and discourses. The ecological investigations and interpretations of the relationship between nature and culture, towards formulating ecologically informed critical principles, inevitably lead to an ecologically oriented critical approach even while analysing visual media. Environment is bound up with our sense of personal and social identity. In this context, the possible relations between the text (advert) and nature are examined in terms of ecological concepts. It attempts to find a common ground between the human and the non-human to show how they can coexist in various ways, because the environmental issues have become an integral part of our existence. The word *environment* is used to mean the surroundings or conditions in which a person, animal or plant lives or operates as well as the setting or conditions in which a particular activity is carried on. The natural environment encompasses all living and non-living things occurring naturally on earth or some region thereof. It is an environment that encompasses the interaction of all living species. A natural environment on earth that has not been significantly modified by human activity is indicated by the word *wilderness*. The human-made surroundings that provide the setting for human activity, ranging in scale from buildings and parks or green space to neighbourhoods and cities that can often include their supporting infrastructure, such as water supply or energy networks forms the built environment. Writing about the relationship between cinema and space in the world-system, for instance, Fredric Jameson (1992) argues that mass culture always involves a secret striving to represent the totality of social space, 'an unconscious, collective effort at trying to figure out where we are and what landscapes and forces confront us ...' (Jameson 1992:3). The most ubiquitous cultural phenomenon in late capitalist society, advertising expresses and influences our spatial consciousness and imagination in a variety of ways.

Critical accounts of the broader cultural and ideological significance of advertising (as opposed to the study of its success or
failure in marketing specific goods or services) usually begin
with the question of representation. The underlying patterns
and consistencies that govern how advertisers portray various
dimensions of our social and natural world need to be evaluated. The normative spatial archetypes that appear in the landscapes of advertising pass by virtually unnoticed, perceived
(if at all) as little more than an idealized backdrop designed to
complement the favourable depiction of commodity or brand.
More than simply serving as an innocent frame for the real action, however, such representations feed into and reinforce an
interlocking network of common sense assumptions and beliefs
that mediate our interaction with space. Adverts displaying appropriate pictures of pleasant natural scenes are said to evoke
emotions that are very similar to those experienced in direct
contact with natural environment. This is based on the assumption that visual representations of nature are equally appropriate
to evoke emotions similar to actual nature. That natural advertising imagery can evoke similar feelings to nature has significant
implications for advertising. Environment may come to denote
(a) the surrounding in which a person lives, (b) setting or conditions
in which a particular activity is carried out, (c) the natural environment encompassing all living and non-living and their interaction
(d) the wilderness as a natural environment on earth that has not
been significantly modified by human activity and (e) the built
environment or the human made surrounding that provide the
setting for human activity. Nature becomes a marketing device in
advertising, a market commodity. The modern estrangement of
man from nature and the industrial technological society changing the natural landscape (wilderness as *disciplined* by reason),
lamenting the destruction of the natural environment is the focus of many adverts. There takes place a denigration of urban
life and idealization of nature and the technology that will get
us *there*. Apart from the restorative power of natural landscapes
its visual splendour (aesthetic value) is also exploited providing
a spectacular visual experience. It is ironic that adverts use the
pristine image of a hyper-pure nature to motivate the use of a
product that consumes excessive amount of natural resources
and emits high levels of pollutants or causes health issues (Coca

Cola or Volkswagen ads). These ads fantasize an escape from the ills and burdens of civilization and presents a demonized urban space (images of dirt and congestion) to an unpredictable nature (nature/natural, a lost Eden/Arcadia, which has to be controlled (man controlling/mastering nature through technology)—most products be it cosmetics, detergents, toilet cleaners insist on being close to nature, having no chemicals and being 100 per cent *natural* (containing kiwi extracts, *badam*, almond, *neem* or something else from nature). There is always a preference for nature as pristine and uncontaminated by civilization. Scarcity breeds value and the more difficult it becomes to *experience* nature, the more appealing natural signifiers become. Fraudulent environmentalist claims are used by corporate to *greenwash* everything. Promotional adverts indicate the environmental issues and concerns (like save water, electricity, those aimed at agriculturists) and promote nature stressing on the interconnected existence of man and his surroundings. The billboards and hoardings that engulf the landscape offer a form of visual pollution. The environment is bound with ones sense of identity which also raises debates as to whether natural imagery has to be standardized or adapted. Man attempts to amputate nature and seeks to assert a human order to a system that follows different orders. The unquestioned use of land animals result in environmental looting and plundering which necessitates a paradigm shift in the thinking pattern. Hence there arises the necessity of socially–ecologically committed advertising and not an advertising that is manipulative. Adverts displaying appropriate pictures of pleasant natural scenes can evoke emotions that are very similar to those experienced in direct contact with natural environment. It is maintained that visual representations of nature are equally appropriate to evoke emotions similar to actual nature. That natural advertising images can evoke similar feelings to nature has significant implications for advertising. Psychology is harvested to enhance advertising effectiveness and affecting reactions to natural scenes in advertising contribute to increasing attitude towards the advertisement and the brand. Nature images in advertising potentially improve attention towards advertising messages and memory. It may instill a beneficial perceptual atmosphere without diverting the attention from advertising messages and the brand.

Ecologically oriented criticism evaluates texts in terms of responses to environmental crisis and seeks a synthesis of literary (here visual text), environmental and social concerns. An interdisciplinary study of text (adverts here) and environment is sought to devise possible solutions for the improvement of the contemporary environmental situation. It analyses representations of nature in works (literary as well as others). Ecocritics investigate such things as the underlying ecological values, what is meant by the word *nature*, and whether the examination of *place* should be a distinctive category, much like class, gender or race. They examine human perception of *wilderness* (signifying nature in a state uncontaminated by civilization), and how it has changed throughout history and whether or not current environmental issues are accurately represented/mentioned in popular culture and modern literature. The ecocritical mode was officially heralded by the publication of two seminal works—*The Ecocriticism Reader* (edited by Cheryll Glotfelty and Harold Fromm) and *The Environmental Imagination* (Lawrence Buell). As Cheryll Glotfelty points out:

> Ecocritics and theorists ask questions like, How is nature represented in this sonnet? What role does the physical setting play in the plot of this novel? Do men write about nature differently than women do? How has the concept of wilderness changed over time? In what ways and to what effect is the environmental crisis seeping into contemporary literature and popular culture? What bearing might the science of ecology have on literary studies? ... What cross-fertilization is possible between literary studies and environmental discourse in related disciplines such as history, philosophy, psychology, art history, and ethics? All ecological criticism shares the fundamental premise that human culture is connected to the physical world, affecting it and affected by it. Ecocriticism takes as its subject the interconnections between nature and culture, specifically the cultural artifacts of languages and literature. (Glotfelty and Fromm, 1996:xix)

While ecocriticism had its official beginnings as a discipline in the 1990s, important critical essays that fall into the ecocritical mould appeared as early as the 1800s. In an article that extends ecocriticism to Shakespearean studies, Estok speaks of ecocriticism also as 'any theory that is committed to effecting change by analysing the function–thematic, artistic, social, historical, ideological, theoretical, or otherwise—of the natural environment, or aspects of it, represented in documents (literary or other) that contribute to material practices in material worlds' (*Shakespeare and Ecocriticism*, 16–17). This echoes the functional approach (of cultural ecology) which analyses the analogies between ecosystems and imaginative texts (even those like adverts) and posits that such texts potentially have an ecological (regenerative, revitalizing) function in the cultural system (Zapf, 2008).

Environmental problems require analysis in cultural as well as scientific terms; being the outcome of an interaction between ecological knowledge of nature and its cultural inflection. As against the *Arcadian* approach of radicals advocating de-urbanization, use of non-synthetic products and low-technology solutions are those proponents of environmental protection which prefer the *Promethian* environmentalism that promotes the decoupling of human economy and natural ecology as far as possible to protect nature. The images of natural beauty emphasize the harmony of humanity and nature. An ecocritical analysis unravels how visual texts interact with and participates in the entire ecosphere. Nature has been used to legitimize gender, sexual and racial norms. It takes up how nature gets represented in works of value. Visuals may take interest in nature as a subject or focus on industrialization changing the natural landscape (lamenting the destruction of the environment). It may furthermore emphasize on the natural setting as done by travellers and natural historians. In a Wordsworthian manner, the beauty and mystery of nature has also been celebrated in adverts. The sense of place tends to take the centre stage. The vital interrelatedness between culture and nature has been a focus of literary/visual culture. This attention to culture–nature interaction continues to be characteristic of the staging of human experience up to the present. Hubert Zapf mentions how literature itself can be described as the symbolic medium of a particularly powerful form of *cultural ecology*. Cultural ecology studies the relationship between a given society and its natural environment as well as the life-forms and ecosystems that support its life ways. Ecocriticism actually launches a call to connect to the issues of today's environmental crisis. New eco-theory responds to the global ecological crisis and addresses important environmental issues, specifically by examining values, in literary texts, with deep ecological implications. This is applicable in examining visual texts (advertisements), too.

Visual media (advertising) can be perceived as an aesthetically and culturally constructed part of the environment. The environmental crisis is a question that cannot be overlooked in studies of the visual culture—the ways in which nature is marginalized, silenced or pushed, in Manes's words, 'into a hazy backdrop against which the rational human subject struts upon'. Ecocritics like Donna Haraway, Diana Fuss, Patrick Murphy and Evelyn Fox Keller urge for a reconception of nature as an active and speaking subject. As William Howarth argues:

> ...in fact texts [visual too] do reflect how a civilization regards its natural heritage ... . Ecocriticism observes in nature and culture the ubiquity of signs, indicators of value that shape form and meaning. (Glotfelty and Fromm, 1996:77)

Fritjof Capra in *The Web of Life* demands the recognition of the intrinsic value in nature (deep ecology) against an anthropocentric/shallow ecology. Contextualizations, in literary/visual texts, of ecological themes, like environmental pollution, extinction of the species, deforestation, toxic waste contamination and destruction of tropical rainforests, would lead to more and more analysis of ecologically informed criticism. William Rueckert clearly states, experimenting with 'the application of ecology and ecological concepts to the study of literature [and other texts] ... has the greatest relevance to the present and future of the world we all live in' (Glotfelty and Fromm, 1996:107). Arguing about the importance of *literary ecology* he also produces a new conceptualization:

> The conceptual and practical problem is to find the grounds upon which the two communities—the human, the natural— can coexist, cooperate, and flourish in the biosphere. All of the most serious and thoughtful ecologists ... have tried to develop ecological visions which can be translated into social, economic, political, and individual programs ... I invoke here ... the first Law

of Ecology: 'Everything is connected to everything else'. (Glotfelty and Fromm, 1996:107–108)

Wilderness is a construction mobilized to protect particular habitats and species, and is seen as a place for the reinvigoration of those tired of the moral and material pollution of the city—having an almost sacramental value, holding out the promise of a renewed, authentic relation of humanity and earth. It is the place of exile—a fall from grace. It indicates freedom as well. With the rise of capitalism, nature was turned into a market commodity. The *wild* was *disciplined* by reason. The politics of wilderness indicates it to be a site of class and gender struggle. Gary Snyder, an advocate of deep ecology, argues that civilization is the locus of chaos and disorder, while wilderness epitomizes the free self-organization of nature. Rather than being simply opposed, the wild ramifies through the civilized and sustains it.

Ecocriticism expands the notion of *the world* to include the entire ecosphere (not just the social sphere). It aims to show how texts with an earth-centred ecocentric approach can be significant in creating an awareness as well as solving real and pressing ecological concerns as well as advocates a rethinking of our commonly held beliefs and perceptions, and our versions of nature, towards creating a 'consciousness of the essential unity of all life'. Present ecological problems are held to be rooted in deep-seated social problems, particularly in dominatory hierarchical political and social systems. Social ecology locates the roots of the ecological crisis firmly in relations of domination between people. In the framework of social ecology, 'the very notion of the domination of nature by man stems from the very real domination of human by human'. While the domination of nature is seen as a product of domination within society, this domination only reaches crisis proportions under capitalism. The notion that man must dominate nature emerges directly from the domination of man by man. However, it was not until organic community relation dissolved into market relationships that the planet itself was reduced to a resource for exploitation. This centuries-long tendency finds its most exacerbating development in modern capitalism. Owing to its inherently competitive nature, bourgeois society not only pits humans against each other, it also pits the mass of humanity against the natural world. Just as men are converted into commodities, so every aspect of nature is converted into a commodity, a resource to be manufactured and merchandised wantonly. The plundering of the human spirit by the market place is paralleled by the plundering of the earth by capital.

Advertising is but one component of ideologies of space that incorporate a jumbled, heterogeneous and often contradictory mix of philosophical fragments and cultural myths, images and symbols, ideas and beliefs, rituals, institutions and practices. They give structure and form to how we experience space, furnishing the categories and concepts through which perception becomes knowledge, thereby legitimating certain forms of awareness and experience while precluding others. They also produce maps of affect which regulate our capacity and desire to make emotional investments in space, shaping how and why certain types of space (or features of particular spaces) come to matter to us in both positive and negative terms, while others are largely ignored. Adverts hint at the modern estrangement from nature. The vital interrelatedness between culture and nature has been a special focus of literary/visual culture from its archaic beginnings in myth, ritual and oral storytelling, in legends and fairy tales, in the genres of pastoral literature/texts, nature poetry. Literary/visual texts have staged and explored, in ever new scenario, the complex feedback relationship of prevailing cultural systems with the needs and manifestations of human and non-human *nature*. Adverts convey a strong ecological emphasis or message. They illustrate a socially recognized sense of community between humans and the natural landscape. In an ethnoecological perspective, it indicates how different groups of people living in different locations understand the ecosystems around them and their relationships with surrounding environments. It seeks valid, reliable understanding of how humans have interacted with the environment and how these intricate relationships have been sustained over time. It indicates not only a localized study of people but also signifies people's understanding and experience of environments around them (a human-focused approach to the interactions between living organisms and their environment). An ecocritical approach to advertising formulates a conceptual foundation for the study of interconnections between adverts and the environment. Literary/visual texts can be perceived as an aesthetically and culturally constructed part of the environment, since it directly addresses the questions of human constructions, such as meaning, value, language and imagination, which can, then, be linked to the problem of ecological consciousness that humans need to attain. Within this framework, ecocritics are mainly concerned with how texts transmit certain values contributing to ecological thinking. The environmental crisis is a question that cannot be overlooked in advertising as well. Consciousness raising in environmental thinking and the ethical and aesthetic dilemmas posed by the global ecological crisis force one to recognize the important role such approaches play in understanding man's position in the ecosphere. The true concern of ecocriticism ought not to be with obsolete representational models, but with how nature gets textualized in texts to create an eco-literary discourse that would help produce an intertextual as well as an interactive approach between literary language (here the language of adverts) and the language of nature. The verbal constructions of nature, either in its romanticized, idealized form, or as hostile wilderness, usually lead to a binary way of either/or thinking that justifies the present catastrophic abuse of nature. To counter this logocentric approach, ecocriticism embarks upon the project of reconceptualizing nature, not as an object of observation or interpretation, but as an active agency in its own right. A reconception of nature as an active and speaking subject is, thus, necessitated. A vision of nature as a self-articulating subject refutes nature/culture dualism inherent in our thinking towards a consciousness of humans valuing both nature and culture in their diversity. However, the assumption that nature speaks for itself creates a discursive problem, for it is again the human subject speaking for nature in a paradoxical attempt to overcome the human/non-human divide within the discourse itself. Apparently, literary/visual culture studies become not something distinct from environment, but an integral part of it by contextualizing the ecological concepts of wholeness, interconnections and interrelatedness of all organisms, human and non-human alike. Natural themes and imagery have been used in advertising to flesh out and concretize two principles of spatial epistemology—the pursuit of spatial novelty and a spatial phenomenology that privileges spectacle—by attaching a utopian flavour to movement through space. The personal hygiene industry relies on ecophobia since capital-driven notions about personal cleanliness assign us preferences for perfumes over natural body odours. The cosmetic industry prefers covering up nature's flaws and blemishes. Every attempt amputates nature and seeks to assert a human order to a system that follows an entirely different order. Psychology is harvested to enhance advertising effectiveness. Positive effective reactions to natural scenes in advertising contribute to increasing affirmativeness towards the advert or the brand. Car advertising has invoked the fantasy of leaving behind the constraints of a crowded, mundane and polluted urban environment for the wide open spaces offered by nature. For both producers and consumers, the association of automobiles with (travel to) pristine natural environments helps to forget the vast resources and infrastructure required to support car-based societies as well as the enormous ecological consequences that accompany their mass production. The dream of escaping the city for the sensual bliss of nature continues to hold on the popular imagination. Cities or, more accurately, the monotonous routines that often seem to dominate urban and suburban existence are regularly targeted by advertisers—a popular formula in marketing discourse. The flip side of this denigration of urban life is the idealization of nature (and the technology to get us *there*) as the antidote to the mind-numbing boredom of daily life. Invoking nature as the endpoint of vehicular travel confirms the belief that spatial mobility can offer access to places, experiences and events that are fundamentally different. Escape to someplace else is both possible and desirable, offering emancipation from the tyranny of the every day. The virtuous character and restorative powers of natural landscapes are invariably linked to their awe-inspiring visual features. Nature's value and significance grows in proportion to the extent that it can be perceived and consumed in a spectacular fashion—the ease with which such wilderness locales can be sharply and quickly differentiated from more prosaic locations is precisely what makes them so attractive to advertisers. Yet the key that unlocks such an experience is almost always the visual splendour of the natural landscape. Signifiers of nature become emblematic of the pursuit of spectacular visual experience that dominates our perceptions and expectations of space. This martial injunction plainly refers not to physical or proprietary control over space nor to the simple mastery of nature for our own ends but instead models a form of spatial agency based on the pursuit of visual stimulation, the art of cleverly positioning oneself in the right place at the right time, thereby maximizing one's subjection to an array of spectacular environments and events. At one level, explaining the appeal of natural imagery as a marketing device (and the ideological implications that flow from such rhetorical strategies) is not especially difficult. The semiotic economy that governs promotional culture ensures that the most highly prized marketing slogans and signifiers are those that enable people to symbolically distance and differentiate themselves from conventional, mainstream forms of social life. Scarcity breeds value, and the more difficult it becomes to experience nature (or places that are culturally sanctified as relatively untouched by human activity), the more appealing natural signifiers become as a means of distinction. As city streets and suburban neighbourhoods give way to the rugged, epic and timeless beauty of landscapes seemingly untouched by humanity, one can fantasize about escaping the collected ills and burdens of history, society and civilization. Not only is urban space demonized in a host of predictable ways, but, more dangerously, urban ills that have an eminently social and historical origin—congestion, smog, suburban sprawl, urban poverty, crime and so on— are naturalized as inevitable features of urban life, reinforcing personalized flight as the only viable and realistic solution to the problem of the city. Just as the distortions of the dream help to accommodate the expression and management of wishes and anxieties that would otherwise be repressed, images of nature can similarly solicit the (distorted) expression of popular hopes and fears about social space. The alienated city, notes Jameson, 'is above all a space in which people are unable to map (in their minds) either their own position or the urban totality' (Jameson, 1992). Images of a ferocious and unpredictable nature are, of course, ideal for dramatizing an automobile's capacity to protect its occupants from inclement driving conditions as well as master the roughest terrain. Such narratives have broader (if unintended) effects upon how we conceptualize and understand the world that lies outside. Among the many attractions of nature—in all of its many guises from terrifying to serene—to advertisers is its seemingly boundless capacity to accommodate the felicitous projection, expression and aestheticization of our thoughts and feelings about social space, from utopian dreams about environments that can delight, inspire and amaze to dystopian nightmares of frightening and dangerous spaces that threaten our safety, security and well-being. The psychological and emotional connection to nature is two-way—specific places and environments can contribute to one's sense of well-being or security, while negative environmental changes can cause feelings of personal loss. These living connections intertwine the natural environment and the human psyche. It concerns the meaning and significance of places for their inhabitants and users.

Images of pleasant nature scenery have been classified as vague, unspecific and possibly ineffective green claims, as opposed to substantive, informational claims. Advertising plays an essential role in the production of consumerist demand by inventing false needs and by stimulating the formation of compulsive consumption habits, totally violating the conditions for maintenance of planetary ecological equilibrium. As capitalism, especially in its current neoliberal and globalized form, seeks to commodify the world, to transform everything existing—earth, water, air, living creatures, the human body, human relationships, love, religion—into commodities, so advertising aims to sell those commodities by forcing living individuals to serve the commercial necessities of capital. Both capitalism as a whole and advertising as a key mechanism of its rule involve fetishization of consumption, the reduction of all values to cash, the unlimited accumulation of goods and of capital, and the mercantile culture of the *consumer society*. Advertising often uses fraudulent environmentalist arguments to greenwash everything. People need to be convinced to abandon consumption habits incompatible with ecological equilibrium imprinted through the continuous pounding by advertising that incites (it tells the consumer that they can affirm their personality only by buying and displaying supposedly exclusive products), encourages and stimulates them night and day to buy and buy again. Advertising is an essential gearing in the infernal neoliberal/capitalist spiral of ever-increasing, ever-expanding production/consumption/accumulation—a spiral that is driving the degradation, increasing at a geometric rate, of the environment—degradation that leads us, by means of climate change, to a catastrophe without precedent in human history. Images of nature are among the most common signifiers of utopia in commercial discourse, tirelessly making the case that a certain commodity or brand will enable an escape from the malaise and drudgery of urban existence. The invocation of natural themes has been especially prominent in the marketing and promotion of sport utility vehicles over the past decade. Speeding through deserts and jungles, fording raging rivers, and even scaling the heights of Mt Everest, the SUV is routinely depicted in the most spectacular and remote natural locations. Here exists the irony of using pristine images of a hyper-pure nature to motivate the use of a product that consumes excessive amounts of natural resources and emits high levels of pollutants. Automobile as a commodity has used natural themes and imagery to attach a utopian flavour to movement through space. Car advertising has often invoked the fantasy of leaving behind the constraints of a crowded, mundane and polluted urban environment for the wide open spaces offered by nature. Invoking nature as the endpoint of vehicular travel affirms one of automobility's most precious and fiercely guarded illusions, namely that spatial mobility offers access to places, experiences and events that are fundamentally different from everyday life, that one can escape to somewhere other than where one is now. The use of nature to frame flight to the countryside summons up a powerful nostalgia for the simpler times and lives connoted by idealized scenes of rural life.

On Translation

Translation communicates the same message in another language. The text to be translated is the source text (ST) and the language that it is to be translated into is the target language (TL). Translators play an important role in the evolution of languages and cultures. Often a TL lacks terms found in a source language (SL). Total translation is what is generally meant by translation; all the linguistic levels of ST (phonology, graphology, grammar and lexis) are replaced by TL material. In the case of restricted translation, there is the 'replacement of SL textual material by equivalent TL textual material at only one level'. Two main types of restricted translation are phonological translation and graphological translation (Baker, 1998:121–122). Restricted translation at the grammatical or lexical level only is difficult if not impossible because of the interdependence of grammar and lexis. Catford stresses that there can be no restricted translation at the inter-level of context because 'there is no way in which we can replace SL "contextual units" by equivalent TL "contextual units" without simultaneously replacing SL grammatical/lexical units by equivalent TL grammatical/lexical units' (Encyclopedia Routledge: 121–122). Adherence to source norms determines a translation's *adequacy* with respect to the ST; adherence to norms originating in the target culture determines its *acceptability* within that culture. Speaking about the strategies of translation Mona Baker (1998:240) says:

> A translation project may conform to values currently dominating the target language culture, taking a conservative and openly assimilationist approach to the foreign text, appropriating it to support domestic canons, publishing trends, political alignments. Alternatively, a translation project may resist and aim to revise the dominant by drawing on the marginal, restoring foreign texts excluded by domestic canons, recovering residual values such as archaic texts and translation methods and cultivating emergent ones (e.g., new cultural forms).

The politics of linguistic transmission has now evolved into a politics of cultural transmission in which translators—and translations—perpetuate or contest values and ideas that represent particular cultures; hence, the necessity for positioning translation within cultural studies. The word and the visual complement each other. Barthes (1977:10) points out that:

> ...the text constitutes a parasitic message designed to connote the image, to 'quicken' it with one or more second-order signifieds.

In other words, and this is an important historical the words; it is now the words which, structurally, are parasitic on the image. It is not the image which comes to elucidate or 'realize' the text, but the latter which comes to sublimate, patheticize or rationalize the image. Image illustrates the text (make it clearer). Now the text loads the image, burdening it with a culture, a moral an imagination.

In order to facilitate global advertising, advertising agencies have begun to conduct cross-cultural research studies of consumer behaviour. Through advertising, the producer informs the innovators that the product exists and makes claims about its quality. To what extent should a company adapt a luxury product or service to meet local conditions? The design of a firm's symbols and icons through the colour and form and often the appearance of specific words and/or numbers act as indicators (even in localized adverts) for people. It was also viewed as acceptable for some promotional and advertising activities to be adapted to some extent to draw a link between the product and the local market—to create the perception that an international product (and associated values) might be relevant and of value at home in an Asian context. It is recognized that while some core elements of foreign products needed to be promoted on the basis of their degree of Westerness, it was important to modify promotional images and messages to build a link or a bridge between the product and local consumers. The level, and degree, of promotional adaptation may be quite discrete but nonetheless important. The advertisements that have been graphically adapted and those that have been adapted textually before looking into the relation between the text and the graphics which is an essential element in advertising. Visual aspects influence perceived similarity of advertising. However, not all types of pictures (though pictures are more universal than words) are universal in their meanings and some may not be an effective means of communicating with non-literate market segments. Hence, international marketers should research their markets before attempting to communicate with them through pictures. Localization processes should not overlook the full range of effects that can be achieved by translation. Linguistic aspects of localization also need to be considered. It is argued that complete localization of the kind that makes the foreign appear domestic risks locking cultures into passive consuming positions.

Descriptive translation studies (Zohar, 1990; Toury, 1981) draw on the historical study of translation to point out that the many different ways of translating depend very much on the cultural situation involved. The translator offers information about certain aspects of the source-text-in-situation, according to the target text (TT) *skopos* specified by the initiator. The selection made from the information offered in the ST, nor the specification of the *skopos*, are determined by the needs and expectations of the target-text receivers. Translation is by definition interlingual and intercultural. It involves both linguistic and cultural transfer; in other words, it is a culture-transcending process. The functionalist approach considers the function (*skopos*) of text and translation rather than equivalence between the two (translation as a communicative act). The *skopos* of the translation depends on the client, who commissions it with a specific purpose or *skopos* in mind and requires that the translator translates for this purpose. As Zohar puts it 'translation involves reformulation of an utterance *a* in a language *A* by means of an utterance *b* in a language *B*' (Even-Zohar 1991:1). Speaking about translated literature as a secondary system (that it does not hold true), Even-Zohar (1978:17) says:

> If one finds that the translated literature keeps to the contemporary norms of the canonized home system or employs literary innovations and more or less 'freely' uses the resources of language, one would tend to conclude that in case translated literature occupies a primary position ... on the other hand if one finds that the translational norms of a certain period represent petrified norms, often simplified, i.e, similar to epigonic and non-canonized norms, then there is no doubt that the translated literature in question constitutes a secondary system.

Peripheral literature may rise to a central position and become a major source of literature, and a central literature may be pushed to the periphery. Both the *original* and *translated* literature should participate in a literary system. Translation supplies *new* literary works to contact with other literatures, import cultural texts from one culture to another. An act of transfer takes place through translation (this process is visible in translation of adverts). Proponents of equivalence-based theories of translation usually define equivalence as the relation between an ST and a TT that allows the TT to be considered as a translation of the ST in the first place (Even-Zohar, 1978:77). A translation is declared free not (only) when it wanders too far from the meaning of individual SL words or sentences, but when it flouts normative rules set up for the ideological policing of meaning transfer. Catford distinguishes full translation as—Where the entire text is submitted to the translation process and the 'every part of the SL text is replaced by TL text material' and Partial translation: Where 'some part or parts of the SL text are left untranslated' (Baker, 1998:121). Catford defines total translation as the 'replacement of SL grammar and lexis by equivalent TL grammar and lexis with consequential replacement of SL phonology/graphology by (non-equivalent) TL phonology/graphology' (Baker, 1998:122). Nabokov speaking about the problems of translation says that the person who desires to turn a literary masterpiece into another language has only one duty to perform, and this is to reproduce within absolute exactitude the whole text, and nothing but the text. The term *literal translation* is tautological since anything but that is not truly a translation but an imitation, an adaptation or a parody (Baker, 1998:125). Toury points out that translation never functions as totally independent texts. The relation between translations and their environment (be it literary or visual advert texts) may vary, but it is always there, shaping translation behaviour and influencing the position of translated literature. In their functional theory of translation, Reiss and Vermeer claim that it is the *skopos* (i.e., purpose of a translation) which is all important. Authors distinguish between equivalence and adequacy. Equivalence refers to the relationship between an original and its translation, where both fulfil the same communicative function. Adequacy is the relation between source and translation where no functional match obtains and the *skopos* of the translation has been consistently attended to. The ST is of secondary importance. Purpose of translation (*skopos*) is crucial. The culture of the intended readers of the TT and of the client who has commissioned it and, in particular, the function which the text is to perform in that culture for those readers is of significance. The outcome of translational action is vera *translatum*, a particular variety of TT. Vermeer postulates that as a general rule it must be the intended purpose of the TT that determines translation methods and strategies. In cases where the *skopos* is the same for the two texts, Reiss and Vermeer speak of *funktionskonstanz* (functional constancy) where as cases in which the *skopos* differ between the two texts undergo *funktionsanderung* (change of function). The ST does not determine genre of the TT, nor does the genre determine *ipsofacto*, the form of the TT, or, indeed, the *skopos*; rather it is the *skopos* of the translation that determines the appropriate genre for the translatum, and the genre, being a consequence of the *skopos*, is secondary to it (Baker, 1998:237). According to *skopos* theory, then, translation is the production of a functionally appropriate TT based on an existing ST, and the relationship between the two texts is specified according to the *skopos* of the translation. The power of localization to influence the development of languages and cultures cannot be neglected. Linguistic aspect of localization is also of significance. Translatability is mostly understood as the capacity for some kind of meaning to be transferred from one language to another without undergoing radical change. Function-oriented descriptive translation studies attempt to describe the function of translations in the recipient sociocultural context (increase sales in the case of adverts). The most used positioning strategy is to associate an object with a product attribute or characteristic—'Cars that make sense'. Advertising adds extra value to the products through the use of adjectives and persuasive language.

Corporate Social Responsibility

A trend in advertising or marketing is the use of corporate social responsibility (the term became rampant around the late 1960s and early 1970s) known as CSR activities (corporate entering into social service activities which they use subtly to get their brand noticed and get goodwill for their products in a subtle way). Defined as social responsibility, it is the responsibility of an organization for the impacts of its decisions and activities on the society and environment through transparent and ethical behaviour that is consistent with sustainable development and welfare of the society. This trend existed way back in the west where companies have adopted it successfully by saving energy in its manufacturing plants and investing in social activities. CSR is understood to be the way firms integrate social, environmental and economic concerns into their values, culture, decision-making, strategy and operations in a transparent and accountable manner, and thereby establish better practices within the firm, create wealth and improve society. Examples like adverts of Malabar Gold (spending a lot to educate people about waste management [by Mohanlal] where it tries to establish itself as a beholder of culture) and Idea (it's save paper messages implying the ecological hazards before mankind) exist in Indian advertising. Tata is also a company that has made use of this strategy and is engaged in a wide variety of activities directed at helping community development in the Indian context. This in turn is also used as a localization tool (drawing on a particular socio-regional situation and appealing to it). Hindustan Unilever has as part of its CSR activities water conservation management (Surf Excel Quick Wash launched as part of it), plastic recycle and rainwater harvesting). Doing good to the society is seen as something positive, irrespective of regional differences. The goal is to leverage the company's unique capabilities in supporting social causes and improve the competitive context at the same time. Advertising plays a key role in the struggle for success in competitive markets. Because market conditions are seldom static, it is important for an alert competitor to learn how to adjust its advertising strategy in response to changes in the market to maintain or improve its position.

Corporate social responsibility (also called corporate conscience, corporate citizenship, social performance or sustainable responsible business/responsible business) is a modern instrument of accountability in the corporate world. Companies are to play an active role in the welfare of society so that they gain an acceptable image, to achieve high performance. Social responsibility (as against the belief that the corporation's sole responsibility is to provide a maximum financial return to shareholders) is the responsibility of an organization for the impacts of its decisions and activities on society and the environment, through transparent and ethical behaviour that is consistent with sustainable development and the welfare of the society. It takes into account the expectations of stakeholders; is in compliance with applicable law and consistent with international norms of behaviour and is integrated throughout the organization (a working definition by ISO 26000 working group on social responsibility Sydney, February 2007). It will often include charitable efforts and volunteering. The issue of the firm's responsibility to its society has come to fore in contemporary times. It is used as a framework for measuring an organization's performance against economic, social and environmental parameters and amounts to building sustainable businesses, which need healthy economies, markets and communities and a sustainable global economy where markets, labour and communities are able to function well together. Corporate executives wrestle to balance their commitments to the corporation's owners with their obligations to an ever-broadening group of stakeholders who claim both legal and ethical rights. In 1960, Keith Davis suggested that social responsibility refers to businesses' decisions and actions taken for reasons at least partially beyond the firm's direct economic or technical interest. CSR refers to the problems that arise when corporate enterprise casts its shadow on the social scene and the ethical principles that ought to govern the relationship between the corporation and society. The term corporate social performance (CSP) is an inclusive and global concept to embrace CSR, responsiveness and the entire spectrum of socially beneficial activities of businesses. It emphasizes the concern for corporate action and accomplishment in the social sphere. Hence, the need for firms to formulate and implement social goals and programmes as well as integrate ethical sensitivity into all decision-making, policies and actions. CSR is a form of corporate self-regulation integrated into a business model. It functions as a built-in, self-regulating mechanism, whereby a business monitors and ensures its active compliance with the spirit of the law, ethical standards and international norms. It aims to embrace responsibility for the company's actions and encourage a positive impact through its activities on the environment, consumers, employees, communities, stakeholders and all other members of the public sphere who may also be considered as stakeholders. CSR has gradually been elevated to the highest pedestal of importance in all aspects of business and production, be it private or public. In modern times, the concept of CSR incorporates and strives to explain and clarify numerous correlated and uncorrelated issues peculiarly, particularly or especially pertinent to social and environmental interests and welfare, keeping in full view the financial interests and benefits of the shareholders.

Consumers today are more aware of the environmental and social implications of their day-to-day consumer decisions and are, therefore, beginning to make purchasing decisions related to their environmental and ethical concerns. This has been absorbed by the corporate and conveyed through the promotional medium of advertisements. A company's business model should be socially responsible and environmentally sustainable. The company's activities should benefit the society and its activities should not harm the environment. Corporate philanthropy includes monetary donations and aid given to local and non-local nonprofit organizations and communities, including donations in areas such as arts, education, housing, health, social welfare, environment and so on (excluding political contributions and commercial sponsorship of events). Corporate success and social welfare are interdependent. A business needs a healthy, educated workforce, sustainable resources and adept government to compete effectively. Benchmarking involves reviewing competitor CSR initiatives, as well as measuring and evaluating the impact that those policies have on the society and environment, and how customers perceive competitor CSR strategy. It is founded on the reciprocal dependence between an organization and society. Three methods that have been identified as contributing towards measuring CSR (McGuire et al., 1988) are specialist evaluations about the policies of corporate (Abbott and Monsen, 1979; Márquez and Fombrun, 2005; Luo and Bhattacharya, 2006), the content investigation and examination of annual reports and documents of corporate (Basil and Weber, 2006), and the performance of corporation in controlling pollution as a proxy measure which focuses on pollution that is one of the significant aspects or dimensions of social responsibility (Chen and Metcalf, 1980; McGuire et al., 1988) because of the increasing environmental awareness, increasing shortage of resources and the demand for transparency. CSR is becoming increasingly important to businesses nationally and internationally. This is evinced in the advertisements of corporates which try to project an image of being socially responsible and committed. As globalization accelerates and large corporations serve as global providers, these corporations have progressively recognized the benefits of providing CSR programmes in their various locations. It is represented by the contributions undertaken by companies to society through its core business activities, its social investment and philanthropy programmes and its engagement in public policy. Corporates understand that a strong CSR programme is essential in achieving good business practices and effective leadership—that their impact on the economic, social and environmental landscape directly affects their relationships with stakeholders, in particular investors, employees, customers, business partners, governments and communities. For many organizations, CSR is an integral part of the way they operate and a key element in productivity and competitiveness. The corporate giants are conversant with CSR or corporate sustainability in today's parlance. It is a commitment to improve community well-being through discretionary business practices and contributions of corporate resources. A balance is struck between economic, social and environmental imperatives on the one hand and the expectations and welfare of the shareholders on the other. Social responsibility, and its execution, thus involves a well-planned strategy—the assessment of the social environment, formulation of objectives, devising operational plans and programmes, monitoring social progress, assessment of social and economic impact, and summary of outcomes and performances are of utmost importance. There is always interdependence between the society and organization in question or rather a cycle of relationship exists between the two in which the society supports and sustains the organization, while the latter is totally committed to the sustenance and development of the former. The awareness level of the society, which in turn is correlated with the literacy level, the standard of living and the preference pattern are determinants—which help individuals to voice their demands and grievances in a systematic manner, ensuring that organizations in the locality practice CSR in a way that truly benefits society. The organizations have to comply with legislation and voluntarily take initiatives to improve the well-being of their employees and their families as well as for the local community and society at large. Many corporate organizations are becoming increasingly active in addressing social concerns (being accountable for the social effects the company has on people, even indirectly), the management's obligation to make choices and take actions that will contribute to the welfare and interests of society as well as those of the organization. Companies become involved in community causes, by providing additional vocational training places, recruiting socially excluded people, sponsoring local sports and cultural events (as aired in commercials) and through partnerships with communities or donations to charitable activities.

Literature as well as visual texts do not float above the material world in some aesthetic ether, but, rather, plays a part in an immensely complex global system, in which energy, matter and ideas interact. All these numerous facets need to be considered while considering advertising. Another significant aspect is that of localization which will be discussed in the coming chapters.

Localization: Issues in Cultural Transmission

A powerful force drives the world toward a converging commonality, and that force is technology.

—*Theodore Levitt*

Advertisements predominantly persuade people to buy a particular product. They convey a distinct message using a collection of signs (words, pictures, sounds) with a particular purpose—a marketing strategy to disseminate the message and inform people about the availability of a product, to promote it and increase sales. With globalization, multinationals need to advertise their products and services throughout the globe, for their consumers speak different languages and have diverse cultural values, tastes and preferences. The print media (newspaper, daily, weekly, business publications, magazines), broadcast media (radio, television) and others like the Internet, ad films, brochures, pamphlets, leaflets and window displays are some of the media through which advertising is done. These communication vehicles convey commercial messages to their target audience. The place of advertising in society goes far beyond this commercial context. In the last 100 years, advertising has developed from the simple announcements of shopkeepers and the persuasive arts of a few marginal dealers into a major part of capitalist business organization. Raymond Williams argues that advertising is both crucial to the economic functioning of capitalism and a form of social communication, offering us new ways of understanding ourselves. Advertising categorizes man as consumers rather than users—the consumption of material goods offering an illusory satisfaction. In advertising's magic system, they are identified with human values and desires, obscuring the real sources of satisfaction. In this society where people imitate popular and cultural images, 'social cohesion is provided by the pseudo-solidarities (pseudo-mediations) of electronic television images' (Kroker, 1988:268). Viewers become mere playthings or ventriloquists' dummies for the technological imposition of commodity culture in late capitalism. Putting forward a general theorization, Baudrillard (1988:270) says:

...that TV is the real world of postmodern culture which has *entertainment* as its ideology, the *spectacle* as the emblematic sign of the commodity-form, *lifestyle advertising* as its popular psychology, pure, empty *seriality* as the bond which unites the simulacrum of the audience, *electronic images* as its most dynamic, and only, form of social cohesion, *elite media politics* as its ideological formula, the buying and selling of *abstracted attention* as the locus of its marketplace rationale, *cynicism* as its dominant cultural sign, and the diffusion of a *network of relational power* as its real product.

Williams considers advertising as 'the official art of modern capitalist society' (Marris and Thornham, 1996:704). Buying an object buys one social respect, discrimination, health, beauty, success as well as power over one's environment. One of the most important weapons used in successful marketing is advertising. Global media create opportunities for global marketing. Graphic and visual advertising approaches can be used to overcome cultural differences. Regardless of the company's form or style of management, the shift from national to international management entails new tools for advertisers including a single language (usually English), one control mechanism (the budget) and one strategic plan (marketing strategy). Modern advertising is largely considered a product of the 20th century.

Advertising has created some of the most recognized symbols in the world—the golden arches (McDonald's), the swoosh (Nike), the apple with the bite out of it (Apple) as well as those of Mercedes Benz and Volkswagen. A consumer/buyer makes a statement in a subtle way when he/she chooses a Pepsi, Tissot, Louis Vuitton, Gucci, Bossini or a Calvin Klein. The choice of brands becomes an expression of self-identity. When a brand is endorsed by a celebrity, it grabs the viewer's attention and becomes a symbol by associating with the celebrity and with an *in group*. By consuming and displaying brand symbols that are associated with these entities, the consumer reinforces in his mind identification and closeness with the person or group it stands for. These are all mechanisms of conveying imagery through language, attracting viewers' attention and also influencing the memorability of advertisements and particular brands. It is not only words that act as verbal communication, but the voice of a speaker, seen or heard, is also relevant. This *tone of voice* of the advertisement tries to recreate the experience of enjoying the product and should match the image of the product. Television allows the advertiser maximum opportunity to develop the most creative and imaginative ad messages as compared to other medium. The integration of sight, sound, motion and colour offers extraordinary flexibility to make dramatic and lifelike portrayals of products and services. The commercials can effectively communicate an image or mood associated with the brand. Language, being the primary system in normal communication, must not be overlooked in visually dependent television advertising. Creatives employ a number of stylistic techniques to draw the attention of the consumer—conventions of design and typography, adjectives, language games and rhetorical devices, such as repetition and sameness, stand out and act as an aid to memory. The form, style and tone of advertisements are manipulated and combinations of music, colour, typography, costume, voice, camera and lighting are used to evoke the right atmosphere. The aim is to create the right kind of reactions in the right target audience. It is not unusual for national companies to divide their advertising and marketing efforts into regional units to respond better to the competition. Localization has to take into consideration all these to make advertising effective. McDonald's uses agency to handle its national advertising and numerous agencies to handle franchise and regional efforts supplementing the national effort. This gives McDonald's the ability to react to the marketplace by cities, regions or individual stores.

Media analysis involves discovering the connotations of objects and symbolic phenomena and of actions and dialogue of the characters in texts (the meanings these may have for the audience) and linking these meanings to social, cultural, ideological and other concerns. The *codes* (highly complex patterns of association that all members of a given society and culture learn) in peoples' minds, affect the ways in which individuals interpret the signs and symbols they find in the media. Cultural codes provide a connotational framework, each term being aligned with a cluster of symbolic attributes. Adverts use shared prior cultural experience to attribute meaning to its symbolic representation of the product. The cultural context is important in recipient perceptions. Cultural context of the advert, font, colours and subject all reinforce the products' intended identity. The *context* in which the ad is situated is important. This has to be taken care of while localizing. As Umberto Eco points out, codes and sub-codes are applied to the message (text) in the light of a general framework of cultural references, which constitute the receiver's patrimony of knowledge—his ideological, ethical, religious standpoints, his psychological attitudes, his tastes, his value system and so on (making necessary cultural knowledge to understand). This is essential to avoid *aberrant decoding* which may result in cultural misunderstanding. The variant cultures make necessary *translation* of the advertisement texts if they are to draw the prospective buyer.

Codes are variable not only between different cultures and social groups but also historically. People read the world in terms of the codes and conventions dominant within the specific sociocultural contexts and roles within which they are socialized. This makes localization crucial. Texts may be produced within and for a different culture (advertisements produced indigenously in a country different from ones own for the domestic market in that country). Interpreting such texts in the

manner intended may require cultural competency relevant to
the specific cultural context of that texts' production, even when
the text is largely visual. Advertisements exhibiting Indian overtones and symbols are understood easily by those who share the
culture.

Companies either try to standardize their products/advertis-
ing to work in many markets or tailor their products and advertising to local markets. Consumer habits vary from country to
country and region to region. Proctor and Gamble (P&G) Global
Marketing Officer Jim Stengel points out how right global branding decision must be made on a case-by-case basis. To ensure
a savvy global marketing, he encourages marketing employees
to serve in P&G's regional organizations at some point in their
careers. A number of internal programmes that enable marketing employees from all around the world to share knowledge
and best practices from their regions are charted. In most countries, markets are composed of local (marketed in a single country), regional (throughout a region) and international (available
virtually everywhere in the world) brands. Global advertising
may be market oriented or culture oriented. Advertising that
promotes the same product in several countries (international
advertising) appeared in the late 20th century. Saturation of the
home country market as well as market potential for products
in other countries makes companies venture outside the home
market. Exporting a product requires placing the product in
the distribution system of another country. When a company is
regionalized, it may focus on its domestic market, but international considerations are equally important. Multinational companies like Coca Cola have several national, regional offices to
support its international markets. A global perspective involves
a corporate philosophy that directs products and advertising
towards a worldwide market. The ultimate goal of any organization in attaining a global perspective is to leverage its operations in such a way that they benefit from advantages offered by
each country's business environment (Moriarty and Duncan,
1990:511–512).

The transmission of product information through advertisements has an informative/persuasive function. Localization is
an important issue for companies looking to communicate to
the global market and achieve competitive edge. Translation

(linguistic/graphic) plays an important role in localization as well as international business communication. It constitutes an interesting and challenging process. In this marketing strategy, a cultural transmission takes place. As a social construction, translation calls for a sociolinguistic approach. Good advertising is the key to the success of any business. Signs are manipulated to produce shared thought. Meaning arises only when signs are shared by advertisers and consumers—when they both interpret the message to mean the same. Communication often breaks down because signs in advertisements do not have the same meaning (also to be addressed while localizing) for the two parties due to their diverse fields of experience. Every targeted group of customers should find it captivating, understandable and inoffensive with respect to their culture. The advertisement translator has to imbibe the culture associated with the native language and the culture followed by the target audience. The translation attempts to produce on its readers/viewers an effect as close as possible to that obtained on the readers/viewers of the SL. The advert in translation should communicate, as much as possible, to TL speakers the same meaning that was understood by the speakers of the SL and evolve the same response as the source text. Advertisement localization, which incorporates both linguistic and graphic translation from one cultural condition to another, is 'a process of intercultural communication, whose end product is a text which is capable of functioning appropriately in specific situations and context of use' (Baker, 1998:3). A social frame of reference has to be recreated for effective advertising. Neglect of certain indications during the localization process can wreck the best of advertising campaigns. Discussing the problems of correspondence in translation, Eugene Nida concludes that differences between cultures may cause more severe complications for the translators than do differences in language structure. Gideon Toury too points to the two languages and two cultures involved when translating (true of advertisement translation also). Translators are permanently faced with the problem of how to treat cultural aspects implicit in a source text and of finding the most appropriate technique of successfully conveying these aspects in the TL. The social and commercial contexts are significant and translation strategies are adopted to deliver the message. A sociolinguistic approach is, thus, a necessity in the analysis of audio-visual translation. As in the case of translated texts, in localization too, texts are reoriented towards a different reader in a different linguistic and cultural environment. The localizer is to have an in-depth knowledge of the SL as well as the culture of its speakers. The same in-depth knowledge is needed to re-encode the meaning in the TL. Knowledge of the SL–TL allows the translator to understand what the text-to-be translated means, of the culture, social conventions, customs and expectations of the speakers of the source and target texts. The increasing interest in cultural values in advertising is said to have emerged in the 1980s and was furthered by the debate over standardization versus localization of international marketing and advertising. Theodore Levitt's and Bill Jordan's *global sell* theory, advocating standardization of advertising messages and suggesting homogenization of the global marketplace, has been challenged by an assumption that globalization of markets will be accompanied by strengthening of local, cultural, ethnic and national individuality. A 1983 *Harvard Business Review* article by Theodore Levitt (a Professor at Harvard Business School) sets alight a debate over how to achieve global coverage. Levitt argued that companies should operate as if there were only one global market. He argued that differences among nations and cultures were not only diminishing but should be also ignored because people throughout the world are motivated by the same desires and wants—'A powerful force now drives the world toward a single converging commonality, and that force is technology. It has proletarianized communication, transport, and travel ... homogenizing markets everywhere' (Levitt, 1967:20). Levitt further argued that business would be more efficient if they planned for a global market. Refuting Levitt's philosophy, Philip Kotler (a Professor at Northwestern University) maintained that Levitt misinterpreted the overseas success of Coca Cola, PepsiCo and McDonald's. Their success, he held, is based on variation, not offering the same product everywhere. However, it was pointed out that the challenge lies in effectively coming up with ways to communicate the same message to a homogenized audience all over the world. The outgrowth of this debate has been three main schools of thought on advertising. The first being standardization which contends that differences between countries are more a matter of degree than directions, so advertisers must instead focus on the similarities of consumers around the world. The standardization school, also known as the universal, internationalized, common or uniform approach, questions the traditional belief in the heterogeneity of the market and the importance of the localized approach. They assume that better and faster communication has forged a convergence of art, literature, media availability, tastes, thoughts, religious beliefs, culture, living conditions, language and, therefore, advertising. Even when people are different, their basic physiological and psychological needs are still presumed to remain the same. The degree of standardization depends in part on corporate policy and strategic planning as well as on the importance of a particular overseas market. A multinational advertiser wishing to use a standardized advertising campaign needs to rely on an advertising agency with a worldwide network to coordinate the campaign across nations. Degree of feasibility varies from country to country, facilitating the implementation of standardization in some countries while creating problems in others. Standardized international advertising is the practice of advertising the same product in the same way everywhere in the world. The controversy of the standardization of global advertising centres on the appropriateness of the variation (or lack of it) within advertising content from country to country. A standardized advertisement is used internationally with virtually no change in its theme, copy or illustration (other than translation). The localization (adaptation) school of thought argues that advertisers must consider differences among countries including culture, economic and industrial development, media availability, legal restrictions and so on. This conventional school holds that advertisers should take particular note of the differences among countries (e.g., culture, taste, media and discretionary income). These differences make it necessary to develop specific advertising programmes to achieve impact in the local markets. The contingency (moderate) school of thought reasons that neither complete standardization nor complete adaptation is necessary and that a combination of the evaluation of factors can affect the effectiveness of such advertising. Most companies use a via media approach or lean towards localization. Companies like McDonald's translate many of their ads into other languages and conform to local standards and regulations. The organizational structure for managing international advertising depends heavily on whether the company is following standardization or localization marketing and advertising strategy. While for highly standardized advertising efforts, there may be one advertising plan for each product regardless of the number of markets entered, for a product using localized advertising, there probably will be a separate advertising plan for each foreign market. The choice of an advertising agency for international advertising is influenced not only by many of the same considerations as the choice of a domestic agency, but also by the standardized versus local decision. A company that takes a highly standardized approach in international markets is likely to favour an international agency that can handle advertising for the product in both the domestic and the international market. A localized advertising effort, by contrast, favours the use of advertising agencies in many countries for both planning and implementation of advertising. Although advertising campaigns can be created for worldwide exposure, advertising is intended to persuade a reader or listener to do something (buy and order). While some advertisers develop tightly controlled global campaigns with minimum adaptation for local markets (the *global* realm against the subjugated *local*), others develop campaigns in every major market. Companies also adopt a middle path, with a global campaign and a standardized strategy that is partially adapted as needed. A successful advertising campaign conceived for national application is modified for use in other countries. The setting and people are localized in most markets. P&G, Philips, IBM and many other companies have taken their successful campaigns and transplanted them around the world. A strong musical theme, typical of Coke and Pepsi, makes the transfer even smoother because music is an international language.

The advertising programmes must adjust to the local market differences. Advertising and sales promotion laws, language and technological differences vary from country to country. Standardizing the copy content by translating the appeal into the language of the foreign market is fraught with possible communication blunders. A copywriter who is fluent in both the domestic and foreign language and familiar with the culture of the foreign market is a prerequisite. Adaptation is especially important if the advertiser wants its products identified with the local market rather than as a foreign import. Problems arise when a foreign brand name is translated into other languages (like Chinese) for the question arises as to whether its pronunciation should be adopted or its meaning should be translated. If the pronunciation is chosen, the meaning might be different due to the fact that the character symbols represent ideas rather than letters. If the meaning of the brand name is translated, it will be pronounced differently. A global perspective poses concerns about the homogenization of cultural differences. A highly successful campaign in one country may not be successful in another. One of the catch phrases of multinational selling is global marketing. Pizza Hut is considered one of the few truly global restaurant brands. To build a unique brand character, the company used the same television commercial throughout Europe featuring its stuffed crust pizza—a single core product, a single brand, a single identity. Local advertising agencies tailor campaigns to each area's culture and needs. Whether it is the golden arches of McDonald's, the swoosh of Nike or the distinctive logo of Coca Cola, companies look for a unique brand identification that is easily understood and meaningful regardless of the language or culture of a specific country. It is impossible, however, to accommodate all the cultural and national differences in any single marketing strategy. Everything from dietary customs, appropriate body language, religion, gender, accepted means of showing respect and expected levels of formality in different settings have to be taken into consideration. The advertiser has to be aware of both linguistic and cultural nuances as literal translations may be filled with a number of disastrous pitfalls.

Becoming popular with Levitt's (1983) famous article in the early 1980s, many companies took the position that viewed advances in technology and communication as leading to a homogenized group of global consumers. It was believed that consumers around the world could be reached with similar products and messages because people's needs and values were converging. Though there exists the benefits of localized flexibility, many marketers strive for the potential savings from campaigns that attempt to reach global consumers with a single message and strategy. Others (like Marieke de Mooij) argue that one message is not enough to effectively connect with consumers. The interplay of the global and the local was also put forward by Roland Robertson through his idea of *glocalization*. A postmodern shift in theorizing globalization suggests that cultural heterogeneity is produced even when local cultures assimilate and adopt Western popular culture. Studies on the universal/localized advertising approaches (first addressed by Elinder in 1961) have been controversial.

Advertisement translations are important in the marketing strategies of companies. It is done either by the company itself or outsourced to a translation agency. The translators of all text types, and not just advertising, need to be aware of the conventions that exist in both their native language and the language with which they are less familiar. While translation of literary texts enables authors to attain recognition among readers (apart from success at home), localization provides a global market/broader perspective to multinational companies. The focus in advertisement translation is more on the special purpose for which it is made rather than on attaining equivalence between source texts and the translation. It is initiated by a client (a company) who commissions it with a specific purpose (to increase the company's share of potential customers) in mind and requires that the translator translates it for this purpose. The translator has to be aware of the *skopos* of the commercial, the norms and the values of both the cultures (source culture/target culture) and its effect on the client's business. The culture in which the translated message is received is important in the advertising campaign and the translator should '[t]ranslate/interpret/speak/write in a way which enables [his] text/translation to function in the situation in which it is used and with the people who want to use it and precisely in the way they want it to function' (Nord, 1997:29). The SL word may express a concept which is totally unknown in the target culture. Like translated literature, which occupies a peripheral position within the literary polysystem, localized adverts too involve a *secondarization*. Replication of situation attended by word equivalence is sought to attain impact on a consumer in the target culture. The greatest challenge is to attain perfect lip synching, else incongruity arises and the audience notes the discrepancy. Such an advert fails to appeal to the consumer.

In localization, translation has to be tailored for a particular market in a particular country. The adaptation (involved in localization) needs careful thinking in the target culture, for at times the visual elements may prove to be offensive to the target audience. Legal action was initiated and the advert pulled off in the wake of severe criticism against Benetton's new global campaign (titled UNHATE, 2011), which contained a series of photo montages of political and religious leaders kissing. The communication strategy to be effective must be moulded to suit the very consumers targeted. Success depends to a large extent on the translator/translation involved in the procedure. The advert is to be understood by (and inoffensive to) the target audience. Translation becomes a business function and an integral part of the marketing process. The translator, being involved in a cross-cultural communication, dons the role of a *cultural mediator/ cultural go-between*. The translation has to fulfil the function of the original advert and has a similar effect on the receiving market for the product to sell. The translator decodes and encodes the cultural signs and uses the cultural codes that sell. Adaptation of the text, image and visual expression is as important as the verbal expression that goes with it. The meaning of colours and symbolism could also be contradictory from one region to another. The cultural stereotypes and social clichés in use in the hosting society, representation of ethnic preferences, religious convictions and so on differ. Localization should take all these into consideration, to enable a good understanding of the advertising message and to ensure its success in the target market.

Advertising engages linguistic/graphic translation (a change, *translatio, to carry across* from one condition/place to another) in its communication/localization (an adjustment to the cultural system of the TL) process. It makes use of the services of specialized translators. The content and layout of the culture of a specific market is made suitable for a given (target) culture. Traditional translation skills combine with technical ability, posing a challenge to the existing definition of translation—translators going beyond just transferring the language element to paper. Localization is more than just a translation and represents a specific combination of language, region and character encoding. Problems arise when advertisements created in one culture have to be translated for use in another culture. It does not merely imply finding linguistic equivalents in the TL. Translating the body text into a foreign language, yet leaving the remainder in English, would be translation but not complete localization. According to the Localization Industry Standards Association (LISA), localization involves taking a product and making it linguistically and culturally appropriate to the target locale (country/region and language) where it will be used and sold. Advertising translation plays an important role in the global marketing. There takes place a conversion/customization of the original message into the linguistic code of the foreign consumer. Country-specific references have to be taken into account. The translation of idiomatic expressions, metaphoric constructions, physical stereotypes, ethical and political arguments, sensibilities and notions of eroticism of the different cultures have to be considered. For a translation to be localized, it must match the cultural requirements of the target market, ensuring cultural appropriateness. Cultural references must fit in seamlessly with the target market. Localization issues arise in countries like India because of the existing subtle differences in culture and language. As researchers point out, the localized advertisement may have a zero effect (in which translation of the original message into the languages of the foreign consumers brings about neither a drop nor increase in sales), a positive effect (in which the translation automatically involves an increase in demand in the market targeted by the translated campaign) or a negative effect (in which translation becomes a disadvantage). The total amount of money the company can spend on the translation of the advertisement, the time devoted, sociocultural factors, the rules and regulations of the foreign market all have an impact on the process of advertising localization.

Language is a major vehicle of sociocultural interaction. Translation plays an indispensable role in transferring messages across languages and cultural barriers. Those who import texts from one culture to another through translation perform an act of transfer. The texts become an integral part of the home repertoire of the target culture. Advertisement (television) translation (linguistic/graphic from one culture to another) also addresses a new audience and cultural situation and involves a *re-writing* of an original *text*. The whole visual presentation has to be *translated* to adapt to the target culture addressed. The translation involves a 'replacement of textual material in one language (Source Language) by equivalent material in another language (Target Language)' (Catford, 1965:20). Two languages and two cultures are involved in advertising localization, and the difference between cultures may cause severer complications for the translators than do difference in language structure. With localization, a displacement from one language to another takes place and a text/advert is made meaningful to its receiver. Besides being indispensable to the process of localization, translation of adverts is 'a new offer of information in the target culture about some information offered in the source culture and language' (Bassnett and Lefevere, 1990:8). Translation needs to be sensitive to the context. Multinational companies' localization of international advertising campaign consists of adapting their communication to the specifications of the local environment of the hosting country targeted by the campaign. The sociocultural component includes the local particularities stemming from religion, social and ethical norms, and so on. The companies adopt different attitudes to the problems of cultural adaptation in the translation process. It may be linked more to the original context (ethnocentric), integrate the cultural specificity of each country (polycentric), adapt its campaign to regions (regiocentric) or transcend geographic/cultural specificities to create universalized messages (geocentric). The text is reoriented towards a different reader in a different linguistic/cultural environment. Translation requires that the full meaning of the source material be accurately rendered into the TL, with special attention paid to cultural nuance and style. It is only one of the activities in localization. In addition to translation, a localization project includes many other tasks.

In localization, there is stronger emphasis placed on translation tools and technology compared to the traditional translation industry. Localization should be achieved in the target culture without losing the spirit or the identity. The image, slogan, catch line and caption pose problems when being transferred from one language to another, for they become cultural issues. It has to be equally catchy, chiming or appealing in the new language as the original was in its language. The cultural factors of the targeted market are important in commercials for the success of the brand. Localization services are available in

India. In India, the last decade of the 20th century has witnessed a phenomenal growth in advertising business. Companies ranging from large global players to small local retailers increasingly rely on advertising to sell their products.

'Culturalizing' Advertisements: Relocating the Ad Message

Translation is not just the stringing together of the most accurate synonyms by the most proximate syntax.

—*Gayatri Chakravorty Spivak*

Adverts need to convey a distinct message using particular meanings and signs with a specific purpose (promote the product). They are predominantly meant to persuade people into buying a particular (often the latest) product. Customers have different tastes and preferences, speak different languages and have different cultural values. Advertising is the most visible manifestation of the globalization of business in general and of brands in particular. With the rise of globalization, multinational companies need to advertise their products and services throughout the globe to appeal to the plural tastes of society. This has resulted in the evolution of a new type of translation targeted towards advertisements (print as well as audio-visual)—Advertisement Localization. According to the LISA, localization involves taking a product and making it linguistically and culturally appropriate to the target locale (country/region and language) where it will be used and sold.

Localization is the process of adapting and manufacturing a product so that it has the look and feel of nationally manufactured piece of goods—customization to a specific region. It enables companies to do business in markets outside their home market. Efficient localization depends on product and service globalization—making all the necessary technical, financial, management, personnel, marketing and other enterprise decisions facilitating localization. The LISA defines localization as 'the process of modifying products or services to account for differences in distinct markets' (LISA, 2000:13). The degree of localization required may vary:

In the real world of business today factors influencing the extent of localization include the nature and scope of the product concerned, the size of the target market and audience, the length of the product life cycle and anticipated update frequencies, competitor behavior, market acceptance and national or international legislation. (Fry, 2003)

Localization should not be taken in isolation. It needs to be an integral part of the entire product design, development and distribution chain. Slogans and advertising claims require recreation in the TL rather than a literal rendition. The Localization Primer lays down the following regarding localization:

Localization allows the benefits of globalization to accrue not only to large companies and powerful nations—localization lets speakers of less common languages enjoy access to the same products that those in major markets use. In addition localization allows the flow of products and information to be two way as dominant countries receive goods and services from smaller countries that have traditionally had no access to their markets. When companies localize their products and services they help to 'level the playing field' and redress economic inequalities, helping to create a better world in which no one is left out. (Fry, 2003)

The LISA defines a *well-globalized product* to mean a product that has been enabled at a technical level for localization. The term *localization* has been defined as a process to facilitate globalization by addressing linguistic and cultural barriers specific to the receiver who does not share the same linguistic and cultural backgrounds as the sender. While localization does not provide all the solutions required for globalization, it clearly holds significant implications. The extensive adaptation of the message normally employed in localization supports the role of translation and *domestication* as opposed to *foreignization*. Localization is part of globalization, and translation is in turn a component of localization. Localization and its associated processes can be considered a new, well-established paradigm within the language industry. Although it has elements of conventional translation, it cannot be explained entirely on the basis of the conventional paradigm of translation. A subtle difference designates internationalization as the adaptation of products (done once) for potential use virtually everywhere, while localization (done once for each combination of product and locale) is the addition of special features for use in a specific locale. The processes are complementary and must be combined to lead to the objective of a system that works globally. The localization phase involves, among other things, the four issues that LISA describes as linguistic, physical, business, cultural and technical issues.

The localization industry has continued to grow and has established its own business models and best practices, largely without reliance on the knowledge of conventional translation. Localization is driven by market forces as well as by the clients who dictate what they want from language support providers. The emergence of the localization industry has had a significant influence through its efforts to quantify and benchmark the quality of translation. Companies have come to rely on localizers to create a given user environment specified by the language and associated cultural conventions of the market. Translators and interpreters are, thus, an essential cog in the globalization process. Several researchers, like Roehrig and Rondinello, have argued that foreign companies (even establishments operating at the *national* level to approach the *local*) need to adapt at least some aspect of their products and services in Asian and associated developing markets while trying to preserve a sense of authenticity and foreign core value. Localized campaigns require adaptation or customization of advertising messages in global markets. There emerges the need to understand cross-cultural differences, in the way the values are conveyed, since they provide situations for interpreting advertisements, are frequently implied by advertisements, vary across countries and may be used for market segmentation. Targeting consumers by using their cultural values is considered a potent marketing tactic in developing successful advertising strategies. Cultural values reflected in advertising messages are considered to have a powerful influence not only on consumers' product choices, but also on their motivations and lifestyles. Global Consumer Culture Positioning (GCCP) is distinguished from the two other strategies that involve cultural meaning transfer—Local Consumer Culture Positioning (LCCP) defined as a strategy that associates the brand with local cultural meanings, reflects the local culture's norms and identities, is portrayed as consumed by local people in the national culture and/or is depicted as locally produced for local people, and Foreign Consumer Culture Positioning (FCCP) defined as a strategy that positions the brand as symbolic of a specific foreign consumer culture (i.e., a brand whose personality, use occasion and/or user group are associated with a foreign culture).

Message development can be a highly complex problem for multinational companies that market their products and services on a global scale. While the proponents of the standardized approach argue that people all over the world share the same basic needs and motivations, and therefore, advertising campaigns can be constructed around these needs and motivations with a universal approach, the advocates of the localized approach attest that standardization of advertising campaigns is not possible because several striking differences—including cultural characteristics, government regulations and consumer behaviour—exist between nations. As a result of these differences, advertisers must tailor their campaigns on a country-by-country basis. Levitt sparked a heated debate when he considered marketing globalization (standardization) as a necessity for a successful global corporation. He asserted that the world is becoming a common marketplace and people all over the world are remarkably alike regarding love, hate, fear, envy, joy and their lives. In the article, Levitt (1983) proposed that companies should move towards creating holistic or global marketing strategies. While Levitt recognizes the growing phenomenon of market segmentation, he argues that these segments are global, rather than local—that increasingly, all over the world, one finds the same market segments repeated over and over again. Following Levitt's proposal, Saatchi & Saatchi (a top international advertising agency with its headquarters in the West) in its 1986 annual report stated that the global corporation operates as if the entire world (or major regions of it) were a single entity; it sells the same things in the same way everywhere. Localization holds that advertisers have to consider insurmountable barriers like differences in culture, taste, media infrastructure and economic development, and consumers' resentment of international corporations' attempts to homogenize their differing tastes and cultures. Consumers grow up in particular cultures characterized by value systems, beliefs and perception processes. Given these considerations, it becomes necessary to design specific advertising programmes to achieve impact in local markets. International advertisers must be cognizant of any resurgence of nationalism, the stage of economic development, media availability and legal restrictions in the targeted nations (an instance being Coca Cola in India—the Plachimada issue in Kerala and the subsequent revamping of its advertisements—indicating the pertinent historical context). International advertisers are often faced with the issue of whether, and to what extent, they should change their advertising messages from one country to another. The relevance and the influence of the local culture are still very substantial in numerous countries around the globe. Localization of international/national advertising campaigns consists of adapting the company's communication to the specificities of the local environment of the hosting countries targeted by the campaign. Doing away with localization implicitly caters to the idea that cultural imperialism via advertising rests on the notion of value's transfer from *Centre* to *Periphery* nations by means of images and explicit copy, the result of which is a substitution of traditional values and beliefs to the detriment of periphery nations.

Advertisement translation (visual/aural/linguistic) plays a significant role in business communications and international marketing. Communication becomes effective in a foreign environment only when the message has been translated. The responsibility for achieving the goals in a competitive market to a large extent, thus, rests with the translator/localizer. The *original* message has to be converted into the linguistic code of the *foreign* consumer. Localization of advertising campaigns consists of adapting the company's communication to the specificities of environment of the hosting countries targeted by the campaigns. Companies create international reputation and aim at cross-cultural communication through it. The sociocultural/politico-legal components/restrictions are to be considered in the process. The brand name/slogan/caption all pose a problem, raising cultural issues when it comes to localization of advertisements. The cultural factor can at no point be overlooked. Cultural codes that sell are to be integrated by the translator. Culturalization of content draws on the knowledge of the TL and cultural conventions relevant to the field to which the text belongs. It also touches on wider commercial considerations, such as the treatment of brand names in a particular market, where the particular name sounds actively offensive or means something completely different in the TL and, hence, would require reconsideration of naming. It, therefore, requires expertise in the commercial field, such as international market research and multicultural advertising, which can provide advice on wider issues than immediate translation problems. Marketing or advertising blunders are caused due to cultural insensitivity on the part of international marketers. Being an intercultural communication, graphic adaptations become a necessity. The people and advertisements communicating within the same culture share the same experience, but when it has to be translated into another language and culture, cultural gaps/barriers may arise. The effect created should be as close as possible to that obtained to the readers/viewers in the original. Idioms and phrases which are culture bound prove an obstacle to translation. They fail to make sense in another culture when a literal translation is resorted to. Correspondence is to be maintained between the source advert and the target advert. Even in cases where the product or service has a very strong international image, some degree of subtle local adaptation might still be required to meet local market needs. The degree of adaptation may vary from product to product and, even, from location to location. Economic factors, time constraint, sociocultural parameter, as well as the political and legal framework affect advertising localization. The relevance and influence of these parameters are certainly varied according to regions and countries. Overlooking them leads undoubtedly to the failure of the campaign. In this context, the translator/ localizer plays a key role in the adaptation of the communication campaign. Although the function of advertising is to influence demand for specific products and services, nevertheless in a cultural context the role of advertising is to reinforce conventional cultural values and help communicate new tastes, habits and customs. The targeted group of customers should find it captivating, understandable and non-offensive with respect to their culture. Professional translators are approached for localization of an advert. Values and beliefs have to be translated with expertise. These translators/localizers are different from other types of translators due to the difference in the nature of their work.

Advertisement is a mode of communication, and translation aids in the communication process. Localization helps in increasing a company's share of potential customers. An advertisement or promotional video is translated into different languages and sometimes the style of presentation is also changed to give it a local look. The main challenge during advertising localization is the dubbing of the original advert into the TL and matching the lip movement of the anchors according to it, to give naturality to the adverts so that it appeals to the consumers. The translator has to analyse the effect of his work on the client's business. Translation (visual/linguistic) is a key factor in localization. Creativity is a must for the translator. Straight translation is not enough in marketing products. It necessitates local intelligence and thorough understanding of the customs and cultures of the country where marketing is intended. For companies looking to communicate their corporate messages to the global markets and achieve competitive edge, effective localization is vital. The contents must be adapted to the linguistic and cultural system of the TL. The graphical component must also undergo any necessary transformation to meet the linguistic and cultural communication requirements. Translation is a communicative act—'a process of intercultural communication, whose end product is a text which is capable of functioning appropriately in specific situations and context of use' (Baker, 1998:3–5). Skopos theorists regard a *text* (here adverts) as 'an offer of information from its producer to a recipient and translation a secondary offer of information about information originally offered in another language within another culture' (Baker, 1998:3–5). Multinational companies' localization of international advertising campaigns consists of adapting the company's communication to the specificities of the local environment of the hosting country targeted by the campaign—sociocultural components (local particularities stemming from religion and social ethical norms), politico-legal components (the local distinctiveness shooting from the nature of the political system) and so on. The translator plays a pivotal role, for he has to be certain that the sociocultural restrictions do not create problems and has to manage the cultural differences between the different hosting countries of a single advertising campaign. Interculturality demands him to convey a single message written in two different languages without losing spirit or identity. Adaptation in content and form is indispensable. Graphic adaptation is required in the case of background which has to be changed to suit the sociocultural environment of the hosting country. Cultural factors of the targeted market take place within the commercial communication (a cultural *mimesis*). Adaptation of text, image, trademark, brand name and slogan with the visual expression is as important as the verbal expression that underlies it. The graphic identity in addition to the verbal identity, thus, has to be relocated. The adaptation of currencies, weights, measures and addresses vary according to countries and languages. The meaning of colours and symbolism of geometrical/architectural forms could be contradictory from one region to another. The cultural stereotypes and social clichés in use in the hosting culture of the advertising message, representation of ethnic preferences, religious convictions, national spirit and so on cannot be overlooked. A good understanding of the advertising message and success in the targeted market is essential. Verbal–graphic localization as well as iconographic localization becomes necessary.

Translation is an important step in the localization process, but localization is not just another word for translation. The content and layout have to be adapted to the culture of a specific market. For a translation to be localized, it must match the cultural requirements of the target market ensuring cultural appropriateness. Cultural references must be adapted to fit in seamlessly with the target market. Localization issues arise even in countries with common language because of the existing subtle differences in culture and language. Country-specific references have to be taken into account. Translation plays a crucial role in transferring messages across languages and cultural barriers. As Itamar Even-Zohar puts it, translation is no longer a phenomenon whose nature and borders are given once and for all, but an activity dependent on the relations within a certain cultural system.

The globalization of economies and trade intensification leads companies to communicate with consumers of different languages and cultures. Concomitant to globalization are the substantial overcoming of spatial barriers and the centrality of knowledge and information, resulting in the increased mobility of people and objects and a heightened contact between different linguistic communities. Globalization addresses the business issues associated with taking a product global. In the globalization of high-tech products, this involves integrating localization throughout a company, after proper internationalization (LISA defines internationalization as the process of generalizing a product so that it can handle multiple languages and cultural conventions without the need for redesign.) and product design, as well as marketing, sales and support in the world market (LISA). Companies will go global when they start developing, translating, marketing and distributing their products to foreign language markets. Globalization is the process by which a company breaks free of the home markets to pursue business opportunities wherever its customers may be located. Within the framework of international marketing strategies, advertising plays a key role. Localization is an integral part of the overall process called globalization. To *globalize* is to plan the design and development methods for a product in advance, keeping in mind a multicultural audience, to avoid increased costs and quality problems, save time and smooth the localizing effort for each region or country. Internationalization and localization are two primary technical processes that comprise globalization. Internationalization encompasses the planning and preparation stages for a product that is built by design to support global markets. This process removes all cultural assumptions and any country- or language-specific content is stored so that it can be easily adapted. Localization refers to the actual adaptation of the product for a specific market. Glocalization (a portmanteau/ linguistic hybrid indicating the compression of the world and the intensification of the consciousness of the world as a whole) was a term invented to emphasize that the globalization of a product is more likely to succeed when the product or service is adapted specifically to each locality or culture it is marketed in. The term *glocal* refers to the individual, group, division, unit, organization and community which are willing and able *to think globally and act locally*. The term (intended for a global or trans-regional market) *glocalization* originated from within Japanese business practices. It comes from the Japanese word *dochakuka* (originally referred to a way of adapting farming techniques to local conditions/now global localization) invented to explain Japanese marketing strategies. It accentuates that the global-ization of a product is more likely to succeed when the product or service is adapted specifically to each locality or culture it is marketed in—globalized, yet fashioned/customized to accom-modate the user or consumer in a local market/culture. Accord-ing to the sociologist Roland Robertson (1992—credited with popularizing it in western social science discourse in the 1990s), the term glocalization describes the tempering effects of local conditions on global pressures. At a 1997 conference on *Global-ization and Indigenous Culture*, Robertson refers to glocaliza-tion as the simultaneity—the co-presence—of both universaliz-ing and particularizing tendencies; 'the interpenetration of the universalization of particularization and the particularization of universalism' (Robertson, 1992:100). The neologism denotes the connecting of the local and the global via information and technology, as well as the global corporate strategy of tailoring commodities to local markets or fetishizing local places for the purposes of product branding. Tendencies towards homogene-ity and centralization appear alongside tendencies towards het-erogeneity and decentralization. Glocalization entails a radical change in perspective pointing to the simultaneity of globaliz-ing and localizing processes, and to interconnectedness of the global and local levels. Local spaces are shaped and local identi-ties are created by globalized contacts as well as by local circum-stances (a two-level system—global and local).

In the marketing context, glocalization means the creation of products or services for the global market by adapting them to local cultures. Local identities are stimulated and shaped primarily by trans-local interaction, comparison and trends. The local is fundamentally shaped by the global and vice versa. The local milieu plays an important role. Taking into consideration the worldwide tendency to increasingly bring the particular into relationship with the universal, the particular, Robertson says, is what makes the universal work. Glocalization may be seen as the ability of a culture, when it encounters other strong cultures, to absorb influences that naturally fit into and can enrich that culture, to resist those things that are truly alien and to compartmentalize those things that, while different, can nevertheless be enjoyed and celebrated as different. It has emerged as the new standard in reinforcing positive aspects of worldwide interaction, be it in textual translations, localized marketing communication, or sociopolitical considerations. Robertson suggested that the global and the local mutually constitute each other, by this he means a process where the global and the local mesh to form the *glocal*. This conjunctive existence renders localization imperative.

The Visual-linguistic 'Relay': Interpreting Advertisement Signs

Translation is the most intimate act of reading.

—*Gayatri Chakravorty Spivak*

Advertisement is a genre shared by several media. An advertisement *text* is an assemblage of signs (such as words, images, sounds and/or gestures) polysemic in nature. Advertising agencies try to use metaphors, signs and symbols that are easily comprehended by the target market. Chandler (2002:53) points out that in advertisements, what matters in *positioning*—a product is not the relationship of advertising signifiers to real world referents, but the differentiation of each sign from the others to which it is related. Those who share the codes are members of the same *interpretative community*. Familiarity with particular codes is related to social position, in terms of such factors as class, ethnicity, nationality, education, occupation, political affiliation, age, gender and sexuality. Man (*homosignificans meaning makers*) makes meanings through the interpretation of signs. Although adverts do not physically represent the product, they provide an important iconic representation of both the product and what the product should stand for. The cryptic nature of adverts makes the text a key to the visual and vice versa. The ambiguity of the written text can often be interpreted only with reference to the image. An advertisement has its own system of meaning. The polysemic visual sign can only be defined in a *context*. Television uses verbal language, visual images and sound to generate impressions and ideas in people. While jingles aid memorability, slogans provide continuity to a series of adverts in a campaign and help in creating a positioning statement. Logotypes and signatures appear in all the company ads, are immediately recognized, are retained while localizing and give the product individuality at the point of sale (like those of Kellogg's, Intel, HP, Apple or McDonald's). The advertising image can condition perception of objects before they are actually seen. It is designed for maximum visual impact (through a blend of text and imagery to promote product/services), has to mould opinion and not offend the market. All these have to be taken into consideration, while localizing, to reach an audience ignorant of the language/ culture in the source advert.

An advert is constructed with the aim of targeting the product at an audience familiar with and sympathetic to its relevant cultural signifiers. Benetton, Cadbury, Renault all have had to cancel advertisements in some countries because of culturally variant meanings. Benetton gathered negative publicity in the United States with an ad depicting a black woman nursing a white child, because of the historical association with slavery. Cadbury upset the Indian sentiment comparing a brand of chocolate to the disputed territory of Kashmir and describing both as *Too Good to Share* (socio-political connotations—a politically incorrect chocolate bar incensed the nation). The Axe Dark Temptation deodorant advert, part of an international campaign by Unilever aired on Indian television, was banned in India for showing an apparently irresistible chocolate man being gnawed on by scantily clad women. Though parts of the offensive advert were censored to appease the regional audience, the Advertising Standards Council of India (ASCI) on receiving complaints decided to remove it. A Pepsi advert was banned in India after child labour complaints were raised. Large cosmetic and beauty companies like L'Oreal have also had to face claims of racial discrimination/misrepresentation of reality in advertising. In their constant quest to attract consumers and associate products with *cool* or luxurious and hedonistic lifestyles, some advertisers have consistently pushed the boundaries of what is ethically and socially acceptable. Campaigns that blur that distinction often arouse controversy and even protests. For two decades, the most notorious purveyor of sensual *cool* was Calvin Klein—beginning in the late 1970s with the *nothing comes between me and my Calvin's* campaign featuring Brooke Shields and culminating in 1998s *kiddie-porn* controversy. Klein's racy advertisements provoked the ire of conservative groups but earned him the respect of edgier critics who viewed his campaigns as artistically ironic. In the end, the controversies benefited Klein, as the media firestorm provided free publicity for his brand name and underscored the sophisticated *cool* of the campaigns. Many parents, for instance, were incensed at Calvin Klein's ads because they perceived them as pornographic, thereby causing a social cost that extended well beyond the limited scope of merely selling clothes. Views of offensiveness vary a great deal from country to country. Clothing retailer Benetton uses the same ads all over the world, and sometimes the ads impinge on the customs and religious beliefs of certain countries. The intended message in this ad, poignantly called *A Kiss from God*, is that love surmounts all conventional taboos. However, the Italian Advertising Authority banned it. In areas where the influence of the church was less strong, the message was better understood. Scantily clad, suggestively portrayed women sell every different type of product on television, in magazines and now on personal computer screens, in increasing numbers.

Advertisements present a *mediated reality* which run counter to the reality that focuses on persuading the audience to believe in the on-going reality of the narrative. Barthes introduced the concept of *textual anchorage* primarily in relation to advertisements—linguistic elements can serve to *anchor* (or constrain) the preferred readings of an image— *to fix the floating chain of signifieds* (Barthes, 1977:39). Visual expression needs a linguistic anchorage to get rid of superfluous meanings. Hence, there almost always exists some kind of linguistic message related to the picture in an advertisement. Barthes goes on to use the term relay to describe text–image relationships which are complementary. To understand an advert, one has to adopt the identity of a consumer who desires the advertised product (a subject position)—has to take on an appropriate ideological identity. Advertisements stress specific visions of society, focus on how products produce happiness in consumers and project a vision of the future. They use various forms of representation and techniques of presentation. The viewer/reader is important and will bring his/her own interpretations to the texts by drawing on their own cultural values and perceptual codes. Chandler in his *Semiotics for Beginners* points out how decoding involves not simply basic recognition and comprehension of what a text *says* but also the interpretation and evaluation of its meaning with reference to relevant codes. The reader has to be accustomed with the relevant social codes and textual codes. The same text may generate different meanings for different readers. The meaning of an advertisement does not float on the surface just waiting to be internalized by the viewer, but is built up out of the ways that different signs are organized and related to each other, both within the advert and through external references to wider belief systems. The meanings generated by a single sign are multiple/multi-accentual, indicating the potential for diverse interpretation of the same sign according to particular social and historical contexts. This occurs in the case of an advert and makes necessary a localized context.

Television commercials try to communicate quickly with a repertoire of visual images that suggest places and feelings associated with them. Through repetition, they make a virtual iconography of them. Culture and communication shape consumer behaviour and perception of the world. Advertising images offer a sense of identity to their so-called target audiences in the form of observable behaviour patterns and in the social connotations of prestige and status (as when one owns a Verito, a BMW, an Audi or an SX4) often attached to ownership of the product. People worldwide share certain needs; these needs are met differently from culture to culture. Although the function of advertising is the same throughout the world, the expression of its message varies in different cultural settings. This necessitates localization. Cultural differences are most likely between countries that are separated by a vast expanse. Expressions in one language may be out of context when translated into another language. In an advertisement, there exists the harmonious relation of explication (by text) and illustration (by image). Commercial semiotics has the aim of making communication work for brands within their competitive and cultural contexts. The individual becomes a receiver as well as a creator of meaning. The *text* may amplify a set of connotations already given in the visual or it produces (invents) an entirely new signified which is retroactively projected into the image, so much so as to appear denoted there. The text can even contradict the image so as to produce a compensatory connotation. The signifieds of the advertising message are formed *a priori* by certain attributes of the product and these signifieds have to be transmitted as clearly as possible in whichever culture targeted. As Barthes (1977:36) puts it, the viewer of the image 'perceives *at one and the same time* the perceptual message and the cultural message'. The text '*directs* the reader through the signifieds of the image, causing him to avoid some and receive others; by means of an often subtle *dispatching*, it remote controls him towards a meaning chosen in advance' (Barthes, 1977:40). Contemporary television commercials are a powerful example of how images may be used to make implicit claims which advertisers often prefer not to make openly in words. These have to be handled/conveyed while and through localization. Each medium has its own constraints and, as Umberto Eco holds, each is already charged with cultural signification. One has to be familiar with the relevant cultural codes when engaged in localization.

A translation is 'a new offer of information in the target culture about some information offered in the source culture and language' (Bassnett, 1991). The translation (visual-linguistic) involved in localization should (be faithful) accurately render the meaning of the source text, not distort it. Translation, as Susan Bassnett stresses, is not just a literary activity but a cultural one as well. It is a crossing over between two worlds in which the recognition of differences and not sameness between cultures is the first step to an honest but unslavish rendering of the original. Localization involves the process of converting the content in a given language (source) to another language (target). The translator/localizer should have a thorough understanding of both the source and the target language (SL–TL) involved. While translating/localizing, the translator/localizer converts the SL content into the TL. Translation is to be as close as possible to the source content, despite the lack of similar words or appropriate phrases, commonly experienced while translating. Advertisement localization is characterized as offering information, to members of one culture in their language (the TL and culture), about information originally offered in another language within another culture (SL and culture). It is a secondary offer of information, imitating a primary offer of information. The normal position assumed by a dubbed (only aural translation) advert tends to be a secondary one—designating a hierarchical relation. A localized (aural and visual translation) advert becomes an integral part of the home target repertoire. Apart from success at home, translation helps to attain popularity among foreign readers/viewers/market. The translation must match its source text in function and employ equivalent situational means to achieve it. As the SL word may express a concept totally unknown to the target culture, the translator/localizer has to be aware of the conventions existing in both (TL–SL) the languages. Only then an equivalent advertisement *text* can be created in a second language. There should be a successful rendering of the meaning.

Companies often market the same product under different names in different countries or tailor the product, packaging or marketing to the character of the market. Localization involves adaptation. Areas of adaptation could include the design, look and shape of a product, the features of the particular product or service, the type of packaging used, various aspects of promotional materials and associated programmes, and many other aspects of product (or service) design, positioning and overall marketing. Each geographic market being distinctive, these differences have to be taken into account when designing a product or service. Aspects such as the colour, shape and name of a product or service may need to be changed to meet local conditions, cultural preferences and viewpoints (like when Coca Cola entered the Chinese market). Adaptations may be with respect to product or language or culture.

The idiomatic expressions, metaphoric constructions, ethical, political arguments and physical stereotypes need to be adapted. In localization, the layout may have to be changed and the sensibility of the people needs to be taken into consideration. Besides translation, the sociocultural restrictions, which could be problematic in the advertising transfer, have to be dealt with. Managing cultural differences between the different hosting countries of a single advertising campaign is a necessity. Representations of the human body may not be acceptable in some cultures. Images and colours can represent different things in different cultures. All these changes aim to recognize local sensitivities, avoid conflict with local culture and habits and enter the local market by merging into its needs and desires. Adaptations of the advertising image include the adaptation of the meaning related to the background and the relation between the chosen background and the product in question. Graphic stratification renders the background elements that are decisive in determining the meaning of the advertising message. Textual adaptation illustrates, among other things, the ideological dimension of advertising message. The text is not only perceived as a verbal entity, but it also has a graphic identity easily detectable that the translator ought to transfer. McDonald's, the largest chain of hamburger fast food restaurants, has maintained extensive advertising campaign, presenting a real slice of life in its adverts. Television has played a central role in the company's advertising strategy. The *I'm Lovin' It* campaign (launched in 2003) was the company's first global marketing campaign made in 12 languages and aired in more than 110 countries. The intent of the campaign was to create a consistent global brand image, while also allowing for local cultures to be represented. Achieving the local flare was undertaken by creating new packaging with pictures of people from around the world as well as providing for local and regional promotional efforts. As a part of globalization is the increasing presence of McDonald's restaurants worldwide, while the restaurant chain's menu changes in an attempt to appeal to local palates (even the currency has been localized in Indian adverts, the Indian Rupee in India). For promotions in France, the restaurant chain chose to use Asterix the Gaul, a popular French cartoon character. The Indian version uses different Indian situations like the father trying to persuade the daughter into marriage and the bollywood star Rajesh Khanna's look alike, which the Indian audience would be able to relate to. Whether it is the trademark, the brand name or the slogan, the visual expression is as important as the verbal expression that underlies it. In this way, the art of the translator/ localizer consists of pushing as far as possible the cultural *mimesis* without losing, however, the identity of the original message. To localize, a product is to adapt the local characteristics of a market on to a standardized product so that it can connect with a wider target audience. A brand like Nike standardizes to create a unique and standard product and to sell it in different regions in the same standardized communication platform. It is communicated all over the world in the same way. Their adverts and products are standardized and they do not localize their product's look or feel. Their target audiences (like adverts for cars) are *up class* who are exposed to international brands and can understand English as part of their day-to-day life. Still they do localize in another way, like in the US, they associate with Baseball and Basketball tournaments, whereas in India, they associate with Cricket and Hockey.

Advertisements may use very little written information and mainly focus on visual elements to convey the message. The visual image supports the verbal appeal to develop a strong and persuasive impression in the audience' mind. Celebrity endorsement advertising has been recognized as a 'ubiquitous feature of modern day marketing [and of localization]' (McCracken, 1989:10). Advertising takes advantage by fusing the celebrity with the product (another localizing strategy adopted). The celebrity's style and image become an endorsement for attitudes and values. Celebrities are employed by advertisers to lend their personality (an absent presence) to a product or brand and have been found to produce more positive responses towards advertising and greater purchase intentions than a non-celebrity endorser. Fair and Handsome has roped in Shahrukh Khan for Hindi and Soorya, the Tamil hero, for the South. Pepsodent presents Shahrukh (an actor with a national/international appeal) who here is reminiscent of the 10-headed Ravana (he appears as a Punjabi in another 2012 Pepsodent advert) from Indian mythology to signify germs and decay that strike the tooth. The same advert has been dubbed into Tamil (linguistic translation only). While certain aesthetic characteristics of a spokesperson get associated with local culture prototypes, a distinct set of characteristics reflects global consumer culture, and the use of such spokesperson characteristics is likely to give the brand a global image. Often actors with a national/Indian (even international) appeal, chosen as brand ambassadors—L'Oreal (Aishwarya Rai, Sonam Kapoor and Freida Pinto), Lux (Aishwarya Rai, Priyanka Chopra and Katrina Kaif), Levi's (Akshay Kumar), Reid and Taylor (Amitabh Bachchan), Airtel (Vidya Balan and Madhavan, Saif and Kareena, the jingle is retained in the Airtel ads, Karthi in Tamil and Ramcharan in Telugu), Garnier (Genelia D'Souza, Priyanka Chopra and Kareena Kapoor), Titan Raga (Katrina Kaif)—appear in Indian commercials. Brand images have been established by those like the Indian cricket team for Nike, Abhishek Bachchan for Omega (counterparts like Pierce Brosnan, Nicole Kidman, George Clooney, Michael Phelps and Zhang Ziyi), Amitabh Bachchan for Reid and Taylor and Deepika Padukone for Tissot. Actors like Amitabh Bachchan also appear in government promotion programmes like promotion of polio eradication (which is regionally carried out by regional actors) as well as promotion of tourism (tourism Gujarat *Khushboo Gujarat ki*). While Coke uses Aamir Khan (the different ways in which Aamir appears and the language [as a *Jatt, Pahadi,* Bengali] he uses is indicative of Indian multiculturalism and the need for localization that is realized here) and Hrithik Roshan for its national audience, the Tamil actor Vijay appears in the Tamil version. Pepsi has actors like Kareena Kapoor, Priyanka Chopra, Deepika Padukone, Saif Ali Khan, Shahrukh Khan and Ranbir Kapoor (Madhavan and Surya in Tamil, Ramcharan in Telugu), to endorse it. Manappuram, a firm from the sleepy town of Valapad in Trissur district of Kerala, roped in the actors Akshay Kumar (Hindi), Venkatesh (Telugu), Puneet Raj Kumar (Kannada) and Vikram (Tamil), along with the Malayalam star Mohanlal, to give a pan-Indian face to its business of lending money against pawned gold. It worked and the brand became a household name all over India. Muthoot Finance, India's largest gold loan company, headquartered in Kochi (its roots can be traced back to Kozhencherry in Pathanamthitta district), roped in the Indian cricketers for promotion purpose. While Jos Alukkas presents Mahesh Babu in Telugu and Vijay in Malayalam and Tamil, Joy Alukkas has the singer Shreya Ghoshal to render its jingle in five different Indian languages. The South Indian culture is represented in Jos Alukkas advert (in both languages) through the *tharavad*, the close-knit joint family, *chechi, akka, paatti, illam, thatha, muthachan*—Tamil–*Thathavude anpillam*/Malayalam–*Muthachante snehaveedu*. To the extent that the spokesperson embodies aesthetic characteristics that reflect the local culture (an Indian businessman/woman driving a Peugeot/Verito/Audi/SX4 in an Indian TVC) or a specific foreign culture (a German engineer spokesperson for Audi in a US television advertisement), consumers are likely to associate the brand with that culture. Indian advertisers, acknowledging the importance of localization, endorse their products through local heroes/language. Levis 501 relaunched globally with a new campaign called *Live Unbuttoned*. Akshay Kumar, Bollywood superstar, was the brand ambassador in India (as Imraan of Signature-Denizen). Akshay Kumar appears in its advertising campaign with a supermodel (international appeal) alongside. As celebrities echo the symbolic meanings and values closely tied to the culture in which they have attained their eminence, the selection of celebrity endorsers and the creative execution of this advertising strategy tend to mirror the fundamental cultural orientations and values of that society (Choi et al., 2005:86). Image values transferred into the communication messages, thus, influence consumers. When a brand is consumed by idols, it becomes a symbol of association with an *in group*. It is important for the advertisers to match the personality of the celebrity with the product or company's image and the characteristics of the target market—use of local personalities would communicate a stronger message. Regio-centred advertisements also exist—Pothys has creatively adapted the idea into Malayalam with Mammootty and Tamil with Sathyaraj-Seetha. The Indian television has Mohanlal (Malabar Gold), Mammootty (South Indian Bank) Prithviraj (Kalyan Silks), or Jayaram and Shreya (Kalyan Sarees) and Aishwarya Rai (Kalyan Jewellers) endorsing products for the Kerala/Malayalee audience. Adverts like Uninor, Malabar Gold and Kalyan Silks aim a national appeal—another way of achieving localization where each region/culture of the country is considered, in a single advert as in Uninor or Idea

Sirji No Language Problem, ads which address different Indian states through a single advert—through its TVCs which cater to the whole of India. Kalyan Silks (and Malabar Gold) presents the varied Indian culture through its Goan, Bengali, Rajasthani, Lucknow weddings, and it does not even leave out Kottayam or Kannur. The world over, advertisements with celebrities drive sales and brand recall (an instance would be rejigging of Slice juice with Katrina Kaif's *Aam Sutra* advert). Adverts may exist for the local market and comprise local/global brand images (adverts like that of Pothys, Jayalakshmi and Seemati which present a global setting in which the Indian sari is placed).

Localization processes should not overlook the full range of effects that can be achieved by translation. In general, localization addresses significant, non-textual components of products or services. In addition to translation (and, therefore, grammar and spelling issues that vary from place to place where the same language is spoken), the localization process might include adapting (the geo-cultural indicators) graphics, adopting local currencies, using proper forms for dates, addresses and phone numbers, the choice of colours and many other details, including rethinking the physical structure of a product. All these changes aim to recognize local sensitivities, avoid conflict with local culture and habits, and enter the local market by merging into its needs and desires. Cultural elements play a decisive role not only in the good understanding of the advertising message, but also in its success in the target market. Translatorship amounts first and foremost to being able to play a social role, that is, to fulfil a function allotted by a community—to the activity, its practitioners and/or their products—in a way which is deemed appropriate. While translating (in advertising), the translator addresses people, their dress code, food habits, customs, tradition, beliefs and feelings, geographical and environmental elements and logos. The range of translation strategies is restricted by the nature of the target culture involved. The structural difference in the languages concerned has to be kept in mind. Different receivers (or even the same receiver at different times) find different meanings in the same linguistic material offered by the text. The Fair and Handsome advert (aired in Hindi, Malayalam and Tamil on different regional channels) presents an instance of localization (linguistic/visual) in the Indian advertisement industry.

(Hindi—Shahrukh Khan, an *akhada* in India, Shahrukh to a wrestler)

Shahrukh Khan: *O pehalwaan, ladkiyom wali fairness cream laga raha hai. Kal nailpolish lagayega, parson lipstick. Langot uthaar (pulling his dress), lehanga lapet le. Pehalwaan, Fair and Handsome lagaa.*

Voice-over: *Mardon ki thwacha hothi hai sakth jis pe ladkiyon-wali fairness cream beasar. Sirf Emami Fair and Handsome mein hai American Lumino Peptide jo kisi bhi saadharan mardom wali fairness cream se zyada asardar, zyada fast.*

(the wrestler appears after using the cream)

...

Shahrukh Khan: *Emami Fair and Handsome, duniya ki number one fairness cream, mardon ke liye.*

*** (Malayalam—Soorya, setting/visuals same, Soorya to a wrestler)

Soorya: *Hey pehalwaan, penkuttikalude fairness cream purat-tukaya. Naale nailpolish, mattannal lipstick...*

Voice-over: *Purusha charmathil penkuttikalude fairness cream-inu prabhavamilla. Emami Fair and Handsomil undu American Lumino Peptide. Ithu purushanmarkkulla mattu saadharana fairness creaminekkal kooduthal bhalapradham, kooduthal fast.*

(the wrestler appears after using the cream)

...

Soorya: *Emami Fair and Handsome, lokathe number one fairness cream, Purushanmarkku.*

While Shahrukh would appeal to most Indians, Soorya would definitely to those who belong to South India. *Lehanga lape-tle, pavada udukku, dhavaniye kett* all (the different cultural indicators) indicate the localization (at the linguistic level) the advert has undergone. It is noteworthy that in all three languages Fair and Handsome as the *number one fairness cream* (not translated) is retained (in English). Translation/localization is an integral part of a business when the target audience has a different culture and speaks a different language. To communicate effectively and achieve the desired result, there arises the need to communicate in the language of the target audience when the audience is not familiar with a common language like English. Pepsi is a standardized product sold all over India in similar looking bottles. However, in Tamil Nadu, the Tamil language is used for promotion of the product. The same is not true of Kerala, for Kerala is seen as having more English educated people and accept English communication easily. Consumers in Tamil Nadu like to see their products in their local language and it helps Pepsi to penetrate even to uneducated class of people. A translation agency bridges the language and cultural barrier by providing accurate and reliable translation of contents.

The culture becomes the operational unit of translation. A translated/localized advertisement addresses a new audience and cultural situation. The translator has to be aware of the cultural codes at play in both languages because advertisement translations are important in the marketing/advertising field. It is an interesting and challenging process and helps to provide access to products in major markets. Communication becomes effective only when the message is correctly translated—adapted for a particular market in a particular country. A translation/transfer/localization takes place. The entire responsibility of effective communication lies on the advertisement translator/localizer. Adaptations, literal translation and partial substitutions are resorted to as the culture in which the translated advert received is important. It needs careful thinking not to create a negative impact on the target culture. Translators are cultural mediators. In the case of adverts, localization should fulfil the function of the original and have a similar effect on the receiving market for the product to sell and be well received by the people. Translation strategies are adopted to deliver the message and overcome geographical barriers in advertising. The transmission of product information has a persuasive/informative function. It is not confined to finding linguistic equivalents in the TL. A social frame of reference has to be recreated in another culture. The sociocultural conditions are to be considered. Fair and Lovely makes use of puja, chanting of mantras and an *Ayurvedic chehra* all connoting the necessity of rootedness

in the traditional values of India. For the Tamil viewers, Genelia appears in the advert (the tune of the jingle is retained). The
retaining of jingles in localized adverts enables continuum and
even before the visual appears one starts humming the familiar
tune. This musical nature is inherently Indian. Each region has its
musical heritage. Though one may not remember the lines, the
tune lingers in the mind. Hindi film songs when used in adverts
(like Nissan Micra, Nano, Estilo) are at times (or tune retained
with the words in translation) replaced with familiar regional
ones (Malayalam ones for Kerala), while the visuals are retained.
The advertisement media also makes use of different cultural
images in its race for catching the viewer's attention in the allotted seconds. The jingle literature of Asian Paints Apex Ultima
shows how the tune is based on the *vanjipattu, thullal, pulluvan pattu* of Kerala (the *Payale vida pooppale vida ennenekum
vida* advert). Here, the ethnomusicology has been revamped to
suit the aural taste of the consumer/viewer and to convey the
qualities of the paint. Though the advert does not have anything to do with *vanjipattu, thullal* or *pulluvan pattu*, the paint
accesses the Indian/Kerala mind through it (in Tamil through
Pongal). The advert creates none of the visual appeal of the
aforementioned folk forms, though the aural significance would
echo in Kerala ears and create a feel *of Kerala*. It is with a sort
of received familiarity that the audience accepts it nostalgically.
The feeling of cultural oneness is conveyed in Kerala-centred
adverts through various signifiers like the *setmundu, pook-
kalam* and bharathanatyam. The polyphonic-multivalent
ethnic music in which these jingles are rooted tends to
be uprooted and exploded to arouse faint ethnic memories, losing its ethnicity—getting reduced to just an imaginary bridge arousing interest in the hearer/audience.
Applied ethno-musicology in adverts does not make use of its
ethnicity but as a seductive pastiche (as citation or quotation in
bits and pieces). This reduces the ethno-musical jingles to mere
instant indexical references, being replaced from one culture to
another, creating a localized ethnic globality.

Most of the Indian adverts involve linguistic translation
(mostly dubbed version) concomitant to localization. As cultures may have different conventions, trans-cultural text production requires substitution of elements of the source text by

elements judged more appropriate to the functions the target text is to serve. The target text receiver differs from the source text receiver in language, culture, world knowledge and text expectations. Like literary translation, translation of advertisements too involve some form of loss (the meaning, the visual appeal which is transferred in translation) when the advertisement is not properly localized. There exists the problematics of interpreting texts across cultural boundaries. The localizer appropriates the text and brings it home in a form palatable to the monolingual TL reader/viewer. Advertisement translation is culture bound. One has to domesticate the SL text. Localization has to capture the sense of the original in an analogous rather than identical form, one that functions in a similar fashion within the target culture. The way the translated text is adapted to TL and cultural norms becomes the yardstick for evaluating the translation/localization. The localized advert is simultaneously bound to the source text and to the presuppositions and conditions governing its reception in the target linguistic and cultural system. Differences in cultural presuppositions of the SL and TL communities may require the translator to apply a cultural filter, that is, a set of cross-cultural dimensions along which members of two cultures differ in sociocultural predispositions and communicative preference. The prospective function or *skopos* of the target text as determined by the initiator's (i.e., client's) need is largely constrained by the target text user (reader/listener) and his/her situation and cultural background. Being an intertextual and intercultural transposition, translation/localization does not simply involve substituting single terms with their alleged synonyms, nor does it involve comparing sign–systems *per se*. Instead it involves confronting textual situations against a background of specific forms of socially and culturally shared knowledge set in different historical situations. Cosmetic companies like Fairever have tried to penetrate the Indian market in numerous ways through its adverts (with the Tamil actress Asin, Coming Home, Doctor [with its Indian rural life ads), drawing on the Indian context. Idea Sirji ad series with Abhishek Bachchan relies on the Indian reality—India and over population, multiculturalism and love for cricket. The same advert has been transposed into regional languages with popular regional actors and linguistic translation. Multinational companies spent a fortune on their marketing strategies. Advertising agencies make use of specialized translators. The translation process is done either by the company itself with its employees/translators or outsourced to the translation agency. It has to be translated in such a way that it is understood by the target audience. The linguistic phrases and culturally equivalent words are to be replaced. Often the translator has no access to the natural environment of the target market as he is away from it. This hampers his understanding of the culture and dynamism of the foreign market. In some of the adverts, the visuals are localized with personalities/situations familiar to the Indian audience and Indian situations (like the mother applying oil on her daughter's hair—Garnier advert). A unique brand identity was developed with Close up positioned as the toothpaste that gives people confidence in very *up close and personal* situations. The commercials depicted youthful adults' idea of fresh breath, white teeth, self-confidence as well as sex appeal. Close up retains its jingle and has set the advert to linguistic adaptation in Tamil, Hindi as well as Malayalam—English/Hindi—*Paas aa, paas aa, paas aaona/paas aa, paas aa, paas aaona.* (Voice-over) *New Close up with active clean mouth wash. For the freshest breath and dazzling white teeth. Close up, the closer the better.* Hindi—*Paas aao meri saason mein samao, paas aaona.* (Voice-over) *Aazmayiye active clean mouthwash aur micro whiteness ki toophani taazgi naye close up mein, ki sabse taazi saans hain aur safedh daanth.* (Voice-over) *Naya Close up paas jitna behatar utna.* Tamil—*Nerungi Varuvai, Nerungi Varuvai, Nerungi Varuvaai.* (Voice-over) *Puthiya Close up active mouthwashukal. Ungalku kidaykum mikavum poothulanjha shvasam matrum venmaypalkal. Close up evalavu nerungumo avalavum nallathu.* Malayalam—*Close up avatharipikunnu petanoru divasam. Akalangale ini akatu aduthuvannate. Aduthu va, aduthu vaa, aduthu vannate.* (Voice-over) *Prathikshikatha nerathanu avasarangal kayarivarunathu. Puthiya Close up, ithile antibacterial mouthwash micro whiteners formula nalkunnu shvaasam, nalkunnu thilangunna pallukal. Ningalkum Close up confidence.* The tune is retained in all versions of the advert. It uses Soorya and a globalized ambience to appeal to the Indian youth. Traditional media has been successful in generating a mass appeal by offering content in Indian languages. They have recognized the potential of Indian language content as a tool to reach out to the masses and increase their user base. Fair and Lovely has the same advert (Fair and Lovely Shade Card ad) in different languages:

English:

(Two girls [here A and B] checking their fairness with a shade card)

A: *Wow! I have become one shade fairer. Let's see yours.*

B: *Mine is clearer.*

A: *But we started off from the same number. So how did you get fairer? Did you cheat? You must have cheated, if you had that result.*

B: *You need to apply Fair and Lovely daily. Not like you, once in a while.*

Voice-over: *Fair and Lovely a day clears marks, evens skin tone and gives up to two times clear fairness. Clear fairness with Fair and Lovely.*

Hindi:

A: *Cheh badgayi* (checking fairness level on a shade card)

B: *Mera dugna*

A: *Dono ne ek hi number se start kiya. Tu aage kaise. Tune cheating ki.*

B: *Cheating nahin. Dugna asar chahiye to roz lagana padta hai. Tere jaise nahin, kabhi kabhi.*

Voice-over: *Fair and Lovely roz lagane se itna zyada gorapan aagaya.*

A: *Unbelievable! Kyon roz lagati ho?*

B: *Ji nahin asar dugna.*

Voice-over: *Fair and Lovely roz lagao, dugna gorapan pao.*

Malayalam:

A: *Wow! oru shade kudi. Ninte kanate.*

B: *Eniku irattiyayi.*

A: *Randalum ore numberila start cheythe, pinne nee engane mumbilayi. Cheating cheytho?*

B: *Cheating nee cheythathanu. Iratti result venamenkil Fair and Lovely divasavum puratanam. Ninnepole vallapozhum pora.*

Voice-over: *Fair and Lovely divasavum purattu, nedu randiratti kooduthal charmakanthi*

A: *Wow! Unbelievable.*

B: *Ennum purattunundu. No cheating, result iratti.*

Voice-over: *Fair and Lovely divasavum purattu iratti charmakanthi nedu.*

Peter England adverts make use of marigolds, *diya* and *diwali* with rich Indian connotations (indicating an auspicious beginning) as well as a mix of English and the regional language; the same advert is dubbed into Tamil and Malayalam. The actor, the theme and caption serve as connecting links between these ads. Another marketing strategy is the use of mixed language in adverts. The different language formats (local language/slang, English or a mix of the two) used also determine the advertising effectiveness. The mixed language becomes an informal mode of communication. The introduction of Hinglish (a mix of Hindi and English)—Uninor (*Ab mera number hai* in Hindi or *Ini yen number* in Tamil), Pepsi, Alpenleibe (subversive and uses a local variant of Hindi), the cars Verito, Estilo (also uses a song familiar to the Indian audience *churaliya hai tumne jo dil ko*)—into the advertising lingo is an instance. The local language conveys a sense of belonging and appeals more to the local population. Cadbury Perk Poppers uses a caption combining English and the regional language—(Hindi) *New Cadbury Perk Poppers, ab chocolatey Perk ka maza chote chote size mein*; (Malayalam) *Cadbury Perk Poppers, ippol chocolatey Perkintey rasam cheriya cheriya sizeukalil*; and (Tamil) *Cadbury Perk Poppers, ippoth chocolatey Perkin khushi chinnanchiruvadivathil*. Airtel advert is another example—*Chai ke liye jaise toast hota hai, waise har ek friend zaroori hota hai.* The code mixing (Hinglish) also becomes indicative of contemporary Indian culture. The Airtel *Har ek friend zaroori hai* song, indicating contemporaneity, is an instance:

Chai ke liye jaise toast hota hai
Vaise har ek friend zaroori hota hai
Aise har ek friend zaroori hota hai

***

Koi effortless, koi forced hota hai
Lekin har ek friend zaroori hota hai

***

Koi bike pe racewala vroom-vroom friend
Shopping mallwala shopping friend
Koi examhallwala copying friend

***

Joke buddy ... poke buddy
Gaana buddy shaana buddy
Chaddi buddy yaar buddy
Kutte ... kamine

***

The Tamil *Har ek friend* advert (*Apni ovvoru friendum theva machan*) uses the same visuals with the audio in Tamil. The English words used in this advert are retained in Tamil version also. The signature tune of Airtel composed by the Indian musician A.R. Rahman became highly popular; its new version released in 2010 as part of the rebranding campaign of the company with a new logo. The Airtel tune accompanies its adverts in all languages, offering continuum and familiarity.

Studies reveal a growing literature on brand name translation which emphasizes the importance of awareness in such translations of sound symbolism. An instance is Chinese language in which sound symbolism and naming are especially important. In such cases, the characters chosen to represent the product produce pronunciation close to the original. A slightly different transliteration (*ke kou kele delicious enjoyable*) which Coca Cola used 10 years after its initial entry into the Chinese market is said to have ushered in success for the company. Phonaesthemes play a significant role in brand naming decisions and advertising and are of significance to translators. Every attempt is made to bridge the cultural gap between the source and the target cultures, and to increase/promote sales. Language's implicit, symbolic meaning is important. Therefore, one way for a brand to communicate global consumer culture is to use English words, written and/or spoken, in its communication. In contrast, a brand manager wanting to use local consumer culture might emphasize the local language. Finally, a brand could associate itself with a specific foreign consumer culture by employing spoken and written words from that culture in its advertising and/or brand name (like Volkswagen). Companies like Nike (*Just do it*) and Reid and Taylor (*Bond with the Best*) retain their English catch line in the regional telecast, while those like Cadbury (English/Hindi), Crompton Greaves (Hindi/Malayalam—*Bharose ki roshni/Vishvasathinte prakasham*), Surf Excel (Hindi/Malayalam—*Daag Ache Hai/Kara Nallathanu*), Fairever (Hindi/Tamil/Malayalam—*Naamumkin kuch bhi nahin/ Mattramudiyathathu ethume illai/Maattan pattatha-thayi onnumilla*), Alpenleibe (Malayalam—*Kothiyoori nunan-jhu nunanjhu*/Hindi—*Lalach aha laplap*. Here, the use of words (cultural signifiers) in the two languages *Kothiyoori/Lalach* and *nunanjhu/laplap* are indicative of the *translation* process) go in for translation. Most Indian regio-centred advertisements go for a literal translation. The Idea advert says, *An Idea can change your life* in English and *Ek Idea jo badal de aapki duniya* in Hindi. While L'Oreal caption *Because you are worth it* becomes *Kyonki hamein naaz hain khud par*, Garnier (cosmetics with several markets around the world) retains its English caption (*Take Care*) in most of its adverts (in very few Hindi adverts, it is adapted to *Apna khayal rakhna*). The graphic components also undergo necessary change. An instance is the Indian Nike (a sportswear supplier based in the US that promotes its products through sponsorship agreements with celebrity athletes and professional teams [like the Indian cricket team]) commercial which captures the familiar spirit of the crowded Indian street with its chaotic traffic jam, familiar Indian street cricket and ordinariness. This along with the presence of Indian cricketers (as against Tiger Woods and Roger Federer, Indian advertising uses Zaheer Khan and S. Sreesanth. The caption and logo are retained in the ads) as onlookers proffers cultural belonging.

Incongruity occurs when the words being broadcast in translation are not properly synchronized with the actors' lip movements on screen. The audiences become aware of the mismatching. Commercials like Surf Excel (from Hindi to Malayalam), Vicks (from Hindi to Malayalam) and Harpic (from Hindi to Malayalam/from Tamil to Malayalam) mostly offer instances of poor lip synching (despite word correspondence) and localization when aired regionally. Cadbury (English/Hindi) has strived for equivalence (sentence/sense) in its translation of the song accompanying its visuals, which does not call for lip synching—*There's something so real in everyone/There's something so real I can want/It's you, it's real/And the feeling is right/There's something so real in the taste of life. Cadbury's Dairy Milk, The Real Taste of Life*. With the same tune (different visuals), this becomes *Kuch khaas hain hum sabi mein/Kuch baat hain hum sabhi mein/Baat hain, khaas hain/Kuch swaad hain/Kya swaad hain zindagi mein. Cadbury's Dairy Milk, Asli Swad Zindagi Ka*. The Cadbury *Shubh Aarambh* series plies on the Indian context by drawing on the traditional Indian custom of having something sweet before any new venture—*Kuch meetha ho jaye*. This is because of the belief that *Kaam acha hota hai*. One of its adverts ropes in Amitabh Bachchan to bring in the point *Muh meetha karo*. The ambience is North India indicated through the local variant of Hindi, the turban, anklets, words like chaudhari sahib, Ms Palanpur and the Indian superstitious belief of *nazar na lagaana* (evil eye). The adverts make use of the same final visual of cocoa flowing from two glasses. Cadbury relies on the Indian joint family, houses full of aunts and uncles, being home for festivals and even when asking a girl out on a date, one starts with what ones mother says. The contemporary Westernized society is projected in the Cadbury ad where a boy meets a girl at the bus stop, at the same time insisting on a rootedness in Indian cultural values. The caption *Kuch meetha ho jaye* is used in Hindi, while in Malayalam the translation becomes *Alpam madhuram pakaru*. A word-for-word correspondence is perceptible in most advertisement localization. The old catchy jingle of Vicks in Hindi *Vicks ki goli lo khich khich door karo* becomes *Vicks gulika kazhiku khich khich akattu* in Malayalam (*khich khich* now *karakarapp* of Strepsils, both indicative of throat congestion). When it comes to verbal equivalence, the literal translation often proves awkward and jarring (Surf Excel—*Daag Ache Hain* [Hindi] to *Kara Nallathanu* [Malayalam]). Some of the adverts also have regional versions (Harpic—Hindi/Tamil, Reid and Taylor—Tamil/Punjabi/ Hindi) with a regional tone. Often the dubbed versions of most adverts are instances of *failed* translation (and hence indicate unsuccessful localization) where word-to-word equivalence is attempted without appropriate lip synchronization. The audience (in the case of such adverts) relates (despite the inappropriateness/mismatching) to the audio-visuals appearing before them because of a prior knowledge/familiarity/with the original/source advert. The audio has to be perfectly synchronized with the action/video that produced it. Synchronizing the movements of a speaker's lips with the sound of his speech is requisite in audio-visual advertising/localization. Only then does it fit into the target culture and contribute towards fulfilling its purpose by appealing to the viewers. Understanding language as well as foreign culture becomes essential. Bilingual copywriters who understand full meaning of the English or concerned text can capture the essence of the message. Marketing is an important aspect of corporate business operations, which plans to enhance its presence through innovative offerings. Examples from the print media too highlight issues of localization that crop up in marketing.

The adverts (Malayalam/English) from the print media too indicate the localization (linguistic/visual) process at work in print advertisements. Here, the same adverts have been adapted to cater to a multicultural nation like India. It hints at the increasing necessity of appealing to the multifarious Indian segments. The shifting polysemic Indian urban–rural context has been drawn upon in the adverts. Localization takes place at numerous levels (in print ads) as in television advertisements—(*Manza*— linguistic adaptation, *IDBI Bank*—linguistic adaptation, *State Bank of India*—linguistic and visual adaptation [targeting different states of India]).

With rising globalization, defined by Robertson as the 'crystallization of the world as a single place' (*Globalization: Social Theory*, 1992) and 'the emergence of the global human condition' (*Globalization: Social Theory*, 1992), advertisements featuring the idea that consumers all over the world consume a particular brand or appealing to certain human universals might invest the brand with the cultural meaning of being a conduit to feeling at one with global culture. Brands that apparently have used such strategies include Sony (*My First Sony*, which positioned one of its products as appropriate for young people around the world), Philips (*Let's Make Things Better*, advertisements explicitly feature people from different countries), Benetton (*The United Colors of Benetton*, slogan emphasizing the unity of humankind) and Blackberry (indicating globality of the *Blackberry family*). The aesthetic construction and display of the brand logos may also reflect alternative consumer culture positioning. Some logos may be tied less to specific cultures in terms of their appearance (like the swoosh of Nike, the star of Mercedes-Benz), others may be more symbolic of specific cultural traditions. Most consumers would view the logo in its aesthetic entirety (including shape, colour, texture and overall design) and form linkages to global, foreign or local consumer culture on the basis of the symbol's gestalt-like familiarity. Certain story themes are likely to be identified generally as symbolic of global consumer culture. Ownership of a brand like Toshiba or Dell signifies that the consumer is a member of the transnational commerce culture. Depending on the story-related themes in an advertisement, consumers are more or less likely to associate the brand with a specific consumer culture. Local culture members recognize whether signs in their country's advertising symbolize global, foreign or local consumer culture, for they are meaningful positioning constructs in television advertising.

The New Media: A Study of the Mobile Online Advertising

Today we are beginning to notice that the new media are not just mechanical gimmicks for creating worlds of illusion, but new languages with new and unique powers of expression.

—*Marshall McLuhan*

Globalization is generally stated as more than an expansion of activities beyond the boundaries of particular nation states. It shortens the distance between people all over the world by the electronic communication, the great development expressed as the *death of distance*. The new media that has emerged is said to radically break the connection between physical place and social place, making physical location much less significant for our social relationships. However, changes in the new media environment create a series of tensions in the concept of *public sphere*. According to Ingrid Volkmer (1999), public sphere is defined as a process through which public communication becomes restructured and partly disembedded from national, political and cultural institutions. This trend of the globalized public sphere is a geographical expansion from a nation to world scale. It also changes the relationship between the public, the media and the state (Volkmer, 1999: 123). *Virtual communities* are established online, thus transcending geographical boundaries and eliminating social restrictions. Howard Rheingold describes these globalized societies as self-defined networks, which resemble what we do in real life. New media has the ability to connect like-minded others worldwide. While this perspective suggests that the technology drives—and therefore is a determining factor—in the process of globalization, arguments involving technological determinism are generally frowned upon by mainstream media studies. While commentators such as Castells espouse a *soft determinism* whereby they contend that:

> Technology does not determine society. Nor does society script the course of technological change, since many factors, including individual inventiveness and entrepreneurialism, intervene in the process of scientific discovery, technical innovation and social applications, so the final outcome depends on a complex pattern of interaction. Indeed the dilemma of technological determinism is probably a false problem, since technology is society and society cannot be understood without its technological tools. (Castells, 1996:5)

Manovich and Castells have argued that whereas mass media 'corresponded to the logic of industrial mass society, which values conformity over individuality' (Manovich, 2001:41), new media follows the logic of the postindustrial or globalized society whereby 'every citizen can construct his/her own custom lifestyle and select his/her ideology from a large number of choices. Rather than pushing the same objects to a mass audience, marketing now tries to target each individual separately' (Manovich, 2001:42). New media advertising is considered the emerging medium of advertisement. As long as value is provided (whether by providing content on a topic, a recipient is interested in or a discount for a product related to one purchased previously), consumers will be willing to be exposed to a few advertisements (be it online, email advertising or any other form of advertising). While some websites prefer a subscription-based model, others rely on banner, box and contextual advertisements. Each and every email sent by the company contains its logo, information of its products and services, and links to its websites. These items are a part of the advertising and should be surrounded on all sides by the items which make the communication actually add value to the lives of its viewers/readers. The media theorist Marshall McLuhan has pointed out in the 1960s that the media are not just passive channels of information. They not only supply the stuff of thought, but they also shape the process of thought. Localization in this context too means adapting all of the content to different local cultures and involves more than just *translation* for it includes all aspects of communication.

An online advertising process involves advertisers, publishers and service companies. They interact with each other to conduct online advertising processes, activities and transactions. Internet marketing and online advertising efforts are typically used in conjunction with traditional types of advertising like radio, television, newspapers and magazines. Internet marketing, or online marketing, a readvertising and marketing effort, uses the Web and email to drive direct sales via electronic commerce. The Web offers many ways for an advertiser to show their ads to potential customers. However, the Web offers an opportunity to tailor display ads in a way that hardcopy media cannot—it is possible to use information about the user to determine which ad they should be shown, regardless of what page they are looking at. Internet marketing may be classified into more specialized areas such as Web marketing, email marketing and social media marketing. While email marketing involves both advertising and promotional marketing efforts via e-mail messages to current and prospective customers, social media marketing involves both advertising and marketing (including viral marketing) efforts via social-networking sites like Facebook, Twitter and YouTube. Online advertising (also called Internet advertising) uses the Internet to deliver promotional marketing messages to consumers. It includes email marketing, search engine marketing, social media marketing, many types of display advertising (including the Web banner advertising) and mobile advertising. Like other advertising media, online advertising frequently involves both a publisher, who integrates advertisements into its online content, and an advertiser, who provides the advertisements to be displayed on the publisher's content. Other potential participants include advertising agencies which help generate and place the ad copy, an ad server which technologically delivers the ad and tracks statistics, and advertising affiliates which do independent promotional work for the advertiser. Display advertising conveys its advertising message visually using text, logos, animations, videos, photographs or other graphics. Display advertisers frequently target users with particular traits to increase the advert's effect. Online advertisers (typically through their ad servers) often use cookies, which are unique identifiers of specific computers, to decide which ads to serve to a particular consumer. Cookies can track whether a user left a page without buying anything, so the advertiser can later retarget the user with ads from the site the user visited. Advertisers collect data across multiple external websites about a user's online activity and create a detailed picture of the user's interests to deliver even more targeted advertising. This aggregation of data is behavioural targeting. Advertisers can also target their audience by using contextual and semantic advertising to deliver display advertisements related to the content of the webpage where the adverts appear. Retargeting, behavioural targeting and contextual advertising are all designed to increase an advertiser's return on investment. Advertisers may also deliver advertisements based on a user's suspected geography through geotargeting. A user's IP address communicates some geographic information (at minimum, the user's country or general region). The geographic information from an IP can be supplemented and refined with other proxies or information to narrow the range of possible locations. With mobile devices, advertisers can sometimes use a phone's GPS receiver or the location of nearby mobile towers. Cookies and other persistent data on a user's machine may provide help narrow a user's location further. Adverts appear in numerous forms online. Web banners or banner ads are graphical adverts displayed within a webpage. Banner ads can incorporate video, audio, animations, buttons, forms or other interactive elements. A pop-up ad is displayed in a new web browser window that opens above a website visitor's initial browser window. A pop-under ad opens a new browser window under a website visitor's initial browser window. A floating ad, or overlay ad, is a type of rich media advertisement that appears superimposed over the requested website's content. Floating ads may disappear or become less obtrusive after a preset time period. An expanding ad is a rich media frame ad (allowing advertisers to fit more information into a restricted ad space) that changes dimensions upon a predefined condition, such as a preset amount of time a visitor spends on a webpage, the user's click on the ad or the user's mouse movements over the ad. A trick banner is a banner ad where the ad copy imitates some screen element users commonly encounter, such as an operating system message or popular application message, to induce ad clicks. Trick banners typically do not mention the advertiser in the initial ad and are a form of bait-and-switch. An interstitial ad displays before a user can access requested content (sometimes while the user is waiting for the content to load) and are a form of interruption marketing. A text ad displays text-based hyperlinks. Text-based ads may display separately from a webpage's primary content, or they can be embedded by hyperlinking individual words or phrases to advertiser's websites. These ads may also be delivered through email marketing or text message marketing and often render faster than graphical ads (and can be harder for ad-blocking software to block). The Internet Advertising Bureau has made available a standard Terms and Conditions document for Internet advertising. Many publishers and advertisers use this document as a foundation for their online advertising agreements. Over the years, the online ad industry has settled on a number of standard ad dimensions that are commonly used for online advertising. This has benefited both publishers and advertisers; publishers do not have to worry about non-standard ad sizes that do not fit into the design of their site, and advertisers can create one set of ads and know that most sites will be able to accommodate the ad dimensions they use. The online advertising industry continues to evolve, as advertisers, publishers and technology vendors attempt to find new ways to come up with new and innovative ways to handle online advertising in a way that provides the most benefit for users, advertisers and publishers. While online advertising is not the same as print or television advertising, it can be used for things that other advertising cannot. With a print or television campaign, there is no direct interaction with the ad itself; the advertiser must hope that the reader or viewer will call a phone number or go to a website they see in an ad. The chances of someone actually getting up in the middle of watching a television show or reading a newspaper are slim. With online advertising, on the other hand, it is not asking nearly as much for someone to click on a banner ad, or at least interact with a banner ad to see what it is about. This is one of the benefits of a more interactive medium. Ultimately, the continued success of online advertising will depend on finding the best ways to take advantage of the unique capabilities of the online medium. There are several types of online advertisements. The common types are banners, rich media banners, emails and game-based advertisements. Static and dynamic banners are the most popular formats for online advertisements due to the low cost in design and posting. Static banners refer to HTML-based regular banners that present advertisements using static images with fixed sizes. Animated banners (or dynamic banners) integrate animations with static banners based on JavaScript and HTML. Both static and dynamic banners are very useful for brand building in online advertising. Interactive banners are popular because they provide users a two-way communication channel to interact with advertisers. They provide a pull-down menu and an edit box for viewers to input information and response with actions. Interactive banners are frequently used in online shopping and online registration. In most cases, these banners are created using HTML, Java Script or/and Java Applets. Online banners now have standardized advertising formats. The rich media banners on the Web use multimedia technology (such as audio, video and graphics) to present advertisements. The major purpose of rich media banners is to draw viewers' attention using dynamic video and graphics and effective images and sounds. Rich media banners not only provide web surfers with new experience, such as advanced animation, audio/video support and advanced tracking, but also invite them to interact with advertisements to gain additional information about the target products or services. They depend on a more complicated multimedia technology. They are very effective and useful for brand building in online advertising. Online classified advertising is advertisements posted online in a categorical listing of specific products or services (like online job boards, online real estate listings, automotive listings, online yellow pages and online auction-based listings). Adware is a software that, once installed, automatically displays advertisements on a user's computer. The ads may appear in the software itself, integrated into webpages visited by the user or in pop-ups/pop-unders. Adware installed without the user's permission is a type of malware. Online advertising, and in particular social media, provides a low-cost means for advertisers to engage with large established communities. Advertising online offers better returns than in other media. Online advertisers can collect data on their ads' effectiveness, such as the size of the potential audience or actual audience response, how a visitor reached their advertisement, whether the advertisement resulted in a sale and whether an ad actually loaded within a visitor's view. This helps online advertisers improve their ad campaigns over time. Advertisers have a wide variety of ways of presenting their promotional messages, including the ability to convey images, video, audio and links. Unlike many offline ads, online ads can also be interactive (some ads let users input queries or let users follow the advertiser on social media). Online ads can even incorporate games. Online advertising may use geo-targeting to display relevant advertisements to the user's geography. Advertisers can customize each individual ad to a particular user based on the user's previous preferences. They can also track whether a visitor has already seen a particular ad in order to reduce unwanted repetitious exposures and provide adequate time gaps between exposures. Online advertising can reach nearly every global market, and online advertising influences offline sales. Once ad design is complete, online ads can be deployed immediately. The delivery of online ads does not need to be linked to the publisher's publication schedule. Furthermore, online advertisers can modify or replace ad copy rapidly. Online advertising has been recognized as one of the efficient and effective means for marketing and advertising due to its global visibility, low cost, effective performance tracking and measurement. With the quick growth of Internet users and the fast advances of Internet technology and e-commerce, more businesses and manufactures pay their attention to online advertising by spending a great deal of money on posting their advertisements over the Web. Online advertising refers to the use of the Internet as a communication media and channel to post online advertisements on the Web. Online advertising has penetrated general population much more rapidly than traditional media in the past. This mode of advertising has its distinct features and advantages over traditional advertising. Online advertisements are interactive ads that support two-way communications between advertisers and ad viewers. Viewers not only receive ads, but are also enabled to send their feedback and questions regarding products back to the advertisers. These adverts have the advantage of providing viewers with a direct link to access the related product information and catalogues. This often leads to product trading and increases business transactions, thus enabling static and dynamic customer targeting. In online advertising, diverse customer targeting methods can be used to support static and dynamic advertisement selection, presentation and display. The methods may be carried out based on page contents, customer profiles and dynamic trading data. Online advertisements can be easily delivered, displayed, maintained and updated because of their digital nature. As a result of this, the lifecycle of an advertising process is reduced. The advertisements are highly traceable and measurable due to digitalization. Diverse methods can be used to track and evaluate the performance and effectiveness of posted online advertisements. Many websites attract advertisers by generating high Internet traffic through interesting dynamic updated web contents. These businesses conduct online advertising by selling their scheduled advertising spaces (such as web banner) based on webpage contents. ISP-based businesses (such as AOL) follow a different online advertising model. They provide various Internet services to customers through consumer-oriented Internet access services, communication and message services (such as email and instant messaging), news, chat rooms and e-commerce retail shopping. Ad-serving businesses provide online advertising services for advertisers to post advertisements on selected websites. They help advertisers in advertising campaign, ad space search, delivery and display, as well as ad tracking and performance measurement. They can even sell their ad tracking data to business marketing groups. Ad-network businesses provide a direct advertising network between publishers and advertisers with a huge supply of advertisements and a large ad space inventory. Whenever an online ad publisher wants to find customers to sale its available ad space, it can interact with an ad-network business to get the potential customers who are not sure where (or which websites) they should post their online ads. The ad-network business collects its share whenever an online advertising business deal is made between its customers. It is very useful for large online ad publishers (or websites) because they usually are not able to sell their surplus ad space inventory by themselves and need ad-network companies to help them sell their unscheduled ad space in a short timeline at reasonable cost. Ad-network businesses may also provide limited services for both advertisers and publishers, such as ad tracking, analysis and reporting. Ad-trading businesses function as intermediaries between advertisers and ad publishers by providing an ad brokerage marketplace, which supports online ad space trading, auction or exchanges over the Internet. They allow online ad publishers (or websites) to post unscheduled ad spaces to attract advertisers to purchase. Whenever a deal is settled between an advertiser and a publisher, the ad trading business gets its commission fee. The online ad spaces are posted on an auction marketplace to allow advertisers to bid based on a predefined auction model and rules or online advertisements and/or ad spaces can be exchanged between advertisers and/or online ad publishers through an interaction channel, such as ad exchanged marketplace.

Email marketing is directly marketing a commercial message to a group of people using email. Every email sent to a potential or current customer could be considered email marketing. It usually involves using email to send ads, request business, or solicit sales or donations, and is meant to build loyalty, trust or brand awareness. Email marketing can be done to either sold lists or current customer database. The term is usually used to refer to sending email messages with the purpose of enhancing the relationship of a company/seller with its current or previous customers, to encourage customer loyalty and repeat business, to sending email messages with the purpose of acquiring new customers or convincing current customers to purchase something immediately. Email advertising is ad copy comprising an entire email or a portion of an email message. Email marketing may be unsolicited, in which case the sender may give the recipient an option to opt-out of future emails, or it may be sent with the recipient's prior consent (opt-in). Email has been used to conduct marketing and advertising for a long time. With the increase of Internet users, email has become another effective means for online advertising. Advertising through emails provides an extremely cost-effective, high-response-rate marketing vehicle. It enables businesses to acquire and retain consumers, sell and promote products, drive loyalty and reinforce branding efforts. There are several types of email advertisements. Email newsletters are created by businesses or their sales representatives to focus on a group of people who share the common interests on product and business news and updates of product services. They are sent out periodically to potential customers with their permission and can be cancelled anytime. Email discussion lists are created among a group of members who are interested in a particular topic. Email messages, made of conversations on a special topic, are sent to the subscribers in a discussion list. Most good email discussion lists have a moderator who reviews all the messages and decides which are appropriate to be sent to the entire list. The subscripted email marketing channels offer subscribed Web surfers real-time broadcasting commercial emails based on their interested channels. Each channel focuses on dynamic product and service news and advertisements for a special business category. The information and messages are updated dynamically at the real-time base. Since commercial emails can be easily created and delivered using Internet email, email-based advertising offers inexpensive and effective advertising opportunities for advertisers to reach a targeted set of audience in a niche market. Moreover, advertising performance analysis and campaign can be easily carried out based on the total number of web users who receive the commercial email messages. However, email-based advertising has its drawbacks. Many web users frequently receive a great number of unsolicited and unwanted commercial emails on the Internet which creates a negative impression on email advertising among web users. Consequently, these commercial emails are deleted by them whenever received. Not all email servers support the HTML format which makes it difficult to implement the click-through capability in email messages. Well-defined online advertising processes not only define the electronic advertising procedures and workflow, but also provide the basis to build automatic cost-effective solutions for online advertising and services.

In comparison to traditional advertising, email marketing has its advantages and disadvantages. Email marketing (on the Internet) is popular with companies for several reasons— Email's immediacy reduces delays in communication, allowing businesses to run more smoothly; it is significantly cheaper and faster than traditional mails, mainly because of high cost and time required in a traditional mail campaign for producing the artwork, printing, addressing and mailing; advertisers can reach substantial numbers of email subscribers who have opted in to receive email communications on subjects of interest to them. However, these may be filtered or rejected too. Email marketing can be carried out through different types of emails. Transactional emails are usually triggered based on a customer's action with a company. Triggered transactional messages include dropped basket messages, purchase or order confirmation emails and email receipts. Transactional emails are a golden opportunity to engage customers, to introduce or extend the email relationship with customers or subscribers, to anticipate and answer questions or to cross-sell or up-sell products or services. Direct email involves sending an email solely to communicate a promotional message (an announcement of a special offer or a catalog of products). Opt-in email advertising, or permission marketing, is a method of advertising via email whereby the recipient of the advertisement has consented to receive it (a newsletter sent to an advertising firm's customers). Such newsletters inform customers of upcoming events or promotions, or new products. A company that wants to send a newsletter to their customers may ask them at the point of purchase if they would like to receive the newsletter. Similar to newspapers, newsletters create certain anticipation in readers. The reader gets into the habit of receiving (and even enjoying the content) the newsletter and is most likely to stay subscribed and look forward to getting the next email. Building a habit in email subscribers enables them to recognize your brand and associate it with a positive sentiment. Diverse content email newsletters give the freedom to include different types of content that might be important. The same newsletter can contain a popular blog post, a new offer, an announcement of an upcoming event, information about a discount and a link to a survey. Dedicated emails (or also known as stand-alone emails) contain information about only one offer. Dedicated sends are generally used to reach out to an entire email database in instances when all of the subscribers should be notified about a specific marketing campaign, such as a timely new offer or an upcoming event. With dedicated sends to an entire email database, it is possible to generate a lot of buzz around a brand. There is an explosion of engagement resulting from the simultaneous forwarding and social media sharing (with Twitter, LinkedIn and Facebook sharing links in the email). In the paid media universe, one has the benefit of being specific when describing the target audience. In the case of double opt-in, people will receive an email asking them to click on a link in order to confirm their registration.

Transactions are also the messages received from e-commerce sites like Amazon that confirm customers' order and give shipment information and other details. Email marketing is a powerful channel for driving real business results. The goal of all marketing is to attract interest in, build desire for and generate sales of your products or services. Email marketing is a perfect medium to pick up where other marketing leaves off. It is still one of the most cost-effective ways to contact prospects and customers, is far cheaper than traditional bulk postage mail and in many cases can have a much larger impact on immediate sales and long-term relationship strength than traditional advertising. When done correctly, email marketing can be an extremely powerful and effective marketing technique. It's a medium that allows a buyer and seller to freely communicate with one another and build a relationship based on value and trust. However, when erroneous, email marketing can be destructive, erode brand equity and turn happy clients litigious. There are two types of email marketing. One can either send unsolicited email promotions or send out emails only to persons who have requested to receive them. Unsolicited email (called spam) will ruin any legitimate organization's reputation and brand value. Permission-based email marketing, on the other hand, is used effectively every day by hundreds of thousands of organizations to build the value of their brands, increase sales and strengthen the relationships they have with their clients and subscribers. The key difference, of course, is that these senders are only sending messages to persons who have requested to receive them. Permission-based email marketing can be an extremely effective way to increase visitor-to-sale conversion rates, build strong relationships with your customers and turn one-time buyers into lifetime product evangelizers who recommend the organization. It allows companies to develop and sustain relationships with their prospects and consumers by creating value. The nature of permission marketing—building a relationship with a prospect or expanding the relationship with an existing customer over time—allows to concentrate on the prospects and customers who are really interested in what is to be sold and are more than willing to become repeat customers.

Mobile media has begun to draw more significant attention from media giants and advertising industry. Mobile advertising (a subset of mobile marketing) is a form of advertising via mobile (wireless wireless mobile devices such as smart phones, feature phones or tablet computers) phones or other mobile devices. It is marketing on or with a mobile device, such as a smart phone.

Mobile advertising may take the form of static or rich media display ads, short message service (SMS) or multimedia messaging service (MMS) ads, mobile search ads, advertising within mobile websites, or ads within mobile applications or games (such as interstitial ads, *advergaming*, or application sponsorship). There are more mobile devices in the field, connectivity speeds have improved (which, among other things, allows for richer media ads to be served quickly), screen resolutions have advanced, mobile publishers are becoming more sophisticated about incorporating ads and consumers are using mobile devices more extensively. A successful mobile advertising campaign is a combination of goals, statistics, creativity and an intuitive knowledge of the mobile consumer. It can provide customers with time- and location-sensitive, personalized information that promotes goods, services and ideas. Marketing through SMS became increasingly popular in the early 2000s in Europe and some parts of Asia when businesses started to collect mobile phone numbers and send off wanted (or unwanted) content. As with all marketing, balancing the timing and frequency of the messages is extremely important. If enough messages are not sent, it is difficult to remain in the forefront of the customer's mind. If too many messages are sent, it may annoy the recipient and cause them to unsubscribe. Over the past few years, SMS marketing has become a legitimate advertising channel in some parts of the world. The Interactive Advertising Bureau (IAB) and the Mobile Marketing Association (MMA) have established guidelines and spread the use of the mobile channel for marketers. Mobile SPAM messages (SMS sent to mobile subscribers without a legitimate and explicit opt-in by the subscriber) remain an issue in many other parts of the world, partly due to the carriers selling their member databases to third parties. Mobile marketing via SMS has expanded rapidly in Europe and Asia as a new channel to reach the consumer. SMS has become the most popular branch of the mobile marketing industry with several 100 million advertising SMS sent out every month. Some see mobile advertising as closely related to online or Internet advertising, though its reach is far greater currently, most mobile advertising is targeted at mobile phones. In some markets, mobile advertising is most commonly seen as a Mobile Web Banner (top of page) or Mobile Web Poster (bottom of page banner), while in others, it is dominated by SMS advertising. Other forms include MMS advertising, advertising within mobile games and mobile videos, during mobile TV receipt, full-screen interstitials, which appear while a requested item of mobile content or mobile web-page is loading up, and audio advertisements that can take the form of a jingle before a voicemail recording, or an audio record-ing played while interacting with a telephone-based service such as movie ticketing or directory assistance. The main measure-ments of the effectiveness of a mobile media ad campaign are impressions (views) and click-through rates. One of the popular models in mobile advertising is cost per install (CPI) in which the pricing model is based on the user installing an App on their mobile phone. In addition to standard mobile display ban-ners, a growing trend is to include rich media execution within the banner ads. This includes banners that would expand to a larger size, offering advertisers a larger display to communicate their message. Games may be integrated within the banner to make the experience more interactive or a video within the ban-ner space. This unobtrusive two-way communication caught the attention of media industry and advertisers as well as cell phone makers and telecom operators. Eventually, SMS became a new media—called the *seventh mass media channel* by several media and mobile experts—and even more. Besides, the imme-diacy of responsiveness in this two-way media is a new territory (a two-way mobile media, as opposed to one-way immobile media like radios, newspapers and television) for media industry and advertisers, who are eager to measure up market response immediately. Additionally, the possibility of fast delivery of the messages and the ubiquity of the technology (it does not require any additional functionality from the mobile phone, make it ideal for time- and location-sensitive advertising, such as cus-tomer loyalty offers (shopping centres, large brand stores) and SMS promotions of events. To power this strength of SMS adver-tising, timely and reliable delivery of messages is paramount, which is guaranteed by some SMS gateway providers. Types of mobile advertising change rapidly, mobile technology coming up with a strong push for identifying newer and unheard-of mobile multimedia. The result being that subsequent media migration will greatly stimulate a consumer behavioural shift and establish a paradigm shift in mobile advertising. However, the rapid change in the technology used by mobile advertisers can also have adverse effect on the number of consumers being reached by the mobile advertisements, due to technical limitations of their mobile devices. Hence, campaigns that aim to achieve wide response or are targeting lower-income groups might be better off relying on older, more widespread mobile advertising technologies, such as SMS. As mobile is an interactive mass media similar to the Internet, advertisers are eager to utilize and make use of viral marketing methods, by which one recipient of an advertisement on mobile, will forward it to another. This allows users to become part of the advertising experience. At the bare minimum, mobile ads with viral abilities can become powerful interactive campaigns. At the extreme, they can become engagement marketing experiences. Targeted mobile marketing requires customization of ad content to reach interested and relevant customers. To customize, such behavioural personal data, user profiling, data mining and other behaviour watch tools are employed, and privacy advocates warn that this may cause privacy infringement. Mobile marketing differs from most other forms of marketing communication in that it is often user (consumer) initiated (mobile originated) message and requires the express consent of the consumer to receive future communications. Irrespective of how well advertising messages are designed and how many additional possibilities they provide, if consumers do not have confidence that their privacy will be protected, this will hinder their widespread deployment. Mobile advertising has raised considerable interest as mobile technology has advanced and companies worldwide are starting to use not only text messages, but also multimedia messages in their mobile commercial communication. The receiver of the message can react by calling the marketer, sending the company a text message or connecting her/himself to the company's webpages (if fitted to the mobile in use). Thus, mobile advertising is much more interactive and personal than traditional advertising. Mobile advertising may lead to a vicious circle of advertisers setting goals according to mass media (e.g., reaching a high number of potential customers), and ad agencies or advertisers designing mobile adverts for mass audiences without personalization and interactivity, which annoys many customers, leading to a failure of the campaign.

The mobile web features text and graphics optimized to match the specific screen resolutions and browser capabilities of each user's mobile phone. A smartphone with a high resolution screen is capable of handling larger, more visually rich ads than a standard-feature mobile phone with fewer resources, which can only be served light-weight advertisements designed for small screens with limited resolution. In order to accommodate the wide range of mobile phone capabilities, advertisers are to produce and provide ads creative in pre-defined dimensions supported by most mobiles, thus ensuring that the ad unit is matched to the mobile phone model's capabilities, and that it best fits the mobile phone's display. This approach helps ensure a good user experience and increases process and campaign effectiveness. Some publishers and markets recommend or require the use of ad indicators (signifiers) when displaying an ad unit. The publisher or local market guidelines define the exact format and placement of the ad indicator. Indicators are used with both text and banner ads. Some publishers and ad-serving solutions provide a capability to re-size the ad creative dynamically to match the mobile phone's screen dimensions and capabilities. It's important that the creative takes into account both the impact of image re-sizing (i.e., certain amount of degradation of image quality) and that automatic resizing may not work well with animated banners. Virtually every mobile phone in the world supports SMS, creating a ubiquitous market for SMS-based advertising campaigns. SMS ads may be delivered as part of an on-going opt-in mobile advertising campaign. The font size is entirely controlled by the mobile phone and is not under the control of advertiser or publisher. Therefore, the message renders differently on different mobile phones. The length of the ad is subject to the space available after the content. There should be a clear separation between the text message content and the ad. The primary design goal should be that the SMS advertising unit is clearly identifiable as an advertisement and is easily understood by the receiver of the message. Many advertisers have looked at creating their own branded applications and uploading these into app stores. These take many different forms depending on the brand and its attributes. They can be entertaining, informative or functional (Duracell running game and a Nestle recipe app). Advertisers are responsible for the infrastructure costs for an advertising website or associated click-through pages including keeping up with traffic demands, communications, hosting, hardware and software, as well as the costs of implementation. Ad-serving infrastructure may be capable of performing automatic resizing, where a standard dimension is dynamically adjusted to match the phone's display while maintaining the aspect ratio of the standard ad unit. Push notifications were popularized with the Android operational system, where the notifications are shown on the top of the screen. It has helped application owners to communicate directly with their end users in a simple and effective way. If not used wisely, it can quickly alienate users as it causes interruptions to their current activities on the phone. SMS and push notifications can be part of a well-developed inbound mobile marketing strategy. With the increasingly widespread use of smart phones, app usage has also greatly increased. Therefore, mobile marketers have increasingly taken advantage of smart phone apps as a marketing resource. This allows for direct engagement, payment and targeted advertising. Brands are now delivering promotional messages within mobile games or sponsoring entire games to drive consumer engagement. This is known as mobile advergaming or ad-funded mobile game. Advertising on webpages specifically meant for access by mobile devices is also an option. The MMA is the premier global non-profit trade association established to lead the growth of mobile marketing and its associated technologies. It is an action-oriented organization designed to clear obstacles to market development, establish mobile media guidelines and best practices for sustainable growth, and promote the use of the mobile channel. The MMA provides a set of guidelines and standards that give the recommended format of ads, presentation and metrics used in reporting. Google, Yahoo and other major mobile content providers have been selling advertising placement on their properties. Quick response (QR) codes allow a customer to visit a webpage address by scanning a 2D image with their phone's camera, instead of manually entering a URL which would include tracking features which would be unwieldy if typed by the customer. MMS is a rich media messaging service that allows mobile users to send and receive messages/media that can include graphics, photos, audio, video and text. Unlike the Mobile Web, this media resides on the user's mobile phone, so a data connection is not required to access the ad content once the message has been received. MMS is not yet universally supported by all operator networks and all mobile phones; however, the advertising opportunity using MMS is significant. The MMS guidelines consist of a set of ad unit dimensions, file formats and maximum file sizes, as well as additional considerations for advertisers and publishers. MMS mobile marketing can contain a timed slideshow of images, text, audio and video. This mobile content is delivered via MMS. MMS short text ad is a supplementary text ad unit appended to the content (or body) portion of an MMS slide containing the primary, non-advertising content of the MMS slide. An MMS Short Text Ad can contain links that are clickable by the end user. An MMS Long Text Ad is a supplementary text ad unit filling all of an MMS slide, whereby the text can contain a link that is clickable by the end user. MMS Banner Ad is a supplementary colour graphics ad unit displayed at the top or bottom of an MMS slide. An MMS Banner Ad can be clickable by the end user, in which case a separate text link can be considered. In mass-market campaigns, the goal is a good user experience across all mobile phone models, network technologies and data bandwidths. Clicking on ad units provide opportunities for the user to receive additional information from the advertiser. Both ad banners and interstitial ad images may be active and link either to places inside the application or to outside the application. This functionality must be consistent with a mobile phone's capabilities and will be limited by both types of mobile phone and mobile phone connectivity.

Sponsored Mobile Application is a publisher's downloadable application which features a sponsoring arrangement at various places across the application (Nike or Adidas sponsoring a football app). Essentially, an advertiser will sponsor an entire site, or at least a section of a site or a specific page on a site. With this type of advertising, it is most common for the sponsorship to be exclusive for a given period of time. An advertiser uses this kind of advertising for branding or for introducing a new product. Since visitors to the site will see the same sponsorship advertising constantly, rather than in rotation with other ads; it is more likely to sink in and be established in their minds. This is perhaps the most basic and traditional form of advertising. With this method, the advertiser essentially buys a run of advertising, usually for a specific period of time. Most commonly, publishers will sell a Banner Run on a specific section of a site or specific ad spots on a page. Affiliate advertising is based on the concept of an advertiser rewarding a publisher (the affiliate) for any business that is brought in. Generally speaking, the publisher will run ads for an affiliate with special tracking code that helps the advertiser to identify which site a visitor came from. Affiliate systems can also often keep track of which visitors actually sign up for or buy something as well, and the affiliate can be rewarded accordingly. Affiliate systems can reward publishers just for clickthroughs, or more specifically for actual sales and leads. Most commonly, Pay-Per-Click advertising is associated with search engines and contextual advertising. Generally, the advertiser pays out to the publisher for each click on an ad. Commonly these ads will be text links and will be shown either as part of a search results page or based on the content of a site (Google's AdSense). Entertainment is a very traditional ad-supported medium. Integrated Ad is an advertisement that is integrated with the application or game experience and is formatted to be compatible with the main content type used in the application context. It can be resized, reshaped and freely positioned as part of the core application content. Unlike online banners, the publishers of game-based online advertisements are online game vendors instead of web publishers. They use two ways to post advertisements to game players. The common approach is to replace online game images by textures having advertisement implemented therein. The game players are visually influenced by advertisements when viewing the virtual world of games. Another approach is to separate the whole game into several episodes. Game players have to view and interact with certain advertisement before going to another episode. In this approach, advertisements usually receive more interactive responses from players because it takes the advantage of the eagerness of players to continue the game. Since most advanced online games are usually multimedia based, game-based advertisements cost more to create and implement due to their dependency on complicated technology.

Although game-based advertising is usually very effective to drive the attention of game players, its audience is limited to game players only. In many cases, game players feel annoyed with advertisements while they are playing games.

In traditional advertising, posting and delivery of advertisements is very simple due to the static one-to-one mapping between an advertisement and an advertising space (or a time slot) and the independence between advertisements. However, the advertisement posting in online advertising becomes more complicated due to the digital implementation in online advertising, the mapping relationship between an advertising space and an advertisement during a scheduled advertising time slot becomes much more complicated than the one in traditional advertising; and due to the advantage of digital advertising, advertisements can be structured in a more complex way to achieve diverse marketing goals and implement complex business roles. Online publishers (or advertising service agencies) post online advertisements on the Web according to pre-contracted schedules. During a scheduled advertising time slot, only one advertisement may be posted in its advertising space (this is easily performed by posting the advertisement onto the corresponding advertising space in a target page based on its schedule. As soon as the posting time is over, it will be replaced by another advertisement), or more than one advertisement will be posted on an advertising space during a given time slot (they share the same space during the time slot, and they would be posted in a sequence on a time-sharing base. Several advertisements share the same advertising space in a scheduled time period), or an advertisement may be bound to more than several advertising spaces, and it will be posted on them during a scheduled time slot (advertisement posting becomes little complicated when there is a one-to-many [or many-to-one] mapping between advertisements and advertising spaces. This becomes complex when the targeted advertising spaces belong to different websites [or publishers]). With the advantage of digital nature of online advertisements, it is possible to easily construct and implement various posting structures for advertisements. Good advertising structures (the posting structures and relationships between advertisements in different advertising spaces) enables advertisers to conduct effective advertising by implementing diverse business marketing techniques.

In traditional advertising, tracking the detailed information of a posting (or posted) advertisement is difficult or even impossible. Online advertising has its distinct advantage on advertisement tracking because advertisements are delivered, posted, viewed and accessed through digital solutions over the Internet. Online advertisement tracking refers to activities and provided services for advertisers to monitor and track the posting status of an advertisement, and collect and report the tracking data. It is used not only for product-oriented advertisements, but also for tracking brand-building advertisements. The purpose is to confirm advertisers about the delivery and posting of their advertisements according to contracted schedules by providing the related posting states, data and reports and to help advertisers to collect the tracked data about advertisement posting, audience viewing and accesses. These data will be very useful for performance analysis and measurement of advertisements. Advertising targeting aims at effective ways to find and deliver the right advertisements to the potential interested customers. In traditional advertising, only the marketing section can perform pre-advertisement targeting during the advertisement planning through historical data analysis, product survey and analysis. Online targeting for advertisements refers to the activities and services that use real-time data and systematic methods to select and post the advertisements to potential or targeted customers at the right time and the right place. The basic task may be to identify potential customers for a product advertisement and deliver it to them based on their subscriptions or memberships or to select, deliver and present the right advertisements to online users with a real-time solution.

The Social Media: Localization and Global Communication

Today we see marketing as transforming once again in response to the new dynamics in the environment. We see companies expanding their focus from products to consumers to humankind issues. Marketing is the stage when companies shift from consumer-centricity to human-centricity and where profitability is balanced with corporate responsibility.

—Phillip Kotler

Advertising introduces a new product to the prospective buyers or draws their attention to the changes/modifications if the product has been revamped. It distinguishes between users and non-users of the products, tries to retain the former and convert the latter into users. Being a means of mass communication, advertising requires a mass medium which will enable the advertisers to get in touch with a large number of people.

Since neither products nor markets are identical, it requires differing modes of advertising. Each marketer tries to create a specific position for its product among many competitive products, and advertising is effectively employed to achieve this end. The effectiveness of the advertisement is important, for a consumer chooses a product intelligently from the several available. Advertising cost is dependent on the nature of the market and the product, the reputation of the company and its competitive environment.

With the creation of increasingly powerful mobile devices, numerous social media applications have gone mobile and new entrants are constantly appearing. Mobile marketing and mobile social media have become a part of the current scenario. Social media depends on mobile- and web-based technologies to create highly interactive platforms through which individuals and communities share, co-create, discuss and modify user-generated content. Social media differentiates from traditional/industrial media in many aspects such as quality, reach, frequency, usability, immediacy and permanence. For content contributors, the benefits of participating in social media have gone beyond simply social sharing to building reputation and bringing in career opportunities and monetary income. Due to the fact that mobile social media runs on mobile devices, it differentiates from traditional social media as it incorporates new factors such as the current location of the user (location-sensitivity) or the time delay between sending and receiving messages (time-sensitivity). While traditional social media offer a variety of opportunities for companies in a wide range of business sectors, mobile social media makes use of the location- and time-sensitivity aspects of it in order to engage into marketing research, communication, sales promotions/discounts and relationship development/loyalty programmes. More consumers are accessing social media content via mobile platforms, especially apps. A common thread running through all definitions of social media is a blending of technology and social interaction for the co-creation of value. People obtain information, education, news and other data from electronic and print media. Social media are distinct from traditional media such as newspapers, television and film as they are comparatively inexpensive and accessible and enable anyone (even private individuals) to publish or access information. It is capable of reaching a global audience.

Social media technologies are capable of reaching a global audience. Social media tools are generally available to the public at little or no cost. Social media can be capable of virtually instantaneous responses. It can be altered almost instantaneously by comments or editing and has provided an open arena where people are free to exchange ideas on companies, brands and products. Social media provides an environment where users and public relations (PR) professionals can converse, and where PR professionals can promote their brand and improve their company's image by listening and responding to what the public is saying about their product.

Social media marketing programmes usually centre on efforts to create content that attracts attention and encourages readers to share it with their social networks. Being a platform that is easily accessible to anyone with the Internet access, the increased communication for organizations fosters brand awareness and often, improved customer service. Additionally, social media serves as a relatively inexpensive platform for organizations to implement marketing campaigns. Social networking websites allow individuals/companies to interact with one another and build relationships. When companies join the social channels, consumers can interact with them. Social networking sites and blogs allow individual followers to retweet or repost comments made by the product being promoted. By repeating the message, all of the users' connections are able to see the message, therefore reaching more people. Social networking sites act as word of mouth. Because the information about the product is being put out there and is getting repeated, more traffic is brought to the product/company. Through social networking sites, companies can interact with individual followers. This personal interaction can instill a feeling of loyalty into followers and potential customers. Also, by choosing whom to follow on these sites, products can reach a very narrow target audience. Social networking sites also include a vast amount of information about what products and services prospective clients might be interested in. Marketers can detect buying signals, such as content shared by people and questions posted online. Understanding of buying signals can help sales people target relevant prospects and marketers run micro-targeted campaigns. Mobile phone usage has also become beneficial for social media marketing. Many cell phones have social networking capabilities: individuals are notified about any happenings on social networking sites through their cell phones, in real-time. This constant connection to social networking sites means products and companies can constantly remind and update followers about their capabilities, uses and importance. Because cell phones are connected to social networking sites, advertisements are always in sight. Also, many companies are now putting QR codes along with products for individuals to access the company website or online services with their smart phones. In the context of the social web, customers and stakeholders are participants rather than viewers. Social media in business allows anyone and everyone to express and share an opinion or an idea. Each participating customer becomes part of the marketing department, as other customers read their comments or reviews. The engagement process is fundamental to successful social media marketing. Social networking sites can have a large impact on the outcome of events. Small businesses also use social networking sites as a promotional technique. Businesses can follow individuals' social networking site use in the local area and advertise specials and promotional deals. Twitter allows companies to promote their products on an individual level. The use of a product can be explained in short messages that followers are more likely to read. These messages appear on followers' home pages. Messages can link to the product's website, Facebook profile, photos and videos. This link provides followers the opportunity to spend more time interacting with the product online. This interaction can create a loyal connection between product and individual and can also lead to larger advertising opportunities. A good marketing strategy for businesses to increase footfall or retain loyal customers includes offering incentives such as discounts or free food/beverages for people checking into their location or special privileges for those of that location. With the development of location-based search services, Google+ allows for targeted advertising methods, navigation services and other forms of location-based marketing and promotion. Companies use blogging platforms for their social media repertoire. Platforms like LinkedIn create an environment for companies and clients to connect online. Companies that recognize the need for information, originality and accessibility employ blogs to make their products popular and unique, and ultimately reach out to consumers who are privy to social media. Blogs allow a product or company to provide longer descriptions of products or services (including reasoning, testimonials and uses). It can link to and from Facebook, Twitter and many social network and blog pages. Blogs can be updated frequently and are promotional techniques for keeping customers. These online environments being accessed by virtually any consumers become a part of the creative process. Promotional opportunities such as sponsoring a video are possible on YouTube. The type of language used in the commercials and the ideas used to promote the product reflect the audience's style and taste, and the ads are usually in sync with the content of the video requested (this is an advantage YouTube brings for advertisers). With social networks, information relevant to the user's likes is available to businesses, who then advertise accordingly. Internet and social networking seeps are one of the issues facing traditional advertising. Video and print ads are often leaked to the world via the Internet earlier than they are scheduled to premiere. Social networking sites allow those leaks to go viral and be seen by many users more quickly. Time difference is also a problem before traditional advertisers.

Advertising is beginning to move viewers from the traditional outlets (traditional advertising techniques included print and television advertising) to the electronic ones. Studies suggest that even those ads ignored by the users may influence the user subconsciously. Social media marketing provides organizations with a way to connect with their customers. However, organizations must protect their information as well as closely watch comments and concerns on the social media they use. Numerous additional online marketing mishap examples exist leading to deterioration of the company's corporate image. Because users have different operating systems, web browsers and computer hardware (including mobile devices and different screen sizes), online ads may appear differently to users than the advertiser intended, or the ads may not display properly at all. Furthermore, advertisers may encounter legal problems if legally required information does not actually display to users, even if that failure is due to technological heterogeneity. Due to ad-blocking, or ad filtering, the ads may not appear to the user because the user uses technology to screen out ads. Many browsers block unsolicited pop-up ads by default. Other software programs or browser add-ons may also block the loading of ads or block elements on a page. Some web browsers offer privacy modes where users can hide information about themselves from publishers and advertisers. By tracking users' online activities, advertisers are able to understand consumers quite well. Advertisers often use technology, such as web bugs and respawning cookies, to maximizing their abilities to track consumers. Scammers can take advantage of consumers' difficulties verifying an online persona's identity, leading to artifices like phishing (where scam emails look identical to those from a well-known brand owner). Consumers also face malware risks when interacting with online advertising. Numerous efforts have been undertaken to combat spam (ranging from blacklists to regulatorily required labelling to content filters), but most of those efforts have adverse collateral effects, such as mistaken filtering. Different jurisdictions have taken different approaches to privacy issues with advertising. Many laws specifically regulate the ways online ads are delivered. It is through a process of building social authority that social media becomes effective. While people are resistant to marketing in general, they are even more resistant to direct or overt marketing through social media platforms. A marketer can generally not expect people to be receptive to a marketing message in and of itself. An increasing number of scholars have sought to study and measure the impact of social media. Studies have suggested that social media services may be addictive, and that using social media services may lead to a fear of missing out. Consumers continue to spend more time on social networks than on any other category of sites. Social networking has become more popular among the old and the young.

Those criticizing the social media contend that it will increase an information disparity between winners, who are able to use the social media actively, and losers, who are not familiar with modern technologies. There is also a huge debate on the ownership of the content on social media platforms since it is generated by the users and hosted by the company. Added to this is the danger to security of information, which can be leaked to third parties with economic interests in the platform, or parasites who comb the data for their own databases. Advertising and promoting products on social media also becomes important in this era. Tweets containing endorsements have become prevalent.

Advertisements combine information and image making. The audience and the culture are important. To be successful in the challenging environment, organizations must adapt their advertisements to give them the look and feel of locally made products. This involves catering to a wide range of linguistic, cultural, content and technical issues. Product presentation (which includes size, shape, language, colours, graphics and icons) and functionality must be adapted to local conventions. Localization is an important issue for companies that aim to market and sell their products in national/international markets.

With the growth of global communications and marketing, there arises the need to adapt social media communication to different cultural audiences and locales. Localization means adapting all of the content to different local cultures. It involves more than just translation as it includes all aspects of communication. Since social media is heavily influencing all of our communications, it is no longer enough just to localize the content. In today's dynamic, social networking-charged environment, one needs to adapt communication to match the intended target markets to make sure that the message and intent is successfully communicated. Companies may shape their message and communication according to their international audiences. Localization in this context also aims at the company's adaptation of its product, brand or message so that it appeals more specifically to small populace with different cultural standards. Large brands with a national presence and multiple locations could benefit by localizing their service or product. Cultural preferences and different cultural characteristics demand that messages be sensitive to the differences. An ad that does not take culture into consideration is bound to fail. Hence, there arises the necessity of localizing social media communication for foreign-language markets as well. This includes transcreating or localizing social media content, developing user engagement and maintaining a visible presence on the web. To ensure that apps have the right impact in each of the markets, they too need to be localized. A global presence is necessary for any organization hoping to connect with customers around the world. Customizing or localizing content for specific markets and cultures dramatically multiplies desired effect. Social media localization is the adaptation of social media content for foreign markets. Linguists monitor and engage in online conversations, in specific foreign language markets, helping to adapt a digital communications to suit different cultural audiences. Social media has become an essential part of customer engagement, with a large number of active Internet users visiting social networks and blogs. With increasing use worldwide, it has become imperative for driven businesses to engage with social media users in multiple languages. Product and service translation and cultural adaptation (for specific countries, regions or groups) to account for differences in distinct markets and societies is true also of other modes of advertising brought under the terms New Media and Social Media. Localization and Internationalization have been described in the *Encyclopedia of Applied Linguistics* as the two key steps in the preparation and translation of digital content for international markets and have formed part of the globalization strategies of multinational digital publishers. The main objective of social localization is the promotion of a demand. It is based on the recognition that it is no longer exclusively the corporations who control the global conversation, but the communities. Social Media Localization pertains to localizing benefits and promotions (through location-based social media channels) to consumers in different places to ensure they engage with a person's social media presence. The approach must change when engaging global audiences. The term localization is used to describe a company's modification of their product, brand or communication so that it appeals more specifically to small populations with different cultural values. This is in contrast to the globalized approach, which is found when a company changes little except perhaps for the language it uses (the IBM international websites and the Pepsi Corporation's international websites). When companies shape their message and communication according to their international audiences, it reduces the whole population into national identities. However, large brands with a national presence and multiple locations benefit by changing their definition of social media localization to include intra-national as well as international efforts. What is needed is an approach to social media management that localizes domestically and not just internationally. Such an approach would accomplish the core targets of social media marketing. It attempts to create a personal experience for the consumer/customer. They elevate the individual voice above the corporate. Creating more focuses, campaigns through localization would obviously boost the potential engagement. It will form a close-knit community of loyal followers/friends/fans, for the community will have many things in common. The community members are loyal vouchers for the particular brand or product. A domestic/localized approach would need a network of small, local social media management firms. An approach specific to each locale becomes a requirement. It becomes essential to have an integrated approach to messaging and the flexibility to change the message as needed. Many large brands do not prefer to spend extra money to shape a message on which they have already spent huge amounts on creating. Cultural preferences and different cultural characteristics demand that messages be sensitive to these differences. Without taking culture into consideration, any message will fail.

The translation services focus on the localization of social media communication for foreign-language markets. They work with professional linguists and copywriters to transcreate or localize social media content, maintaining a visible presence on the web. Smart phones have dramatically increased the popularity of web-enabled local information. There are scores of locally oriented apps on iPhone. Experience and expertise are essential to adapt the marketing content to suit international audiences. In-country subject matter experts, translation memory processes and in-house quality assessment systems all work to ensure that language, message and functionality are of great quality across all media. To target a global market, the website will require a multimedia localization comprehensive service. Localizers provide full translation and localization of website intending to widen the reach. Streamlined localization of apps (e.g., Apple) for iPhones, Android and Windows phones and cross-cultural site design are provided. In order to ensure that apps have the right impact in each of the markets, they need to be localized. The mobile apps too need to be localized to reach a larger audience. As large majority of the audiences employ mobile devices, mobile technology is currently a leading source of advertising. Therefore, the importance of localization and translation of mobile apps and the reason why many companies (despite the extra expenditure involved in offering multilingual content) have made their apps available on a global scale. The value of the localized content as well as the quality of the screens and functionality has to be ensured. Multimedia localization services need to incorporate functionality, user experience and cross-browser testing for websites and online media to ensure that they really meet the standards and are consistent across devices and locales. It is about giving the audience the best possible user experience and leaving them with a positive brand perception. With social media contributing to a globally connected society, businesses that continue to take a global approach to social content and engagement tend to make use of localization for greater resonance and relevance. A global presence is necessary for any organization hoping to connect with customers around the world. In any web strategy, including social and also mobile media, localization is sovereign.

Even websites cannot escape the influence of culture. The online world is quickly becoming more globalized, and the fewer the language options provided, the fewer the downloads. Website localization is the process of adapting/modifying an existing website to make it accessible, usable and culturally suitable to the local language and culture in the target market. It has become one of the primary tools for business global expansion and, being a multilayered process, requires programming expertise and linguistic/cultural knowledge. Else localization is prone to encounter problems. The incidence of this mode is the result of the popularity of computer and Internet users. People all over the world consider the Internet as their main site for information and services. These people do not speak the same language. Website localization is more than mere translation which only solves partial language problems. Going global means that measurement units, layout, symbols, colours, images (carry many subtle cultural messages within them, speaking volumes about the company or the product) and texts (all loaded with cultural meaning) are to be modified to appeal to the target culture. It is crucial that companies involved in internationalization of their business consider website localization and take care to use effective cross-cultural analysis. The use of Twitter is very different from one country to another and even from one region to another. Differences between users in different countries include trends heavily influenced by news and major global events. Twitter usage is heavily affected by language. Facebook supports most languages, which gives it an advantage to cover many locales. A significant number of businesses employ English-driven initiatives across the Web. As customers grow increasingly depended on social networks, data shows that customizing or localizing content for specific markets and cultures dramatically multiplies desired effect. Localization also helps customers feel better about the resulting clicks they make following each engagement. The pages that feature localized content, in addition to the global initiatives, fostered interaction and illustrate the point of why localized strategies are important. Now, with social and mobile commerce becoming pivotal in defining and activating customer relationships within their channels of preference, localized initiatives will only enhance opportunities. Social media marketing in different cultures and different languages requires an understanding of the target audience as well as several important factors like the most popular local social media networks (which varies from one country to another), the languages used in the communication on the local social networks (some are bilingual and some are not), the modern languages and dialects used for communication on the local network (those like the Arabic regions have a lot of dialects), the significant topics in each country and what the local market segments are talking about. It is important to be always up-to-date on locale-based trends because they can change swiftly and frequently. The target culture is extremely important and it will always be necessary to have professional localization candidates to localize communication and to provide advice about the content that is being posted or shared. With good research and an efficient localization team, it will be possible to have an effective strategy and social media policy for each locale that is joined through social media tools and channels.

Unlike the conventional one-way media like television, radio and newspaper, web media has enabled two-way transfer, thereby introducing a new phase of interactive advertising, regardless of whether static or mobile. Location-based services are offered by some cell phone networks as a way to send custom advertising and other information to cell-phone subscribers based on their current location.

The rise of the social media (the process of gaining website traffic or attention through social media sites) has introduced substantial and pervasive changes to communication among organizations, communities and individuals. It refers to the means of interactions among people in which they create, share and/or exchange information and ideas in virtual communities and networks (Geocities, Facebook, etc., are examples of a social media sites). Social network advertising is a form of online advertising that focuses on social networking sites. One of the major benefits of advertising on a social networking site (Facebook, Myspace, Orkut, etc.) is that advertisers can take advantage of the users' demographic information and target their ads appropriately. Social media marketing is commercial promotion conducted through social media websites. Many companies promote their products by posting frequent updates and providing special offers through their social media profiles. Social networks such as Facebook and Twitter provide advertisers with information about the likes and dislikes of their consumers. This technique is crucial, as it provides the businesses with a *target audience*. Social media applications—including collaborative projects, micro-blogs/blogs, content communities, social networking sites and virtual worlds—have become part of the standard communication repertoire for many companies. Social media is used to document memories, learn about and explore things, advertise oneself and form friendships.

'Ad'apting to Markets: Means to the Consumer's Heart and Purse

Connectivity doesn't just mean you get a lot more chances to deliver messages about customer service and pricing plans. This isn't one-sided. It enables people to talk back.

—*James Murdoch*

Televisual constructions contribute towards creating a sense of social and cultural identity. Advertising, especially on the television, is becoming more attentive to the *look* of the advertisement than to the product it sells. An influential figure within television studies, Baudrillard mentions how the ecstasy of communication in the postmodern era has caused *reality* and *fiction* to coalesce. His concept of the *ecstasy of communication* suggests that society has entered an information overload, and that the only powerful mode of resistance left to us lies in a rejection of the commodified images which invade our consciousness. The televisual media are postmodern in their emblematic status owing to their *implosion* of meaning. According to Baudrillard (1988), the meaning has *imploded* because of the extensive exposure to the mass media (Woods, 2010:226). Television commercials pull apart cultural signifiers and allow them to float around in a loose space (which Baudrillard calls *hyperreality*) where they attach themselves to commodities. Judith Williamson (1978:227) in her study of advertising demonstrates how the very structures of advertisements—the play of signifiers, the manipulation of history and the erasure of temporal differences to evoke nostalgia, the use of linguistic and visual puns, the arrangement of fragments, absences, substitutions and synecdoches—themselves suggest a postmodern medium. Drawing on Baudrillard's theories of the collapse of *fiction* and *reality* into a single realm of *simulacra*, Kaplan (1987:44) argues:

> The new postmodern universe, with its celebration of the look-the surfaces, textures, the self-as-commodity-threatens to reduce everything to the image/representation/simulacrum. Television, with its decentred address, its flattering out of things into a network or system, the parts of which all rely on each other, and which is endless, unbounded, unframed, seems...

Television, with its ability to combine visual images, sound, motion and colour, is an ideal medium for advertising. It allows the advertiser the maximum opportunity to develop and convey/disperse the most creative and imaginative advertisement messages as compared to any other medium. Advertising, an integral part of a business plan, is employed to communicate information and ideas to groups of people in order to change or reinforce an attitude and increase the demand for a product. The marketers communicate the uniqueness of their brands to their prospects. It is a source of information which establishes reputation and familiarizes public with the product. A feasible means for communicating with the millions of ultimate consumers, creativity is essential in the designing/localization of advertisements. It has to avoid use of objectionable appeals, technique, excessive repetition of messages, loud volume and silliness of presentation. Through words and visuals, it creates in the mind of many a desire to buy one particular product in preference to a number of others. The advertiser pays the medium to deliver the message used to promote the sale of a product or service, to influence public opinion. It hastens the trial and acceptance of new products and modifies the consumer perception of goods and services. The advertising strategy must be adapted to markets (local/global) that are ever changing and to competition that is ever threatening. To successfully interpret the want-satisfying qualities of products and services in terms of consumer needs and wants, the advertiser must have a thorough knowledge of the consumer, the product and the structure of the market. This becomes more important when an advertisement calls for localization. Consumer research, product and market analysis are essential in any product launch. The special layout, colour, size and location of the advertisement influence its sales. Believability is important to build a brand image. The visual content should work with the verbal and aural elements for the planned localization strategy to succeed. The layout should be designed to provide a logical, clear and unified presentation of the advertising message. Reach of the advertisement is important for the promotion of the product. Only when the target consumers easily understand what the advertisements mean, can they be possibly interested in its information and accept what is advertised and be convinced to take certain action as the advertiser and translator intend. The cultural value systems of different national populations vary widely. This is shown by the way people receive and interpret communications, including advertising, and is reflected in recognizable national advertising styles. Advertising that fails to tune into the nuances of the national character and of the subgroup within the culture that is being targeted will by definition be suboptimal. Translation requires skilled and expensive creative talent. Human needs and wants may be universal, but their expression is deeply rooted in cultural differences. Some form of local autonomy is necessary. Words, symbols and sounds work differently in different cultures. Brands work differently as a result of different values in different markets. The hegemonic assumption that advertising does things to people needs to be challenged, for the text is not all powerful or all encompassing in its reach, and consumers are not merely passive receivers of advertising messages. The strategy of advertisers has been changing over the years. It has moved from promoting the product directly to adverts which say less and less about the item for consumption and more about the cultural representations of the advertisement itself as against its referential product. Advertisements frequently quote and allude to other ads, and emphasize style and surface as opposed to utilitarianism. Often these alterations can be traced to shifts in social and cultural taste.

Localization helps sellers to compete for a share of the diverse market by encouraging people to try new products, to maintain product loyalty or to switch brands. In India, the last decade of the 20th century has witnessed a phenomenal growth in advertising business. Localization is an indispensable part of this scenario. In most cases, there is a need to adapt to the local language. Companies ranging from large global players to small local retailers are increasingly relying on advertising to sell their products. Print as well as television advertising makes use of film stars or fashion figures for international/national/regional products as these icons help to build a bridge between the local world and the foreign products. They appear as international citizens of a globalized culture where one has unprecedented access to wealth, success and power. In considering the totality of advertising in the context of consumer culture and as a major vehicle of ideology, language must be seen as integral to the images that flow from advertising. Applied to advertising, consumers make sense of advertising by interpreting the interplay of verbal and visual representation within a meaningful cultural context to form some type of meaningful impression. In the Indian–Kerala–Malayalam advertisement context, localization is mostly confined to the linguistic domain—the advert linguistically adapted to the regional language without any visual adaptation. In most cases, such dubbed adverts present poor lip synching which, though unaesthetic, is overcome by the viewers' existing familiarity with the advert (in the case of a viewer who is familiar with both the languages). Some adverts attempt to achieve localization through a single advert (like Uninor which appeals to the different regions of Kerala/Tamil Nadu through a single advert. Through a single Malayalam/Tamil advert, it aims the Malayalam/Tamil audience) aiming a regio-centric compass. Adverts (like Cadbury) may go for a total translation of its jingle where the problem of lip sync does not arise. Visual (mostly partial like incorporating a regional celebrity) and linguistic translation occurs in adverts like Fair and Handsome and Idea (Hindi/Tamil/ Telugu) with regional actors and the regional language. Regio-centred adverts like Manappuram linguistically and visually (use different actors and other cultural indicators, like *mundu,* in its regional versions) localize their ads to appeal to the viewers— Akshay Kumar in Hindi, Mohanlal in Malayalam, Vikram in Tamil and Venkatesh in Telugu. In most advertisements, the same caption, slogan, dialogue, voice-over or jingle goes through linguistic adaptation. It is the need to create a differential advantage through local sensitivity and increased communicative effectiveness that necessitates adapted advertising programmes. It is more dependent on cultural influence and, hence, the visual and verbal parts of advertising are in particular sensitive, and use of local language, models and scenery increase the probability for the advertisement to be effective.

Thinking and behaving are equally influenced by culture. Paradoxically, someone who thinks globally is still a product of his/ her own culture. The local is often more meaningful than global to the consumers. The basic structure of the global–foreign–local positioning framework, namely language, aesthetics and story themes, is etic (an *etic-emic* approach [Poortinga and Malpass, 1986]) and applies to advertising around the world. However, the detailed expression of that structure can be influenced by local culture (emic). Nescafe's advertising projects the image of a brand consumed globally. However, in the Netherlands, this positioning is executed by featuring an old man from South America enjoying the coffee. In Greece, the advertisement setting portrays several young people on a raft with a small hut for a cabin at the seashore. Global marketers suggest a global youth segment with homogeneous desires. However, when global youth cultural styles are readily available, a localized version of youth culture emerges. Although there is a convergence of technology and media, behaviour of consumers does not appear to converge. The way people think and perceive is to a large extent guided by the framework of their own culture. Globalization entails a comprehensive and well-structured product development lifecycle that starts with a global and local product analysis and moves through product globalization and localization to end with support for and feedback on localized products. The modern market makes necessary a global (polycentric) vision—the need to design products and services for global distribution at the same time keeping in vision the regional variation. Hence, there arises the need for localized products and services which are adapted to meet specific local needs, making them available in the local language, and provide a local look and feel—though budgetary allocation may not always allow region to region total visual/graphic localization. Indian advertising relies more on (dubbed) linguistic/aural translation of adverts than a visual one. There occurs only partial localization/translation in most television adverts. This is perceivable more in the case of Malayalam television adverts (the original Hindi dubbed into Malayalam). It does have its regio-centered adverts which are localized into other languages. Tamil (even Telugu) adapts/localizes adverts to suit their cultural specificity on a larger scale. Aural as well as visual localization (though not possible in all cases) is necessitated at times to get across the message. Gestures are also important cultural signs. Gestures that in one culture have a positive meaning can be embarrassing to members of another culture. Signs and symbols are an important part of association networks in one's memory—package, colour, letters and signs. Advertising displays the rituals around products and brands. It reflects how people behave and interact, how they are dressed, what their language and eating habits are, and how their houses look. These elements are the expressions or artefacts of culture. A global culture refers to the expressions of culture, the symbols, converging eating habits and global heroes. The language a person speaks is part of the culture in which he/she grows. It reflects all manifestations of culture. Culture-specific words reflect the specific values of a culture. They cannot be easily translated into words of other cultures. Untranslated concepts are so meaningful to members of a specific culture that they are effective elements of advertising copy. They refer to collective memory. Monolingual people generally find it difficult to understand this. The values included in the words cannot be translated and often conceptual equivalence cannot be attained. Words and sentences as well as pictures have different meanings depending on the context in which they are embedded. Advertising is a symbolic artefact constructed from the conventions of a particular culture. The sender crafts the message in anticipation of the audience' probable response using shared knowledge of various conventions. Receivers of the same message use the same body of cultural knowledge to read the message, infer the sender's intention, evaluate the content and formulate a response. Cultural knowledge provides the basis for interaction. If advertising crosses the culture of interpersonal communication styles, it also reflects the different roles of advertising across cultures. Differences in perception and visual processing result in a range of differences in the use of pictures in advertising. Localization in the Indian advertisement industry shows tendencies to go beyond the language question to address issues of content and *look and feel*. Translation plays an important role in localization. The linguistic process as well as cultural and content issues is pivotal. In many cases, the information and functionality contained in products need to be adapted for local audiences. Cultural issues concerning the presentation of information (icons, graphics, colours, forms of address, and so on) also need to be considered. A movement towards creative audio-visual localization in adverts is an imminent notable trend. There arises the necessity to concentrate on the linguistic translation involved herein (which unless in the hands of linguistically well-equipped translators can give rise to unnecessary amusing moments for the viewer). The degree of localization required may vary. Successful globalization is a combination of internationalization and localization. *Thinking global* from the outset is a necessity in advertising. Advertising involves visual persuasion, which makes localization (also a creative process) essential in television advertising. Most companies need to adapt at least some aspects of a product or service to meet local market needs, but the degree of adaptation might depend on a range of internal and external factors and issues as well as the target audience. While it is not possible, or indeed logical, to adapt a product or service to meet every local market need, it is equally not always viable or sensible to sell a completely standardized product everywhere. Companies have to consider this issue in terms of their company objectives, the nature of the market(s) they wish to target and the value and power of their brand (there may be brands that are so dominant and powerful that they can be sold with less degree of adaptation). Companies need to think very carefully about the degree to which they plan to adapt or standardize their products or services in global markets. Speaking about the emergence of global consumer culture, Hannerz notes that *world culture* is emerging as a result of the 'increasing interconnectedness of varied local cultures as well as through the development of cultures without clear anchorage in any one territory' (1996:102–111)— indicated by Indian regional adverts like Seemati and Jayalakshmi presenting the South Indian sari along with a national/global setting. This makes necessary a Levittian style *global plan* and Kotlerian *variations* nationally or locally.

Cultural sensitivity (to be sensitive to the context) is essential in the case of advert translation. Localization involves a visual/linguistic adaptation to the local market. The product is conceived from a broader international perspective though complete localization does not involve making the foreign appear domestic and pushing cultures into passive consuming positions. Localization is an integral part of globalization (indicative of simultaneity), for *to go Global* the product has to be made available to *foreign* language markets. The advertising has to accommodate the consumer in the local market. Localization is the process of professional product translation and cultural adaptation, allowing a company to adjust to the differences within distinct markets (like McDonald's, Nike, Idea or Pepsi). Professional localization is not just straightforward translation as it involves a comprehensive analysis of the target culture in order to correctly adapt the company's product and marketing material. Localization is a vital way of recognizing local sensitivities, avoiding conflict with local culture and habits and addressing the needs and desires of local markets. In the Indian context, a localization specialist must take into account not only the linguistic/cultural differences, but also the physical layout of the text, any business and cultural implications and the technical variations between areas. It is important to research the cultures targeted so that the content is understood and does not cause offense (some images may be fine in Western cultures but could cause offence elsewhere in the world). Launching a brand in a market can cause a complex communication issue, beginning with something as simple as the brand name. To be effective, the advertising message must recognize the cultural differences. This makes necessary a good creative team (and a good translator) with sufficient knowledge of the source–target language culture as well as adept in translation. There arises the need to come up with a creative solution that meets the communication objectives on a case-by-case basis.

A creative idea can be appropriate and effective only when it is relevant to the target audience's needs, wants or aspirations. Localization on a regional basis when/if required should be seriously considered. It is made necessary when the target audience is not familiar with the language/visualization used in the advert. A well thought out advert idea tends to perform reasonably well in multiple markets without a great deal of adjustments. A geocentric campaign requires an advertisement to be designed for the worldwide audience from the outset in order to appeal to shared common denominators while allowing for some modification (even if linguistic, it is not to be a casual dubbed version, as mostly seen in Indian television advertisements) to suit each market. It combines the cost reduction advantage of standardization and the advantages of local relevance and effective appeal of individualization—simultaneously catering to the local and the global. In the context of countries like India, regio-centricity becomes crucial. While international advertising ventures tend to be polycentric (or geocentric), national/local ones move towards a region-centric approach.

In addition to his technical skills and semiotic training, the translator/localizer (in India as elsewhere) is a decoder and encoder of cultural signs within the advertising communication. His role has become all the more important since globalization has paradoxically exacerbated the feelings of local identity in a culturally globalized era. The translator has changed into an expert in intercultural communication because he/she masters the cultural codes that *sell*. Localization plays an important role in advertising and product marketing. All translations/localized adverts consequently become *new texts* fashioned after an original. Analysis indicates that in the process there is always the danger of its loosing the *spirit* of the original, thus pushing it to a peripheral position within the polysystem—a secondarization (especially when not properly localized/when has pitfalls of localization). Translated (in the Indian context) advertisements (with poor lip synching and literal translation) become instances of *failed translations* when there is no equivalent (and no creative) linguistic/visual translation. They come to constitute a *secondary system*. The advert is an offer of information from its producer to a recipient and the localized advertisement a *secondary* offer of information about information *originally* offered in another language within another culture. The possible existence of translated adverts as a particular visual/linguistic system also exists. More locally, sensitive global advertising or *glocal advertising* is the need of the hour. By involving creative staff from around the world in the development and modification of a global advertising concept or image, advertising can be more easily adapted to particular places. Many companies have adopted a global and unadapted strategic stance in the market place. Others have adopted a localized approach to the design and associated marketing of their products in the Indian markets. An approach to advertising globally that is inherently flexible, yet highly strategic, is essential. Advertising succeeds or fails depending on how well it communicates the desired information and attitudes to the right people at the right time and at the right cost. The goal of effectiveness remains paramount regardless of country.

Bibliography

Aaker, David A. *Managing Brand Equity*. New York: The Free Press, 1991.

Aaker, David A., and Alexander L. Bowl (eds). *Brand Equity and Advertising: Advertising's Role in Building Strong Brands*. Hillsdale: Lawrence Erlbaum Associates, 1993.

Aaker, David A., and John G. Myers. *Advertising Management*. New Jersey: Prentice Hall, 1975.

Abbott, W., and R. Monsen. 'On the measurement of corporate social responsibility: Self-reported disclosures as a method of measuring corporate social involvement'. *Academy of Management Journal*, 22(3):501–515, 1979.

Abercrombie, Nicholas. *Television and Society*. Cambridge: Polity Press, 1996.

Ackerman, R.W., and R.A. Bauer. *Corporate Social Responsiveness*. Reston, VA: Reston Publishing, 1976.

Adab, B. 'The translation of advertising: A set of guidelines'. *Investigating Translation*. A. Beeby (ed.). Amsterdam: Benjamins, 225–237, 2000.

Adorno, T. *The Culture Industry*. London: Routledge, 1991.

Advertising. Available at http://en.wikipedia.org/wiki/Advertising, accessed on 3 April 2013.

Agrawal, Madhu. 'Review of a 40 year debate in international advertising'. *International Marketing Review*, 12(1):26–48, 1995.

Aguilera, R., D. Rupp, C. Williams and J. Ganapathi. 'Putting the S back in corporate social responsibility: A *Productivity and Performance Management*, 59(3):229–254, 2004.

Ahuja, B.N., and S.S. Chhabra. *Advertising and Public Relations*. New Delhi: Surjeet Publications, 1989.

Albers-Miller, N. 'Appealing to values in advertising across cultures: Results from a distorted mirror'. Available online at www.sbaer.uca.edu/research/sma/1997/PDF/15.pdf, accessed on 3 March 2015.

Alexa, Bezjian-Avery, Bobby Calder and Dawn Iacobucci. 'New media interactive advertising vs. traditional advertising'. *Journal of Advertising Research*, 38(4):23–32, 1998.

Andreas M. 'If you love something, let it go mobile: Mobile marketing and mobile social media 4×4'. *Business Horizons*, 55(2):129–139, 2012.

Appadurai, Arjun. *Modernity at Large: Cultural Dimensions of Globalization*. Minneapolis: Univertsity of Minnesota Press, 1996.

Arun Lal, K., and Sunitha Srinivas C. 'Commodity fetiche: Adverts and the postcolonial consumer, *Diotemas*, 2:97–104, 2010.

Aunger, Robert. *Darwinizing Culture: The Status of Memetics as a Science*. Oxford: Oxford University Press, 2000.

———. *The Electric Meme: A New Theory of How We Think*. New York: Free Press, 2002.

Aupperle, K., A. Carroll and Hatfield J. 'An empirical examination of the relationship between corporate social responsibility and profitability'. *Academy of Management Journal*, 28(2):446–463, 1985.

Baalbaki, Imad B., and N.K. Malhotra. 'Marketing management bases for international marketing segmentation: An alternative look at the standardization/customization debate'. *International Marketing Review*, 10(1):19–44, 1993.

Baker, Mona (ed.). *Routledge Encyclopedia of Translation Studies*. London: Routledge, 1998.

Bandura, A. *Social Learning Theory*. Englewood Cliffs, NJ: Prentice Hall, 1977.

Banerjee, Sy., and R.R. Dholakia. 'Mobile advertising: Does location-based advertising work?' *International Journal of Mobile Marketing*, 3(2):68–75, 2008.

Bansal, P., and K. Roth. 'Why companies go green: A model of ecological responsiveness. *Academy of Management Journal*, 43(4):717–736, 2000.

Baran, Paul, and Sweezy Paul. 'Monopoly capital, the rise of professional journalism, and its subsequent decline'. In *The Political Economy of Media: Enduring Issues, Emerging Dilemmas*. Robert W. McChesney (ed.). New York: Monthly Review Press, 2008, pp. 25–66.

Barnes, S.J. 'The mobile commerce value chain: Analysis and future developments'. *International Journal of Information Management*, 22(2):91–108, 2002.

———. 'Wireless digital advertising: Nature and implications'. *International Journal of Advertising*, 21:399–419, 2002.

Barnes, S.J., and Scornavacca E. 'Mobile marketing: The role of permission and acceptance'. *International Journal of Mobile Communication*, 2(2):128–139, 2004.

Barnhurst, Kevin, and Ellen Wartella. 'Young citizens, American TV newscasts and the collective memory'. *Critical Studies in Mass Media*, 279–305, 1998.

Baron, D. 'Private politics, corporate social responsibility, and integrated strategy'. *Journal of Economics and Management Strategy*, 10(1):7–45, 2001.

Barry, Duncan. *Mass Media and Popular Culture*. Canada: HBJ, 1988.

Barry, Peter. 'Ecocriticism'. *Beginning Theory: An Introduction to Literary and Cultural Theory* (3rd edition). Manchester: Manchester UP, 2009.

Barthes, Roland. *Elements of Semiology*. Annette Lavers and Colin Smith (trans.). London: Jonathan Cape, 1967.

_____. *Image-Music-Text*. London: Fontana, 1977.

_____. *Mythologies*. New York: Hill and Wang, 1987.

_____. *S/Z: An Essay*. Richard Miller (trans.). New York: Hill and Wang, 1974.

Barton, Roger (ed.). *Handbook of Advertising Management*. New York: McGraw Hill, 1970.

Barwise, P., and J.U. Farley. 'The state of interactive marketing in seven countries: Interactive marketing comes of age'. *Journal of Interactive Marketing*, 19(3):67–80.

Barwise, P., and C. Strong. 'Permission-based mobile advertising'. *Journal of Interactive Marketing*, 16(1):14–24, 2002.

Bauer, H.H., S.J. Barnes, T. Reichardt and M.M. Neumann. 'Driving consumer acceptance of mobile marketing: A theoretical framework and empirical study'. *Journal of Electronic Commerce Research*, 6(3):181–192, 2002.

Bing, John. 'Hofstede's consequences: The impact of his work on consulting and business practices'. *Academy of Management Executive*, 18(1), 2004.

Briggs, Rex, and Nigel Hollis. 'Advertising on the web: Is there response before clickthrough?' *Journal of Advertising Research*, 33–45, 1997.

Basil, D., and D. Weber. 'Values motivation and concern for appearances: The effect of personality traits on responses to corporate social responsibility'. *International Journal of Nonprofit and Voluntary Sector Marketing*, 11(1):61–72, 2006.

Bassnett, Caroline, Paul Marris and Sue Thornham (eds). *Media Studies: A Reader*. New York: New York University Press, 2000.

Bassnett, Susan (ed.). *Translating Literature*. Cambridge: D.S. Brewer, 1997.

_____. *Translation Studies*. London: Routledge, 1991.

Bassnett, Susan, and Andre Lefevere (eds). *Translation, History, and Culture*. London: Pinter Publishers, 1990.

Baudrillard, Jean. *Selected Writings*. Mark Poster (ed.). Stanford: Stanford University Press, 1988.

Bellafante, G. 'Feminism: It's all about me'! *Time*, 54–60, 1998.

Benitez-Bribiesca, Luis. Memetics: A dangerous idea. *Interciecia*, 26:29–31, 2001.

Benjamin, W. *Illuminations*. London: Fontana, 1923.

Benkler, Yochai. *The Wealth of Networks*. New Haven: Yale University Press, 2006.

Berger, Arthur Asa. *Media and Communication Research Methods: An Introduction to Qualitative and Quantitative Approaches*. New Delhi: SAGE Publications, 2011.

Berman, Ronald. *Advertising and Social Change*. Beverly Hills: SAGE Publications, 1981.

Bernstein, David. *Creative Advertising*. London: Longman, 1974.

Berthon, Pierre, Leyland F. Pitt and Richard T. Watson. 'The world wide web as an advertising medium: Toward an understanding of conversion efficiency'. *Journal of Advertising Research*, 36(1):43–54, 1996.

Bhabha, Homi. *The Location of Culture*. London: Routledge, 1994.

Bielsa, Esperanca, and Susan Bassnett. *Translation in Global News*. New York: Routledge, 2009.

Blackmore, Susan. *The Meme Machine*. Oxford: Oxford University Press, 1999.

Blackwell, Roger, R. Ajami and K. Stephan. 'Winning the global advertising race: Planning globally, acting locally'. *Journal of International Consumer Marketing*, 3(2):97–120, 1991.

Boddewyn, J.J., Tobin Soehl and Jacques Picard. 'Standardization in international marketing: Is Ted Levitt in fact right?' *Business Horizons*, 69–75, 1986.

Boehmer, Elleke. *Empire, the National and the Postcolonial 1890–1920*. Oxford: Oxford University Press, 2002.

Booth, A. 'The mother of all cultures: Camille Paglia and feminist mythologies'. *The Kenyon Review*, 21(1):27–45, 1999.

Bootwala, Shaila, M.D. Lawrence and Sanjay R. Mali. *Advertising and Sales Promotion*. Pune: Nirali Prakashan, 2007.

Boyd, Robert, and Peter J. Richerson. *Culture and the Evolutionary Process*. Chicago: Chicago University Press, 1985.

_____. *Not by Genes Alone: How Culture Transformed Human Evolution*. Chicago: Chicago University Press, 2005

Boyer, R., and D. Drache. *States against Markets: The Limits of Globalization*. London: Routledge, 1996.

Brand, J.E., and B.S. Greenberg. 'Commercials in the classroom: The impact of channel-1 advertising'. *Journal of Advertising Research*, 34(1):18–27, 1994.

Brierley, Sean. *The Advertising Handbook*. London: Routledge, 1995.

Briggs, Rex, and Nigel Hollis. 'Advertising on the web: Is there response before click-through?' *Journal of Advertising Research*, 37(2):33–45, 1997.

Brodie, Richard. *Virus of the Mind: The New Science of the Meme*. England: Integral Press, 1996.

Buell, Lawrence. *The Environmental Imagination: Thoreau, Nature Writing, and the Formation of American Culture*. Cambridge, MA, and London, England: Harvard University Press, 1995.

———. 'Toxic discourse'. *Critical Inquiry*, 24(3):639–665, 1998.

———. *Writing for an Endangered World: Literature, Culture, and Environment in the U.S. and Beyond*. Cambridge, MA, and London, England: The Belknap Press of Harvard University Press, 2001.

———. *The Environmental Imagination: Thoreau, Nature Writing, and the Formation of American Culture*. Cambridge, MA, and London, England: Harvard University Press, 1995.

Bullis, Douglas. *Selling to India's Consumer Market*. Westport: Quorum Books, 1997.

Butch, Rice and Richard Bennett. 'The relationship between brand usage and advertising tracking measurements: International findings'. *Journal of Advertising Research*, 38(3):58–66, 1998.

Buzzell, Robert D. 'Can you standardize multinational marketing?' *Harvard Business Review*, 46(6):102–113, 1968.

Cambria, Erik, Marco Grassi, Amir Hussain and Catherine Havasi. 'Semantic computing for social media marketing'. *Multimedia Tools and Applications*, 59(2):557, 2011.

Capra, Fritjof. *The Web of life: A New Synthesis of Mind and Matter*. London: Flamingo, 1997.

Carroll, A. 'A three-dimensional conceptual model of corporate performance'. *Academy of Management Review*, 497–505, 1979.

———. 'Corporate social responsibility'. *Business and Society*, 38(3):268, 1999.

Carson, Rachel. *Silent Spring*. London: Penguin, 1999.

Castells, Manuel. *The Rise of the Network Society, the Information Age: Economy, Society and Culture*, vol. 1. Massachusetts: Blackwell Publishing, 1996.

Catford, J.C. *A Linguistic Theory of Translation: An Essay in Applied Linguistics*. London: Oxford University Press, 1965.

Chandler, D. *Semiotics: The Basics*. London: Routledge, 2002.

Chen, K., and R. Metcalf. 'The relationship between pollution control record and financial indicators revisited'. *Accounting Review*, 55(1):168–177, 1980.

Choi, S.M., W. Lee and H.J. Kim. 'Lessons from the rich and famous: A cross-cultural comparison of celebrity endorsement in advertising'. *Journal of Advertising*, 34:85–98, 2005.

Chunawalla, S.A., and K.C. Sethia. *Foundations of Advertising Theory and Practice*. Bombay: Himalaya Publishing House, 1985.

Clark, Terry. 'International marketing and national character: A review and proposal for an integrative theory'. *Journal of Marketing*, 54:66–79, 1990.

Cleveland, Charles E. 'Semiotics: Determining what the advertising message means to the audience'. In *Advertising and Consumer Psychology*, vol. 3. Jerry Olson and Keith Sentis (eds). New York: Praeger Publishers, 1986.

Cloak, F.T. Jr. 'Is a cultural ethology possible?' *Human Ecology*, 3:161–182, 1975.

Cobley, P., and L. Jansz. *Introducing Semiotics*. Royston: Icon Books, 2004.

Cochran, P., and R. Wood. 'Corporate social responsibility and financial performance'. *Academy of Management Journal*, 27(1):42–56, 1984.

Colvin, Michael, R. Heeler and J. Thorpe. 'Developing international advertising strategy'. *Journal of Marketing*, 44(4):73–79, 1980.

Cook, G. *The Discourse of Advertising*. London: Routledge, 1992.

Cosmetics Advertising. Avaialbe online at http://en.wikipedia.org/wiki/Cosmetics_advertising., accessed on 23 August 2014.

Coupe, Lawrence (ed.). *The Green Studies Reader: From Romanticism to Ecocriticism*. London: Routledge, 2000.

Cox, K.R. (ed.). *Spaces of Globalization: Reasserting the Power of the Local*. London: Guilford Press, 1997.

Croteau, David, and William Hoynes. *Media Society: Industries, Images and Audiences*. Thousand Oaks, CA: Pine Forge Press, 2003, p. 303.

Culture Jamming. Available at http://en.wikipedia.org/wiki/Culture_jamming., accessed on 28 July 2014.

Curran, J., and M. Gurevitch (eds). *Mass Media and Society*. London: Edward Arnold, 1991.

Davis, Keith. 'Can business afford to ignore corporate social responsibility?' *California Management Review*, 2:70–76, 1960.

Dawkins, Richard. *The Selfish Gene*. New York: Oxford University Press, 1976.

———. 'Replicators and Vehicles'. *Current Problems in Sociobiology*. King's College Sociobiology Group (ed.). Cambridge: Cambridge University Press, 1982, pp. 45–64.

De Mooij, Marieke K. *Advertising Worldwide: Concepts, Theories and Practices of International, Multinational and Global Advertising*. New York: Prentice Hall, 1994.

De Mooij, Marieke K. *Consumer Behavior and Culture: Consequences for Global Marketing and Advertising.* Thousand Oaks, CA: SAGE Publications, 2004.

―――. *Global Marketing and Advertising: Understanding Cultural Paradoxes.* London: SAGE Publications, 2010.

De Mooij, Marieke K., and Geert Hofstede. 'The Hofsted model applications to global branding and advertising strategy and research'. *International Journal of Advertising,* 29(1):85–110, 2010.

Denk, M., and M. Hackl. 'Where does mobile business go?' *International Journal of Electronic Business,* 2(5):460–470, 2004.

Dennett, Daniel C. *Darwin's Dangerous Idea: Evolution and the Meanings of Life.* New York: Simon and Schuster, 1995.

Dennis E.E., and M.L. DeFleur. *Understanding Media in the Digital Age: Connections for Communication, Society, and Culture.* New York: Allyn & Bacon, 2010.

Dentchev, N. 'Corporate social performance as a business strategy'. *Journal of Business Ethics,* 55(4):395–410, 2004.

Derrida, Jacques. *Positions.* Alan Bass (trans.). London: Athlone Press, 1981.

Detomasi, D.A. 'The political roots of corporate social responsibility'. *Journal of Business Ethics,* 82:807–819, 2008.

Distin, Kate. *The Selfish Meme: A Critical Reassessment,* Cambridge: Cambridge University Press, 2005, p. 238.

Domzal, Teresa J., and Jerome B. Kernan. 'Mirror, mirror: Some postmodern reflections on global advertising'. *Journal of Advertising,* 22(4):1–20, 1993.

Douglas, Mary. 'Deciphering a meal'. In *Myths, Symbol and Culture.* Clifford Geertz (ed.). New York: Norton, 1971.

Drumwright, M.E., and P.E. Murphy. 'The current state of advertising ethics: Industry and academic perpectives'. *Journal of Advertising,* 38(1):49–61, 2009.

Duncan, Tom, and Jyotika Ramaprasad. 'Standardized multinational advertising: The influencing factors'. *Journal of Advertising* 24(3):55–68, 1995.

Dunn, S. Watson, and Arnold M. Barban. *Advertising: Its Role in Modern Marketing* (5th edition). New York: CBS College Publishing, 1982.

Durham, M., and Douglas Kellner. *Media and Cultural Studies.* UK: Blackwell Publishing, 2001.

Dyer, G. *Advertising as Communication.* London: Routledge, 1982.

Eagle, L. 'Commercial media literacy: What does it do, to whom-and does it matter?' *Journal of Advertising,* 22 June, 2007. Available from accessmylibrary.com

Eco, Umberto. *A Theory of Semiotics.* London: Macmillan, 1976.

Eells, R., and C. Walton. *Conceptual Foundations of Business.* Homewood: Illinois, 1961.

Elinder, Erik. 'How international can European advertising be?' *Journal of Marketing* 29(2):7–11, 1965.

Elliott, R. 'Symbolic meaning and postmodern consumer culture'. In *Rethinking Marketing: Toward Critical Marketing Accountings.* D. Brownlie, M. Saren, R. Wensley and R. Whittington (eds). London: SAGE Publications, 1999, pp. 112–125.

Elliott, R., and Ritson M. 'Post structuralism and the dialectics of advertising: Discourse, ideology, resistance'. *Consumer Research: Postcards from the Edge.* S. Brown and D. Turley (eds). New York: Routledge, 1997, pp. 190–219.

Engles, Jack. *Advertising: The Process and Practice.* New York: McGraw Hill, 1980.

Englis, Basil D. (ed.). *Global and Multinational Advertising.* Hillsdale: Lawrence Erlbaum Associates, 1994.

English, B. 'A long way from spin the bottle'. *Boston Globe,* 26 January 2003.

Enzensberger, Hans Magnus. *Consciousness Industry: On Literature, Politics and the Media.* New York: Continuum Books, 1974.

Esselink, Bert. *A Practical Guide to Localization.* Philadelphia: John Benjamins, 2000.

Estok, Simon C. 'Shakespeare and Ecocriticism: An Analysis of "Home" and "Power" in King Lear'. *AUMLA,* 103:15–41, 2005.

Evan, W.A., and George Allen. *Advertising Today and Tomorrow.* London: Uncoses, 1974.

Evans, J., and David Hesmondhalgh (eds). *Understanding Media: Inside Celebrity.* UK: Open University Press, 2005.

Even-Zohar, Itamar. *Papers in Historical Poetics.* Tel Aviv: Porter Institute, 1978. Available online at http://www.tau.ac.il/~itamarez/, accessed on November 2008.

———. *Polysystem Studies.* Durham: Duke University Press, 1990.

———. 'Translation Theory Today: A Call for Transfer Theory'. *Poetics Today,* 2(4):1–7, 1991.

Even-Zohar, Itamar and Gideon Toury (eds). *Translation Theory and Intercultural Relations.* Cambridge: Schenkman, 1981.

Ewert, James H. 'Adbusters' Ads Busted'. *In These Times.* Available online at http://inthesetimes.com/article/3581/adbusters_ads_busted, accessed on 3 March 2015.

Facchetti, A., A. Rangone, F.A. Renga and A. Savoldelli. 'Mobile marketing: An analysis of keysuccess factors and the European value chain'. *International Journal of Management and Decision Making,* 6(1):65–80, 2005.

Fast Food Advertising. Availabe online at http://en.wikipedia.org/wiki/Fast_food_advertising., accessed on 17 August 2013.

Fanon, Frantz. *The Wretched of the Earth.* Constance Farrington (trans.). New York: Grove Press, 1968.

Farbay, A.D. *Successful Advertising.* New Delhi: Crest Publishing, 2004.

Fatt, Arthur C. 'The danger of "local" international advertising'. *Journal of Marketing,* 31(1):60–62, 1967.

Featherstone, Mike (ed.). *Global Culture: Nationalism, Globalization and Modernity.* London: SAGE Publications, 1990.

Featherstone, Mike, Scott Lash and Roland Robertson (eds). *Global Modernities.* London: SAGE Publications, 1995.

Feldman, Tony. *An Introduction to Digital Media.* Routledege: London, 1997.

Ferguson, J.H., P.J. Kreshel and S.F. Tinkham. 'In the pages of Ms.: Sex Role Portrayals of Women in Advertising'. *Journal of Advertising,* 191:40–51, 1990.

Fern L. Johnson. *Imaging in Advertising: Verbal and Visual Codes of Commerce.* London: Routledge, 2007.

Fiske, John. *Television Culture.* London: Routledge, 1989.

Fiske, John, and John Hartley. *Reading Television.* London: Methuen, 1978.

Fitch, H. 'Achieving corporate social responsibility. *Academy of Management Review,* 1(1):38–46, 1976.

Flew, Terry. *New Media: An Introduction.* UK: Oxford University Press, 2002, p. 13.

Forceville, C. *Pictorial Metaphor in Advertising.* London: Routledge, 1996.

Ford, J.B., M.S. Latour and W.J. Lundstrom. 'Contemporary women's evaluation of female role portrayals in advertising'. *Journal of Consumer Marketing,* 8(1):15–27, 1991.

Foster, Hal (ed.). *Postmodern Culture.* London: Pluto Press, 1985.

Foucault, Michel. *Foucault Live.* New York: Semiotext(e), 1996.

Friedman, M. 'The social responsibility of business is to increase its profits'. *New York Times Magazines,* 13 September, 32–33, 1970.

Friedman, T. *The Lexus and the Olive Tree: Understanding Globalization.* USA: Farrar, Straus and Giroux, 1999.

Friedmann, R. 'Psychological meaning of products: A simplification of the standardization vs. adaptation debate'. *Columbia Journal of World Business,* 21:97–104, 1986.

Fry, Deborah. *The Localization Primer* (Revised 2nd edition). Arle Lommel. Available online at http://www.lisa.org/interact/LISAprimer.pdf.2003/

Galbreath, J. 'Corporate social responsibility strategy: Strategic options, global considerations'. *Corporate Governance,* 6(2):175–187, 2006.

Garrard, Greg. *Ecocriticism.* New York: Routledge, 2004.

Garrett, William R. 'Thinking religion in the global circumstance: A critique of Roland Robertson's globalization theory'. *Journal for the Scientific Study of Religion,* 31(3):297–303, 1992.

Garriga, E., and D. Mele. 'Corporate social responsibility theories: Mapping and territory'. *Journal of Business Ethics,* 53:51–74, 2004.

Gentle, Anne. *Conversation and Community: The Social Web for Documentation* (2nd edition). Laguna Hills, CA: XML Press, 2012.

Gerbner, G., L. Gross, M. Morgan and N. Signorelli. 'Living with television: The dynamics of the cultivation process'. In *Perspectives on Media Effects.* J. Bryant and D. Zillman (eds). Hillsdale, NJ: Lawrence Erlbaum, 1986.

Gleason, Philip. 'Identifying identity: A semantic history'. *The Journal of American History,* 69(4):910–931, 1983.

Glotfelty, Cheryll, and Harold Fromm (eds). *The Ecocriticism Reader: Landmarks in Literary Ecology.* Athens and London: University of Georgia, 1996.

Godin, Seth. *Permission Marketing: Turning Strangers into Friends, and Friends into Customers.* New York: Simon & Schuster, 1999.

Goffman, Erving. *Gender Advertisements.* Harvard: Harvard University Press, 1979.

Goldfarb, Avi Tucker, and E. Catherine. 'Privacy regulation and online advertising'. *Management Science,* 57(1):57–71, 2011.

Grafen, Alan, and Mark Ridley (eds). *Richard Dawkins: How a Scientist Changed the Way We Think.* New York: Oxford University Press, 2006.

Graham, Gordon. *Genes: A philosophical Inquiry.* New York: Routledge, 2002, p. 196.

Green, Robert T., W.H. Cunningham and I. Cunningham. 'The effectiveness of standardized global advertising'. *Journal of Advertising,* 4(3):25–30.

Gruber, E., and J.W. Grube. 'Adolescent sexuality and the media: A review of current knowledge and implications'. *Western Journal of Medicine,* 172(3):210–214, 2000.

Grunert, Klaus G. 'Automatic and strategic processes in advertising effects'. *Journal of Marketing,* 60(4):88–101, 1996.

Hall, Stuart. *Culture, Media, Language.* London: Hutchinson, 1980.

———. (ed.). *Representation: Cultural Representation and Signifying Practices.* London: SAGE Publications, 1997.

Hannerz, Ulf. 'Cosmopolitans and Locals in World Culture'. *Global Culture: Nationalism, Globalization and Modernity.* Mike Featherstone (ed.). Thousand Oaks, CA: SAGE Publications, 1990, pp. 295–310.

———. *Transnational Connections: Cultures, Peoples, Places.* London: Routledge, 1996.

Harris, G. 'The globalization of advertising'. *International Journal of Advertising*, 3(3):223–234, 1984.

Harvey, Michael G. 'Point of view: A model to determine standardization of the advertising process in international markets'. *Journal of Advertising Research*, 33(4):57–64, 1993.

Haug, W.F. *Critique of Commodity Aesthetics: Appearance, Sexuality, and Advertising in Capitalist Society*. Minneapolis: University of Minnesota Press, 1986.

―――. *Commodity Aesthetics, Ideology & Culture*. New York, Bagnolet: International General, 1987.

Heikki, Karjaluoto, and Leppäniemi Matti. 'Factors influencing consumers' willingness to accept mobile advertising: A conceptual model'. *International Journal of Mobile Communications*, 3(3):198, 2005.

Henthorne, T.L., and M.S. Latour. 'A model to explore the ethics of erotic stimuli in print advertising'. *Journal of Business Ethics*, 14(7):561–69, 1995.

Heylighen, Francis. 'Selfish memes and the evolution of cooperation', *Journal of Ideas*, 2(4):77–84, 1992.

Heylighen, Francis, and K. Chielens. 'Evolution of culture, memetics'. In *Encyclopedia of Complexity and Systems Science*. Robert A. Meyers (ed.). New York: Springer, 2009.

Hill, S. 'To choose or not to choose: A politics of choice'. *The Humanist*, 53(3):3–6, 1993.

Hill, Ronald P., and Michael B. Mazis. 'Measuring emotional response to advertising'. In *Advances in Consumer Research*, vol. 13. Richard J. Lutz (ed.). Provo, UT: Association for Consumer Research, 1986, 164–169.

Hite, Robert E., and C. Fraser. 'International advertising strategies of multinational corporations'. *Journal of Advertising Research*, 28:9–17, 1988.

Holmes. *'Telecommunity' in Communication Theory: Media, Technology and Society*. Cambridge: Polity, 2005.

Hussain B., and M. Hussain. 'Corporate social responsibility: Do customers get what they expect?' *Journal of Business Studies, Southeast University*, 1(1):133–139, 2005.

IAB Mobile Advertising Guidelines. Available online at http://www.iab.net/iab_products_and_industry_services/508676/mobile_guidance., accessed on 7 March 2015.

Jain, Subhash C. 'Standardization of international marketing strategy: Some research hypotheses'. *Journal of Marketing*, 53:70–79, 1989.

Jameson, Fredric. *The Geopolitical Aesthetic: Cinema and Space in the World System*. Bloomington: Indiana University Press, 1992.

Jameson, Fredric. *Postmodernism, or the Cultural Logic of Late Capitalism.* London: Verso, 1991.

James, William L., and John S. Hill. 'International advertising messages: To adapt or not to adapt (that is the question)'. *Journal of Advertising Research,* 31:65–71, 1991.

Jansen, B.J., and T. Mullen. 'Sponsored search: An overview of the concept, history, and technology'. *International Journal of Electronic Business,* 6(2):114–131, 2008.

Jeannet, Jean-Pierre, and H. David Hennessey. *Global Marketing Strategies* (3rd edition). Boston: Houghton Mifflin, 1995.

Jefkins, Frank. *Introduction to Marketing, Advertising and Public Relations.* London: Macmillan, 1982.

Jethwaney, Jaishri N. *Advertising.* New Delhi: Phoenix, 1999.

Jhully, Sut. *The Codes of Advertising Fetishism and the Political Economy of Meaning in the Consumer Society.* London: Routledge. 1990.

———. *The Spectacle of Accumulation: Essays in Culture, Media, & Politics.* Available online at http://www.sutjhally.com/books, accessed March 2015.

Johansson, Johny K. *Global Marketing: Foreign Entry, Local Marketing, and Global Management.* Chicago: Richard D. Irwin, 1997.

Johnson, Steven Berlin. *Everything Bad is Good for You.* New York: Riverhead Books, 2005.

Jones, John Philip (ed.). *International Advertising: Realities and Myths.* California: SAGE Publications, 2000.

Jue, Arthur L., Jackie Alcalde Marr and Mary Ellen Kassotakis. *Social Media at Work: How Networking Tools Propel Organizational Performance.* San Francisco, CA: Jossey-Bass, 2010.

Kalevi Kull, 'Copy versus translate, meme versus sign: Development of biological textuality'. *European Journal for Semiotic Studies,* 12(1):101–120, 2000.

Kapferer, Jean-Noel. *Strategic Brand Management.* New York: The Free Press, 1992.

Kapferer, Jean-Noel and Laurent. 'Consumer involvement profiles: A new practical approach to consumer involvement'. *Journal of Advertising Research,* 25(6):48–56, 1985.

Kaplan, Andreas. *Rocking Around the Clock: Music, Television, Postmodernism and Consumer Culture.* London: Methuen, 1987.

Kaplan, Andreas, and Haenlein Michael. 'Users of the world, unite! The challenges and opportunities of social media'. *Business Horizons,* 53(1):61, 2010.

Kaptan, Sanjay, and V.P. Subramanian. *Women in Advertising.* Jaipur: Book Enclave, 2001.

Kennedy, Randy. 'Giving new life to protests of yore'. *The New York Times*, 28 July 2007.

Kernan, Jerome B., and T.J. Damzel. 'International advertising: To globalize, visualize'. *Journal of International Consumer Marketing*, 5(4):51–71, 1993.

Kerr, Gayle, Kathleen Mortimer, Sonia Dickinson and David S. Waller. 'Buy, boycott or blog: Exploring online consumer power to share, discuss and distribute controversial advertising messages'. *European Journal of Marketing*, 46(3/4):387–405, 2012.

Keveney, B. 'There's more sex on TV, but little about risks'. *USA Today*, 7 February 2001.

Khondker, H.H. 'Glocalization as globalization: Evolution of a sociological concept'. *Bangladesh e-Journal of Sociology*, 1(2):12–20, 2004.

Kietzmann, Jan H., and Kristopher Hermkens. 'Social media? Get serious! Understanding the functional building blocks of social media'. *Business Horizons*, 54:241–251, 2011.

Kim, Ellen, A. Mattila and S. Baloglu. 'Effects of gender and expertise on consumers' motivation to read online hotel reviews'. *Cornell Hospitality Quarterly*, 52(4):399–406, 2011.

Kincy, Jason. 'Advertising and social media'. *ABA Bank Marketing*, 43(7):40, 2011.

Klein, Benjamin. 'Brand names'. In *Concise Encyclopedia of Economics* (2nd edition). David R. Henderson (ed.). Indianapolis: Library of Economics and Liberty, 2008.

Korhonen, J. 'Should we measure corporate social responsibility?' *Corporate Social Responsibility and Environmental Management*, 10:25–39, 2003.

Korten, David. *When Corporations Rule the World* (2nd edition). San Francisco, CA: Berrett-Koehler, 2001.

Kotler, Philip. 'Behavioral models for analyzing buyers'. *The Journal of Marketing*, 29(4):37–45, 1965.

———. 'Global standardization-courting danger'. *Journal of Consumer Marketing*, 3(2):13–15, 1986.

———. 'Marketing mix decisions for new products'. *Journal of Marketing Research*, 1(1):43–49, 1964.

Kotler, Philip, and Gerald Zaltman. 'Social marketing: An approach to planned social change'. *The Journal of Marketing*, 35(3):3–12, 1971.

Kotler, Philip, and Sidney J. Levy. 'Broadening the concept of marketing'. *The Journal of Marketing*, 33(1):10–15, 1969.

Kroker, Arthur, and David Cook. *The Postmodern Scene: Excremental Culture and Hyper-aesthetics*. Basingstoke: Macmillan, 1988.

Kuczynski, A. 'She's got to be a macho girl'. *New York Times*, 3 November 2002.

Labi, N. 'Girl power'. *Time*, 29 June 1998.

Lane, Richard J. *Jean Baudrillard*. New York: Routledge, 2003.

Lechner, Frank J., and John Boli (eds). *The Globalization Reader* (2nd edition). London: Blackwell, 2004.

Leiss, William, Stephen Kline and Sut Jhally. *Social Communication in Advertising: Persons, Products, and Images of Well-being*. Toronto: Methuen Publications, 1986.

Leppäniemi M., and Karjaluoto H. 'Factors influencing consumers' willingness to accept mobile advertising: A conceptual model'. *International Journal of Mobile Communications*, 3(3):197–213, 2005.

Levitt, Theodore. 'Communications and industrial selling'. *The Journal of Marketing*, 31(2):15–21, 1967.

———. 'The globalization of markets'. *The Marketing Imagination*. New York: Free

Press, 1983.

———. Levitt, Theodore. 'The morality(?) of advertising'. *Harvard Business Review*, 89, 1970.

Levy, Sidney J. 'Meanings in advertising stimuli'. In *Advertising and Consumer Psychology*, vol. 3. Jerry Olson and Keith Sentis (eds). New York: Praeger Publishers, 1986.

Li, Charlene, and Josh Bernoff. *Groundswell: Winning in a World Transformed by Social Technologies*. Boston: Harvard Business Press, 2008.

Lievrouw, Leah A., and Sonia Livingstone (eds). *The Handbook of New Media*. New Delhi: SAGE Publications, 2002.

Lim, Gerrie. *Idol to Icon: The Creation of Celebrity Brands*. London: Cyan Books, 2005.

LISA. *The Localization Industry Primer*. Fechy: Localization Industry Standards Assocation (LISA), 2000.

Lister, Martin, Jon Dovey, Seth Giddings, Iain Grant and Kieran Kelly. *New Media: A Critical Introduction*. London, Routledge, 2003.

Logan, Robert K. *Understanding New Media: Extending Marshall McLuhan*. New York: Peter Lang Publishing, 2010.

Lull, James. *Media, Communication, Culture: A Global Approach* (2nd edition). New York: Columbia University Press, 2000.

Lundstrom, W.J., and D. Sciglimpaclia. 'Sex role portrayals in advertising'. *Journal of Marketing*, 41(3):72–79, 1977.

Luo, X., and C. Bhattacharya. 'Corporate social responsibility, customer satisfaction, and market value'. *Journal of Marketing*, 70(4):1–18, 2006.

Lysonski, S. 'Female and male portrayals in magazine advertisements: A re-examination'. *Akron Business and Economic Review*, 14(2):45–50, 1983.

MacArthur, Kate. 'Pop Star Leads McDonald's Global Ad Campaign Launch', 2 September 2003. Available online at http://adage.com/article/news/justin-timberlake-leads-mcdonald-s-advertising-campaign/38262/, accessed March 2015.

Mahapatra, Arun. *Art of Advertising*. New Delhi: Lotus Press, 2009.

Maignan, I., and D. Ralston. 'Corporate social responsibility in Europe and the US: Insights from businesses self-presentations'. *Journal of International Business Studies*, 33(3):497–514, 2002.

Malmkjaer, Kirsten. *Linguistics and the Language of Translation*. Edinburgh: Edinburgh University Press, 2005.

Manovich, Lev. *The Language of New Media*. Cambridge, MA: The MIT Press, 2001.

———. 'New media from borges to HTML'. *The New Media Reader*. Noah Wardrip-Fruin and Nick Montfort (eds). Cambridge, MA: The MIT Press, 2003, pp. 13–25.

Margolis, J., and J. Walsh. 'Misery loves companies: Rethinking social initiatives by business'. *Administrative Science Quarterly*, 48(2):268–305, 2003.

Márquez, A., and C. Fombrun. 'Measuring corporate social responsibility'. *Corporate Reputation Review*, 7(4):304–308, 2005.

Marris, Paul, and Sue Thornham. *Media Studies: A Reader*. Edinburgh: Edinburgh University Press, 1996.

Marx, K. 'The fetishism of commodities'. *The Portable Karl Marx*. Eugene Kamenka (ed.). London: Penguin, 1983.

Mathur, Navin. *Advertising Consumer Reaction in India*. Jaipur: Printwell, 1986.

Mattelart, A. *Advertising International: The Privatization of Public Space*. London: Routledge, 1991.

Mayne, I. 'The inescapable images: Gender and advertising'. *Equal Opportunities International*, 19(2–4):56–62, 2000.

McAllister, M.P., and S.R. Mazzarella (eds). *Advertising and Consumer Culture*. London: Routledge, 2000.

McChesney, Robert W. 'The political economy of media: Enduring issues, emerging dilemmas'. New York: Monthly Review Press, 2008, pp. 43–281.

McClintock, Anne. 'Soft-soaping empire: Commodity racism and imperial advertising'. In *The Visual Culture Reader*. Nicholas Mirzoeff (ed.). London: Routledge, 1998.

McCracken, G. 'Who is the celebrity endorser? Cultural foundations of the celebrity endorsement process'. *Journal of Consumer Research*, 16:10–12, 1989.

McDonald's Sick of It. Available online at http://www.billboardliberation.com/SickOfIt.html., accessed on 8 March 2015.

McDonald, Loren. 'Transactional emails: Make your first impression count', 23 April 2009. Available online at http://www.mediapost.com/publications/article/104687/transactional-emails-make-your-first-impression-c.html, accessed March 2015.

McGuire, J.B., A. Sundgren and T. Schneeweis. 'Corporate social responsibility and firm financial performance'. *Academy of Management Journal*, 31(4):854–872, 1988.

McLuhan, Marshall. 'McLuhan's Laws of the Media'. *Technology and Culture*, 16(1):74–78, 1975.

———. *The Medium is the Message: An Inventory of Effect*. London: Random House, 1967.

———. *Understanding Media: The Extensions of Man*. New York: McGraw Hill, 1964.

McNamara, Adam. 'Can we measure memes?' *Frontiers in Evolutionary Neuroscience*, 3:1, 2011.

McWilliams, A., and D. Siegel. 'Corporate social responsibility and financial performance: Correlation or misspecification?' *Strategic Management Journal*, 21(5):603–609, 2000.

McWilliams, A., D. Siegel and P.M. Wright. 'Corporate social responsibility: Strategic implications'. *Journal of Management Studies*, 43(1):1–18, 2006.

Meehan, J., K. Meehan and A. Richards. 'Corporate social responsibility: The 3C–SR model'. *International Journal of Social Economics*, 33(5/6):386–398, 2006.

Mehta, Abhilasha. 'Advertising attitudes and advertising effectiveness'. *Journal of Advertising Research*, 40(3):67–71, 2000.

Messaris, Paul. *Visual Persuasion*. Thousand Oaks, CA: SAGE Publications, 1997.

Mittal, B., and W.M. Lassar. 'Sexual liberalism as a determinant of consumer response to sex in advertising'. *Journal of Business and Psychology*, 15(1):111–126, 2000.

MMA Global Code of Conduct. Available online at http://www.mmaglobal.com/files/codeofconduct.pdf, accessed March 2015.

MMA U.S. Consumer Best Practices Guidelines for Cross-Carrier Mobile Content Programs. Available online at http://www.mmaglobal.com/bestpractices.pdf, accessed March 2015.

Mobile Advertising. Availabe at http://en.wikipedia.org/wiki/Mobile_advertising., accessed on 16 July 2014.

Mobile Advertising Guidelines. Available at www.mmaglobal.com/mobileadvertising.pdf., accessed on 5 March 2015.

Mohr, L.A., D.J. Webb and K.E. Harris. 'Do consumers expect companies to be socially responsible? The impact of corporate social responsibility on buying behavior'. *Journal of Consumers Affairs*, 35:45–72, 2001.

Montabon, F., R. Sroufe and Narasimhan R. 'An examination of corporate reporting, environmental management practices and firm performance'. *Journal of Operations Management*, 25(5):998–1014, 2007.

Moriarty, S., and T. Duncan. 'Global advertising: Issues and practices'. *Current Issues and Research in Advertising*, 13(2):313–330, 1990.

Motti Neiger, Oren Meyers and Eyal Zandberg. *On Media Memory: Collective Memory in a New Media Age*. New York: Palgrave MacMillan, 2011.

Mueller, Barbara. 'Degrees of globalization: Analysis of the standardization message elements in multinational advertising'. *Current Issues and Research in Advertising*, 12(1–2):119–134, 1990.

———. *Dynamics of International Advertising*. New York: Peter Lang Publishing, 2004.

———. *International Advertising: Communicating Across Cultures*. Belmont: Wadsworth Publishing, 1996.

———. 'Multinational advertising: Factors influencing the standardized vs specialised approaches'. *International Marketing Review*, 8(1):7–8, 1991.

Muntinga, Daniel, M. Moorman and E. Smit. 'Introducing COBRAs exploring motivations for brand-related social media use'. *International Journal of Advertising*, 30(1):13–46, 2011.

Musto, Ken, and Van Nostrand. *Breaking into Advertising: Making Your Portfolio Work for you*. New York: Reinholt, 1988.

Nelson Michelle. 'The hidden persuaders: Then and now'. *Journal of Advertising*, 37(1):113–126, 2008.

Nida, E., and C. Taber. *The Theory and Practice of Translation*. Leiden: Brill, 1982.

Nigel Morgan, Graham Jones and Ant Hodges. 'Social Media'. *The Complete Guide to Social Media from the Social Media Guys*. Available online at https://rucreativebloggingfa13.files.wordpress.com/2013/09/completeguidetosocialmedia.pdf, accessed on 12 December 2012.

Nord, Christiane. *Translating as a Purposeful Activity: Functionalist Approaches Explained*. Manchester: St.Jerome Publishing, 1997.

Nyilasy G., and L.N. Reid. 'Agency practitioner theories of how advertising works'. *Journal of Advertising*, 38(3):81–96, 2009.

Nylen, David W. *Advertising: Planning, Implementation and Control*. Ohio: South-Western Publishing, 1993.

O'Connor, James. 'International Advertising'. *Journal of Advertising*, 3(2):9–14, 1974.

Ogilvy, David. *Ogilvy on Advertising*. New York: Vintage, 1983.

Okazaki, S. 'Mobile advertising adoption by multinationals: Senior executives' initial responses'. *Internet Research*, 15(2):160–180, 2005.

Oksman, V., and J. Turtiainen. 'Mobile communication as a social stage'. *New Media and Society*, 6(3):319–339, 2004.

Olson, Jerry. 'Meaning analysis in advertising research'. In *Advertising and Consumer Psychology*, vol. 3. Jerry Olson and Keith Sentis (eds). New York: Praeger Publishers, 1986.

O'Mahony, S., and Meenaghan, T. 'The impact of celebrity endorsements on consumers'. *Irish Marketing Review*, 10(2):15–24, 1998.

Onkvisit, Sak, and John J. Shaw. 'Global advertising: Revolution or myopia'. *Journal of International Consumer Marketing*. 2(1):97–112, 1990.

———. 'Standardized international advertising: Some research issues and implications'. *Journal of Advertising Research*, 39(6):19–24, 1999.

Online Advertising. Available at http://en.wikipedia.org/wiki/Online_advertising., accessed on 23 August 2014.

Orr, L.M., and W.J. Hauser. 'A re-inquiry of Hofstede's cultural dimensions: A call for 21st century cross-cultural research'. *The Marketing Management Journal*, 18(2):1–19, 2008.

Ottesen, O. *Marketing Communication Management: A Holistic Approach for Increased Profitablity*. Copenhagen: Copenhagen Business School Press, 2001.

Paglia, C. *Sex, Art, and American Culture*. New York: Vintage Books, 1992.

Patti, Charles H., and John H. Murphy. *Advertising Management, Cases and Concepts*. Ohio: Grid, 1978.

Peebles, Dean, J.K. Ryans and I.R. Vernon. 'A new perspective on advertising standardization'. *European Journal of Advertising*, 2:567–576, 1977.

Phillips, Barbara J., and Edward F. McQuarrie. 'Impact of advertising metaphor on consumer beliefs: Delineating the contribution of comparison versus deviation factors'. *Journal of Advertising*, 38(1):49–61, 2009.

Pollay, Richard W. 'Measuring the cultural values manifest in advertising'. *Current Issues and Research in Advertising*, 6(1):71–92, 1983. Available online at http://works.bepress.com/richard_pollay/25, accessed March 2015.

———. 'The distorted mirror: Reflections on the unintended consequences of advertising'. *Journal of Marketing*, 50:18–36, 1986.

———. 'On the value of reflections on the values in the distorted mirror'. *Journal of Marketing*, 51:104–110, 1987.

Pollay, Richard W., and Katherine Gallagher. 'Advertising and cultural values: Reflections in the distorted mirror'. *International Journal of Advertising*, 9(4):359–372, 1990.

Porter, Michael E. 'The strategic role of international marketing'. *Journal of Consumer Marketing*, 3:17–21, 1986.

Poster, Mark (ed.). *Jean Baudrillard: Selected Writings*. Cambridge: Polity Press, 1985.

Powell, Guy R., Steven W. Groves and Jerry Dimos. *ROI of Social Media: How to Improve the Return on Your Social Marketing Investment*. New York: John Wiley & Sons, 2011.

Powell, Helen, Jonathan Hardy and Sarah Hawkin (eds). *Advertising Handbook*. London: Routledge, 2009.

Presbrey, Frank. *The History and Development of Advertising*. New York: Doubleday, 1929.

Preston, Paschal. *Reshaping Communications: Technology, Information and Social Change*. London: SAGE Publications, 2001.

Pringle, Hamishl. *Celebrity Sells*. New York: John Wiley & Sons, 2004.

Pura, M. 'The role of mobile advertising in building a brand'. In *Mobile Commerce: Technology, Theory and Applications*. B.E. Mennecke and T.J. Stader (eds). Hershey: Idea Group Publishing, 2002, pp. 291–308.

Pym, Anthony. *The Moving Text: Localization, Translation and Distribution*. Amsterdam: Benjamins, 2004.

———. 'What localization models can learn from translation theory'. *The LISA Newsletter, Globalization Insider*, 12(2/4), 2003.

Quelch, John A., and E.J. Hoff. 'Customizing global marketing'. *Harvard Business Review*, 64:59–68, 1986.

Ramaprasad, Jyotika. 'Standardized multinational advertising: The influencing factors'. *Journal of Advertising*, 24:55–68, 1995.

Rau, Pradeep A., and J.F. Preble. 'Standardization of marketing strategy by the multinationals'. *International Marketing Review*, 4:18–28, 1987.

Reichert, T., J. Lambiase, S. Morgan, M. Garstarphen and S. Zavoina. 'Gheesecake and beefcake: No matter how you slice it, sexual explicitness in advertising continues to increase'. *Journalism and Mass Communication Quarterly*, 7(1):7–20, 1999.

Rheingold, Howard. *Smart Mobs: The Next Social Revolution*. Cambridge, MA: Perseus, 2002, p. 288.

Rick Dedrick. 'A consumption model for targeted electronic advertising'. *IEEE Multimedia*, 2(2):41–49, 1995.

Riesenbeck, Hajo, and A. Freeling. 'How global are global brands?' *The Mckinsey Quarterly* 4:3–18, 1991.

Robert, H. Ducoffe. 'Advertising value and advertising on the web'. *Journal of Advertising Research*, 36(5):21–35, 1996.

Robertson, Roland. 'Globalization and societal modernization: A note on Japan and Japanese religion'. *Sociological Analysis*, 47:35–43, 1987.

———. Robertson, Roland. 'Globalization theory and civilization analysis'. *Comparative Civilizations Review*, 17:20–30, 1987.

———. 'The globalization paradigm: Thinking globally'. In *Religion and Social Order*. Greenwich: JAI Press, 1991, pp. 207–224.

———. *Globalization: Social Theory and Global Culture*. London: SAGE Publications, 1992.

Robertson, Roland. 'Globalization: A brief response'. *Journal for the Scientific Study of Religion*, 31(3):319–323, 1992.

Robertson, Roland, and K. White. *Globalization: Critical Concepts in Sociology*. London: Routledge, 2003.

Rogers, Emily. 'Branding: McDonald's packaging in "I'm Lovin" It' revamp'. *Marketing*, 18 December 2003, p. 10.

Rorty, James. *Our Master's Voice—Advertising*. McMaster Press, 2008.

Rossiter, John R., and Larry Percy. 'Attitude change through visual imagery in advertising', *Journal of Advertising*, 9(2):15–16, 1980.

Russell, Bertrand. *The Analysis of Mind*. London: George Allen & Unwin, 1921.

Rutigliano, A. 'The debate goes on: Global vs local advertising'. *Management Review*, 75(6):27–31, 1986.

Ryan, J.K. Jr., and D.G. Ratz. 'Advertising standardization: A re-examination'. *International Journal of Advertising*, 6:145–58, 1987.

Ryans, John K., and J.H. Donnelly. 'Standardized global advertising: A call as yet unanswered'. *Journal of Marketing*, 33:56–60, 1969.

Ryan, M.K., and B. David. 'Gender differences in ways of knowing: The context dependence on attitudes toward thinking and learning survey'. *Sex Roles* 49(11/12):693–99, 2003.

Said, Edward. *Orientalism*. New York: Random House, 1978.

Sampson, Henry. *History of Advertising*. London: Chatto and Windus, 1930.

Sandage, C.H., and Vernon Fryburger. *Advertising Theory and Practice*. London: Longman, 1989.

Saussure, Ferdinand de. *Course in General Linguistics*. Albert Riedlinger (trans.). La Salle, IL: Open Court Publishing, 1983.

Schivinski, Bruno, and D. Dąbrowski. 'The effect of social-media communication on consumer perceptions of brands'. Working Paper Series A, Gdansk University of Technology, *Faculty of Management and Economics*, 12(12):2–19, 2013.

———. 'The impact of brand communication on brand equity dimensions and brand purchase intention through Facebook'. Working Paper Series A, Gdansk University of Technology, *Faculty of Management and Economics*, 4(4):2–23, 2013.

Scholte, Jan Aart. *Globalization: A Critical Introduction*. New York: St. Martin's Press, 2000.

Schorr, A., M. Schenk and W. Campbell. *Communication Research and Media Science in Europe*. Berlin: Mouton de Gruyter, 2003, p. 57.

Schultz, Don E., Martin Dennis and P. Brown William. *Strategic Advertising Campaign* (2nd edition). Chicago: Crain Books, 1984.

Schwartz, M., and A. Carroll. 'Corporate social responsibility: A three-domain approach'. *Business Ethics Quarterly*, 13(4):503–530, 2003.

Scissors, Jack Z., and Bumba Lincoln. *Advertising Media Planning* (5th edition). Illinois: NTC Business Books, 1996.

Scoble, Robert, and Shel Israel. *Naked Conversations: How Blogs are Changing the Way Businesses Talk with Customers.* Hoboken, NJ: John Wiley, 2006.

Secchi, D. 'Utilitarian, managerial and relational theories of corporate social responsibility'. *International Journal of Management Reviews,* 9(4):347–373, 2007.

Sengupta, Subir, and Kartik Pashupati. 'Advertising in India: The winds of change'. In *Advertising in Asia.* Katherine Toland Frith (ed.). Iowa: Iowa State University Press, 1996.

Shamiyeh, Michael (ed.). *What People Want. Populism in Architecture and Design.* Boston: DOM Research Laboratory, 2005.

Sherry, J.F. Jr. 'Advertising as a cultural system'. In *Marketing and Semiotics: New Directions in the Study of Signs for Sale.* J. Umiker-Sebeok (ed.). Berlin: Mouton de Gruyter, 1987.

Shirky, Clay. *Here Comes Everybody.* New York: Penguin Press, 2008.

Sinisalo, J., J. Salo, M. Leppäniemi and H. Karjaluoto. 'Initiation stage of a mobile customer relationship management'. *The E-Business Review,* 5:205–209, 2005.

Soley, L., and G. Kurzbard. 'Sex in advertising: A comparison of 1964 and 1984 magazine advertisements'. *Journal of Advertising,* 15(3):46–64, 1986.

Stanwick, P., and S. Stanwick. 'The relationship between corporate social performance, and organizational size, financial performance, and environmental performance: An empirical examination'. *Journal of Business Ethics,* 17(2):195–204, 1998.

Sterelny, Kim. *Dawkins vs. Gould: Survival of the Fittest.* Cambridge: Icon Books, 2007, p. 83.

Surowiecki, James. *The Wisdom of Crowds.* New York: Anchor Books, 2004.

Swanson, D.L. 'Addressing a theoretical problem by reorienting the corporate social performance model'. *Academy of Management Review,* 20(1):43–64, 1995.

Tai, H.C. 'Advertising in Asia: Localize or regionalize?' *International Journal of Advertising,* 16:48–61, 1997.

Tapscott, Don, and Anthony D. Williams. *Wikinomics.* New York: Portfolio, 2006.

Targeting Local Markets. Available online at http://www.iab.net/guidelines/508676/targeting_local., accessed on 7 March 2015.

Tharp, M., and Marye Tharp. *Marketing and Consumer Identity in Multicultural America.* Thousand Oaks, CA: SAGE Publications, 2001.

Tharp, M., and L.M. Scott. 'The role of marketing processes in creating cultural meaning'. *Journal of MacroMarketing,* 48:47–60, 1990.

The BLF Manifesto. Available online at http://www.billboardliberation. com/manifesto.html., accessed on 8 March 2015.

The Routledge Encyclopedia of Translation Studies. New York: Routledge, 1998.

The Media Awareness Network 2010. 'Special issues for young children: Junk food advertising and nutrition concerns'. Available online at www.media-awareness.ca/english/parents/marketing/issues_kids_marketing.cfm

Theoharakis, V., and A. Hirst. 'Perceptual difference of marketing journals: A worldwide perspective'. *Marketing Letters,* 13(4):389–402, 2002.

Thomson, C.J. 'Marketing mythology and discourses of power'. *Journal of Consumer Research,* 31(1):162–180, 2004.

Thompson, John B. *The Media and Modernity.* Cambridge: Polity Press, 1995, p. 150.

Tiwari, Sanjay. *The (Un)Commonsense of Advertising.* NewDelhi: Response Books, 2003.

Toy Advertising. Availabe online at http://en.wikipedia.org/wiki/Toy_advertising., accessed on 21 April 2014.

Trattner, C., and F. Kappe. 'Social stream marketing on Facebook: A case study'. *International Journal of Social and Humanistic Computing,* 2(1):86–103, 2013.

Triandis C. Harr. 'The many dimensions of culture'. *Academy of Management Executives,* 18(1):88–93, 2004.

Tulloch, Mitch, Jeff Koch and Sandra Haynes (eds). *Microsoft Encyclopedia of Security.* Redmond, Washington: Microsoft Press, 2003, p. 16.

Turban, D., and W. Daniel. 'Corporate social performance and organizational attractiveness to prospective employees'. *Academy of Management Journal,* 40(3):658–672, 1996.

Turner, Bryan S. 'The concept of "the world" in sociology: A commentary on Roland Robertson's theory of globalization'. *Journal for the Scientific Study of Religion,* 3(3):311–318, 1992.

Turow, Joseph, and P. Mcallister Mathew. *The Advertising and Consumer Culture Reader.* New York: Routledge, 2009.

Udayasankar, K. 'Corporate social responsibility and firm size'. *Journal of Business Ethics,* 83(2):167–175, 2008.

Understanding Mobile Marketing: Technology and Reach. Available online at http://www.mmaglobal.com/uploads/MMAMobileMarketing102.pdf, accessed March 2015.

VanBoskirk, Shar, Christine Spivey Overby and Sarah Takvorian. 'US interactive marketing forecast 2011–2016'. *Forrester Research,* 24 August 2011. Available online at https://www.forrester.com/US+Interactive+Marketing+Forecast+2011+To+2016/fulltext/-/E-res59379, accessed March 2015.

Varshney, U. 'Issues, requirements and support for location-intensive mobile commerce applications'. *International Journal of Mobile Communications,* 1(3):247–263, 2003.

Venuti, Lawrence (ed.). *The Translation Studies Reader.* New York: Routledge, 2000.

Volkmer, Ingrid. *News in the Global Sphere: A Study of CNN and its Impact on Global Communication.* Luton: University of Luton Press, 1999.

Voloshinov, Valentin N. *Marxism and the Philosophy of Language.* Ladislav Matejka and I.R Titunik (trans.). New York: Seminar Press, 1973.

Waddock, S., and S. Graves. 'The corporate social performance–financial performance link'. *StrategicManagement Journal,* 18(4):303–319, 1997.

Wang, S., and Wang H. 'A location-based business service model for mobile commerce'. *International Journal of Mobile Communications,* 3(4):339–349, 2005.

Wardrip-Fruin, Noah, and Nick Montfort (eds). *The New Media Reader.* Cambridge, MA: The MIT Press, 2003.

Wartick, S.L., and P.L. Cochran. 'The evolution of the corporate social performance model'. *The Academy of Management Review,* 10(4):758–769, 1985.

Waters, Malcolm. *Globalization.* London: Routledge, 1995.

Watts, Duncan J. *Six Degrees: The Science of a Connected Age.* London: Vintage, 2003, p. 368.

Waxman, S. 'Sex on TV: Study finds more, sooner but safer'. *The Washington Post,* 7 February 2001.

Weber, Robert Philip. *Basic Content Analysis.* Newbury Park, CA: SAGE Publications, 1990.

Weilbacker, William M. *Advertising* (2nd edition). New York: Macmillan, 1984.

Wellman, Barry. *Networked: The New Social Operating System.* Cambridge, MA: The MIT Press, 2012.

Wells, William, John Burnett and Sandra Moriarty. *Advertising Principles and Practice* (5th edition). NJ: Prentice Hall, 2000.

Westfall, Ralph, and Harper W. Boyd, Jr. 'Marketing in India'. *The Journal of Marketing,* 25(2):11–17, 1960.

Wikipedia. 'Corporate social responsibility'. Available online at http://en.wikipedia.org/wiki/Corporate_social_responsibility, accessed on 12 December 2008.

Williams, Raymond. *Television: Technology and Cultural Form.* London, Routledge, 1974.

Williamson, Judith. *Decoding Advertisements: Ideology and Meaning in Advertising.* London: Boyars, 1978.

Williams, Raymond. *The Country and the City.* London: Chatto and Windus, 1973.

Wilmshurst, John. *The Fundamentals of and Practice of Marketing.* William Heinman: London, 1978.

Wood, D.J. 'Corporate social performance revisited'. *The Academy of Management Review,* 16(4):691–718, 1991.

Woods, Tim. *Post Modernism* (2nd edition). New Delhi: Viva Books, 2010.

Wright, John. S., Daniel S. Warner, L. Willis Winter, Jr. and Sherilyn K. Zeigler. *Advertising* (4th edition). New Delhi: McGraw Hill, 1978.

www.wikipedia.com.

Young, James Webb. 'Writing for media'. *MCJ* 101. n.d. Web. 20 November 2007. Accessed on 6 May 2010.

Zahra S.A., and M.S. LaTour. 'Corporate social responsibility and organizational effectiveness: A multivariate approach'. *The Journal of Business Ethics,* 6(6):459–467, 1987.

Zapf, Hubert. 'Literary ecology and the ethics of texts'. *New Literary History,* 39(4):847–868, 2008.

Zobel, J. *Mobile Business and M-Commerce.* Munich, Wienna: Hansa, 2001.

Index

About the Author

Sunitha Srinivas C. is Assistant Professor, Govt. College of Mokeri, Calicut, Kerala. She obtained her MA (English) and PhD from University of Calicut, Kerala.

Dr Srinivas is the recipient of the Editors' Choice Award from Home of Letters, Bhubaneswar. She has published research papers on advertising and media studies in peer-reviewed journals and is the author of *Functionalism and Indian English Fiction: From Cradle to Grave*. She has authored numerous poems. Apart from this, Dr Srinivas has also been a resource person for academic programmes organized by various institutions and universities.